Preparing for Electronic Commerce in Asia

Preparing for Electronic Commerce in Asia

DOUGLAS BULLIS

Q

QUORUM BOOKS
Westport, Connecticut • London

Library of Congress Cataloging-in-Publication Data

Bullis, Douglas.
    Preparing for electronic commerce in Asia / Douglas Bullis.
      p. cm.
    Includes bibliographical references and index.
    ISBN 1–56720–206–3 (alk. paper)
    1. Electronic commerce—Asia.   2. Information technology—Economic
aspects—Asia. I. Title.
    HF5548.325.A78B85   1999
    382′.45004′095—dc21   98–7576

British Library Cataloguing in Publication Data is available.

Library of Congress Catalog Card Number: 98–7576
ISBN: 1–56720–206–3

First published in 1999

Quorum Books, 88 Post Road West, Westport, CT 06881
An imprint of Greenwood Publishing Group, Inc.

Printed in the United States of America

The paper used in this book complies with the
Permanent Paper Standard issued by the National
Information Standards Organization (Z39.48–1984).

10 9 8 7 6 5 4 3 2 1

To all those who wouldn't go on record for these pages
for fear of what their governments would do to them

Contents

Acknowledgments

Almost all of this book's information was sourced from original interviews, supplemented with information from the Internet and via e-mail. Many thanks to the many people whose ideas and assessments went into this book:

Mr. Saw Ken Wye, Mr. Michael Yap, Ms. Tay Lay Kheng, and Julie Tan; Tan Chin Tuan; Adrian Chia; MDC Malaysia; MTDC Malaysia; A. Shukor Rahman, Industry Watch, *CompuTimes*; Francis C. Nantha, *New Straits Times*; Meeta Bhar, Arthur Andersen & Co.; Zoraini Wati Abas, educational writer; Kesh Mahinder Singh, CN Eminent Systems Sdn Bhd.; Rajah Singham, Corporate Network; Gerard Lim, Chairman, Interactive Multimedia Association of Malaysia; Michael Foulds, A.D. Little Malaysia; Torryn P. Brazell, Internet Society; April Cheah, Oracle Malaysia; Tan Sri Dr. Othman Yeop Abdullah Multimedia Development Corporation; Ong Chui Koon, Senior Research Officer Patent Information Unit; Dato' Mustapa bin Mohamed, Minister of Entrepreneurial Development; Bill Tarrant, Editor, Reuters; McKinsey & Company; Fiona Cameron of Public Relations Survey Research Malaysia (SRM); Iain Bell of Frank Small & Associates; Ms. Chin Suit Fang of Price-Waterhouse; Subha Segaram of Coopers & Lybrand; Tan Chin Tuan, Assistant Director, Infrastructure Development, Multimedia Development Directorate; Ms. Evelyn Goh Choong Eng, Project Officer, Infrastructure Development, Multimedia Development Directorate; Telecommunication Authority of Singapore; Ms. Michelle Khor, Communications, NSTB—National Science & Technology Board; Gerald Woon Tai Hwee, Senior Officer, Corporate Communications EDB / Economic Development Board.

And to the many others who didn't want me to reveal who they were or what they said.

Introduction

The 1997 Asian economic crisis sprang from poor practices in the financial and real estate sectors of several countries' economies, exacerbated by poor oversight at the government and corporate directorship levels.

The bad news from these countries tended to obscure the fact that several other aspects of their economies were doing rather well, all things considered. Manufacturing practices, trade efficiency, and investment in technology were healthy production engines for economies whose banking and finance sectors left much to be desired.

In particular, information technology and its spin-off applications of electronic commerce and electronic business were just beginning to show considerable promise for Asian business efficiency, as they have elsewhere. These advances are not likely to go away simply because of a monetary crisis. Certain companies and governments will invest in their future, using information technology as their fulcrum.

This book addresses what businesses can expect from the Asian marketplace for information technology and electronic commerce in the next five to seven years.

Look at Western economies today and it seems hard to remember that disastrous October of 1929—or for that matter, the one in 1982. Some Asians feel that by the time a regional information infrastructure is in place around 2005, people will be saying the same about 1997. Recall that a number of countries were doing things right (Singapore, Hong Kong, the Philippines, and Taiwan) and one major player began to get it right just in time (China). These are the countries likely to lead Asia out of its identity slump.

Most economists now feel that region will undergo three to five years of recession, tapering off between 2001 and 2003, led by some lighthouses in the storm. Then what?

No knowledgeable institutional investor or business leader believes Asia is going to wither away because of a massive credit overextension. Already in March 1998 as this book was being readied for press, investors were pouring into the basket cases of Thailand and South Korea looking for bargains.

It appears likely that information technology will be a solid investment area in Asia for some years to come. Yet Asia is no market for the unwitting. There are long cultural antecedents that work against the free flow of information—face, denial, secrecy, disinformation, autocracy, hierarchy, cronyism.

The Asian countries that prosper and advance from the information era will be those that successfully remove these hindrances. This book is about which they are and how they are doing it.

PART I
Asia's Electronic Commerce Era

1

Meet Your New Market—I

Mat and E.J.

Mat and E.J. are in their early thirties. Both have careers. Mat's is in software design for a medium technology manufacturing company in "P.J." or Petaling Jaya outside of Kuala Lumpur. E.J.'s is in editing, advertising, client services, and marketing (yes, all of these; it is a small company) for a Singaporean technology trade journal published out of a cramped office down by Orchard Road.

Mat is E.J.'s "K.L." (Kuala Lumpur) stringer for news about SME (Small and Medium Enterprise) investments in Malaysia. E.J. in turn sends Mat news about product ideas produced by overseas high-tech companies that may or may not eventually be interested in offshore manufacturing in countries like Malaysia, where markets are modest but so are labor costs.

They network with each other. Gradually, over a "VSOP" cognac (for E.J.) and tea (for Mat) at the Hotel Vistana in K.L., where E.J. stays when he's in Malaysia, or the Oxford Inn on Queen Street, which is Mat's hangout in Singapore, they got to be friends. They talk about their wives (both are newly married) and what to do about the kids when those arrive. They have little interest in politics, but inexhaustible interest in their jobs. They see themselves not as careermen, not as salarymen, but as professionals.

There are thousands like Mat and E.J. in Southeast Asia. They are simply two young, energetic professionals making their own kind of Asian life. They don't think of themselves as unique or special, though the life they lead runs very much counter to the world's (and indeed, Asia's) idea of "Asian."

Mat's wife is named Cik (his nickname for her is "Ciku," the name of a delicious Asian fruit whose taste is a mix of honey and dates). She designs decorative pewterware for one of Malaysia's oldest and most prestigious crafts firms. They live in a modest apartment in Setapak, a gritty steppingstone neighborhood of old-line working-class folks now being mixed with newcomers like Mat and Cik buying into the kind of block high-rises they can afford—fifth floor on a six-floor walk up; bedroom, bath, kitchen, and living room; blessedly aloof from the raspy motos and screeching kids that is the background music from below. The impossible parking is a moot issue for Mat and Cik because they haven't saved the down payment for a Proton yet. No relatives in residence, no live-in servants, not much automated anything. Mat has earmarked space for his computer room in what will in due time be the baby's room. Mat has no idea how distracting a crying baby can be two meters from his keyboard.

Mat and Cik can't afford most of these things because in Malaysia everything related to computers costs twice as much as the prices he sees on-line through Taiwan vendors and Dell. There is little sense of competition among importers and retailers, most of whom own monopolies or exclusive distributorships on the goods they vend. Besides, Cik tells him, why buy it when the electricity goes off so frequently (Sunday evening is the worst) and the life cycle of a modem is three per year, given Malaysia's unprotected phone cables and fierce afternoon electrical storms. There is much truth to her argument. There is also much truth to the fact that Cik wants a father around the house when the children come, not a telehusband in the computer room. She knows what overwork and underpay do to men.

Their house decor is a few Islamic inscriptions in gold embroidery on a green background, plus a calendar featuring palmy, people-empty beach scenes. They buy just about everything at the Jaya Jusco a short walk away, a supermarket chain owned (distantly) by the overseas retailers (as are many Malaysian malls), though you'd never know that to look at the staff which is almost 100 percent Malay.

Mat and Cik do no home entertaining, even with relatives. They are embarrassed at the look and condition of their apartment block. It hasn't been painted in years; laundry drips off the balconies at all hours; bicycles are chained to the rail that fronts the apartments; everyone has two or more huge locks on the door; and trash litters everything, despite a regular trash collection service. Given their salaries, it is the best they can do. It is one reason why they escape to their work as often as they can and eat out for almost every meal. Theirs are not so much long hours at work as long hours away from home.

E.J. in Singapore truncated his name from Ellis Jeffrey because one of the Chinese equivalents of Ellis is Yǎ Lí, which can be translated "correct person," and E.J. long ago parted company with his parents' sixties-Singapore middle-class-Mao political views. His and his wife Pammy's apartment door in the Tampines area of Singapore is guarded by two shrines. These are testimonies of their acceptance of each other's ways—her deep religiosity and his sense for family ancestors. Her shrine is a standard Hindu *puja* (worship) box packed top to bottom with myriad deities and reeking of incense and moldy oranges. His (which Pammy keeps for him) is a traditional Chinese dragon-roofed red ancestral shrine presided over by a cream-and-gold Kuan Yin ceramic tile votive shrine wafting clouds of smoking incense. Chinese-Hindu marriages aren't that common in Singapore, but to the neighbors, they are simply E.J. and Pammy, the computer couple. The main reason for that appellation is that computers are what they mostly talk about.

Their apartment complex might have been a feature in the industrial-architecture press in its heyday; now it looks like the anteroom of a dowager past the days of distinguished visitors. Jade statues stare from windows of one neighbor. Old men dawdle away their retirements picking up bits of trash from the fronts of their steps. One shop has a collection of antique Chinese foo dogs that might have once guarded the entrance to a palace. Most other shops are devoted to sundries and electrical appliances and seem forever in a sign war over prices. Amid these, girls work on their skip-rope rhymes. Everything is painted, kept up, clean, neat.

Like the majority of middle-class Singaporeans, E.J. and Pammy live comfortably on $3000 a month. E.J. is preoccupied with getting the "Five C's"—cash in the bank, credit card, condominium, car, and country club membership. So far E.J. has the first two, but then, so does just about everybody in Singapore. Pamela doesn't really care about money; she knows E.J. will earn it. Her part is contributing whatever finances she can till the children come.

Pamela is office manager for an interior decoration firm. Their house shows it. "We furnished it from the bare walls," she will proudly tell you. "We chose our own furniture, beds, the dining room table, fridge. We started with a secondhand black and white TV, then E.J. got his job and we got a color TV. Now with my job we have a VCR. We save to get what we want." E.J. chimes in, "Our first car will be a Toyota. We'll have the BMW by 2005."

They will, too.

E.J. and Pammy entertain friends and business contacts at home whenever they can. One reason is Pammy's considerable taste in design and decor matters. She never studied it formally (her degree is in management), but she is blessed with a vivid sense of color. She keeps up with Singaporean interior design magazines (subscribing to *Interior Living* and *ID*) and goes to the library once a month to check out the internationals.

Theirs is very different from the older Singaporean tradition of dramatically separating family from the world. A nice dinner with a good bottle of wine (beer if it's one of Pammy's wine-killing curries) and an evening of worldly aware conversation that touches on business subjects, films, the latest in-things to buy, cricket, soccer, and casual wear from California. No one they know is much interested in politics.

"We love what's fashionable and most people our parents' age don't," Pammy informs you. What is fashionable includes American (and some French) slang, voting, makeup, jewelry, movies, higher education, imported ice cream, women managing their own incomes, smoking, drinking, and wild colors. They are worldly, practical, neither idealistic nor cynical, ready for anything.

Mat and Cik up in K.L., and E.J. and Pammy in Singapore are charter members of a new class the demographers haven't really paid much attention to yet. Yet they are a true class—greater than an occupation but not quite an income stratum.

Nearly all of their respective countries' traditional classes are tied to occupation and birth status. Mat and E.J. and their wives are almost defiantly beholden to neither. Without being able to define their views in sociological terms (in fact, largely unconcerned that sociology exists), they simply do not adhere to the idea of *varnas*, the paleo-castes that are the most ancient social hierarchy in Asia: priest-politicians, warrior-business people, providers, and workers.

The reason is that their careers as technocrats and lifestylers do not fit into Asia's previous categories. They are in fact a new *varna* that did not exist before: infopreneurs.

Mat and E.J.'s peers are software developers in Bangalore; architects in Shanghai working with industrial park development; the public relations executive in Jakarta whose wardrobe is nine-tenths Western; the young Thai property manager with (at least until late 1997) a nonstop social life; the "office-lady" in Penang who trudges through her work while waiting for the marriage her parents have arranged; or the woman executive in the high-rise overlooking Marina Bay who does not serve coffee to her boss as her cohorts do in Tokyo, but rather the latest shares prices to a investment analysis group in which she is one of the experts. During coffee breaks she racks her brain trying to figure out how to court a contact at Bloombergs.

Few of these identify with what they see on local TV. Instead their role models are who and what they see on CNN, especially the people who talk to Lou Dobbs. When on vacation, it is to Hawaii or Mauritius, not *balik kampung* ("dear old home town") like their parents.

The real-life Mat and E.J. live in Setapak and Tampines. But those addresses could also be Bangalore, Hyderabad, Hsinchu, Bangsar, Kebayoran Baru, Pudong, or Suzhou—anywhere from whence their new *varna* fraternity sends out website and e-mail announcements of its existence. But where they work is places like http://www.idg.com/, http://www.newspage.com, http://www.cmp.com, and http://www.infospace.com. They haven't yet discovered http.//www.minds.com and http://www.dejanews.com, but watch what happens when they do.

These are not cyberspace, they are cybercolonies. Space is something that can be inhabited by anybody. Cybercolonies are colloquies with a common informational need. They markedly resemble the maritime colonies of Ancient Greece, the Gujarati trade enclaves in old Srivijayan days, the Funan/Khmer settlements before even that. The Malacca sultanates organized their ports under four harbormasters called by their lovely Persian title, *Shahbander*, who were selected from the four principal merchant communities of China, Java, Bengal, and Gujarat. That knowledge results when cultural needs and trade needs merge is not news to Asia.

But cybercolonies aren't quite fully formed yet. Mat and E.J. have never heard of gopher. They do not use http://www.pointcast.com, http://www.idcresearch.com, or http://interactive.wsj.com/public/current/summaries/small.htm. They are unconcerned with financial or commercial websites. They are after the latest developments in procedure technology for their respective interests. They start the day with http://www.idg.net, the gateway site to several hundred computing websites around the world, and surf from there.

The management chat rooms that mesmerize Pammy and the product design news and craft technique sites Cik consults all have one thing in common with the sites visited by their husbands: information is process; it is what they need to get their jobs done. It may come on-line, but it is the equivalent of a trade journal. Their interests are procedure, task, result. They have little interest in analysis, projection, prediction, strategy. They want facts they can use. When the two couples fall into the man-man woman-woman conversation of all couples after dinner, Mat and E.J. trade site news (including the occasional sports and X-rated site) and Cik and Pammy swap tips about Intuit and design.

The members of this foursome, so adventuresome and yet restrained, are nodes in a cybercolony that reaches everywhere in the world. Behaviorally and economically, Mat and E.J.'s use of information to better perform the tasks of the hour much resembles the ancestral trading colonies of Greece, the Muscovy traders, China, the Straits entrepôts, Gujaratis, the Hanseatic League, the junk and the dhow and the schooner and the camel and the mule and the horse. How did cyberspace get turned into infocolony, this collection of occupational niches with its new-wave air of shoptalk and identifying emblems, yet its age-old patterns of doing things the way they have always been done? Data communications merely fulfills in today's complex world some very old and very constant human activity.

Word processing is the record of the mind shaping and clarifying its point of view. Its function is no different than the carving on stone in a temple or the calligrapher's pen. All word processing does is reflect the way we now think.

Spreadsheeting is as old as village chieftains standing before the granary trying to figure out what to provide each person from the annual harvest and what to hold in reserve.

Databases go as far back as the clay cuneiform merchant's records of Mesopotamia and the tally censuses of the ancient Chinese.

Graphics satisfy our urge to beautify and decorate the communications we want people to understand.

There is nothing new in these. They are simply being accomplished in a very sophisticated way. It is the fact of sophistication that is important. Why should we rely on archaic commercial behaviors any more than we should rely on archaic alphabets? The world is not becoming merely a global village, it is becoming a better village.

Information blends modern times with timeless times. Technology changes culture, but blindly. Information is the only thing we have that can successfully bridge the gap between what our minds would like us to do and what our experience says we can do. Information isn't how the world should be, it is how the world is.

Malaysia and Singapore have set their rudders of economy in very different directions. Yet both Mat and E.J. start their day with http://www.idg.net, just as the bankers of Augsburg and the Medicis of Firenze began their days with the news couriered by horseback from their distant money enclaves from Lisbon to Stockholm. What is different between Mat and E.J. and their ancestors, who likewise thought of fact as the grease of getting the job done?

Back in their hacker days—meaning five years ago—Mat and E.J. were doing something that a computer technician would spot immediately but an academic, psychologist, or sociologist would probably miss.

When Mat and his Malay friends got hold of a computer game, their first response after playing it a few times was to dive into its binhex and start modifying the code strings so that they could alter in their favor the way the game came out. At a certain moment the hulking bearded karate goon (amazingly agile for all that body mass) would now emerge from only one door, and Mat and his friends made sure they knew which door. Having suitably tinkered with the rules, they would then invite others to play (for money if possible) and beat the socks off them.

When E.J. and his Chinese friends got the same game, their response after a few plays was to go into the binhex and write down the Boolean sequences of every code string so they could play the game perfectly just the way it was shipped. They didn't know which door the goon would use, but they knew which kick he would use when he did. They too challenged their friends (money was obligatory) knowing the odds were in their favor because they had mastered the rules.

Where did Mat and E.J. acquire these particular responses to technology?

They were brought up in an economic era that, while Mat and E.J. might not have heard it expressed in so many words, was attuned to the fact that Southeast Asia could evolve out of the 1980s value-added ladder model of economic development by embracing a digital economy model. Computers would improve things but not change them.

The notion of a digital economy came from their governments, who wanted the value-adding virtues of processing speed and productivity enhancement but did not want the idea of social change to accompany it. A digital economy is not an information economy; it can be controlled. So Mat and E.J, as well as Cik and Pam, came to understand the digital economy in terms of technique and improvement, not idea and invention. This mentality was reinforced in pricey management seminars that would regularly jet in some guru like Tom Peters or Elizabeth Moss Kanter, who would serve up a peppy appetizer to a meal of spiceless palate-flattening lectures by locals on subjects like "Improving Object Transmission in ATM Telephony" or "Achieving ISO 9001 Standards in the Cement Industry." Peters and Kanter would fly home having left behind a flowery bouquet of pretty phrases like "excellence" and "world class" but leaving the vase pretty much what it was to start with.

Only in 1997 did people discover the problem wasn't their lacking the right buzzwords, it was the time chasm between the culture their decision makers were raised in and the culture that today has to deal with the consequences of their decisions. Throughout the late 1980s and most of the 1990s, information technology was the new buzzword. It was value mimicking. When E.J. sat down at his editor's desk he sought out articles that described how to improve, not to change. When he sat at his marketing desk he sought advertisers who sold the products he described in his articles. When Mat up in Petaling Jaya sent out his e-mails, he was after optimizers, the tidbits of improvement that tinkered with doors in the dungeon but did not perceive any need for a new castle. The result for both was a cheerful conviction that progress is a delivery system.

The principal reason for Mat and E.J.'s absence of concern with pattern is that although Southeast Asia's governments may have shed their monopolistic attitude about owning business sectors, they retained their monopolistic attitude about owning information and power.

Young people today don't see it that way. They don't see themselves as seventy just yet. They are too family-focused to think in terms of power, place, and history. They shun the traditional image paths of bureau, government, and the judiciary. Where they do see themselves is in the adult version of the video arcade, with its values of quick surprise, quick reaction, quick results. The gut-response, no-time-to-think clock speed at which video games run is hugely demanding but at odds with traditional career styles that plod, dote, defer.

So, indeed, is the Internet.

Their parents abhor all this. They do not realize that the areas in which their young people are learning to excel are the very ones most needed in an information economy. Today's teensomethings and twentysomethings are attuned to objects, applets, virtual reality, morphing, and ultra-3D. Their fathers are attuned to analysis, projection, benchmarking, and critical path. Young people think about speed. Their fathers think about predictability.

Indeed, video youngsters have a very different set of thought patterns than one would expect, given their recently comfy middle-class discretionary affluence. On the plus side, they don't think in space, they think in time. Their aesthetic impulses are triggered by event, not thing. One result is that they see themselves as the primary market for the things they do.

They are heirs of a bubble and they know it. They enjoy wealth and social standing they didn't earn. In comparing themselves with their parents they often have low self-esteem. It is hard for them to take much satisfaction in their own accomplishments. They don't have the conquer-all drive of their parents. They can't foresee themselves building the empires their parents did because there are very few empires left. The shipping, timber, land, transport, telecommunications, gambling, lodging, and service industries are so far along the infrastructure curve that the only opportunities that remain lie in greasing the gears.

They read *Business Times Singapore* and *Asia Inc.* for model phrases to use at meetings but dress from the pages of *GQ*. The Malaysia menswear designer Edmund Ser has got them to a T: "Every country has its James Deans. The newer managers accept the fact that the younger ranks are dressing with more flair. After the old guard passes on there will be an explosion in innovative men's wear. Who knows, that may really be an explosion in innovative men. We are seeing the start of it right now."

Their societies are largely unaware that these young people have some useful talents. Like all young living things, they thrive on play. The forms of their play have made them unafraid of high clock speed, high-load input, and instant output. These are the talents required of the information age.

But more than these, they have learned how to take the game apart and win it at binhex level.

That is where they plan to make their future.

2

Asia Needs More Information, Not More Money

History has an uncanny knack for turning brilliant ideas into memories people would rather not remember. Recent Asian economic developments have shown that neither dreams nor denial make for particularly palatable reality. In business terms, even the very word "Asian" has to be used advisedly, for there is no "Asia." Geographers agree where the political borders begin and end, but cultural geographers have a much more difficult time deciding where Asia stops and somewhere else begins.

"Asia" consists of a number of complex cultures with considerably different histories and assumptions. If we stick to the common business and political use of the term, we are on firm ground by simple virtue of common agreement. When we deal with values, however, we are on much shakier territory.

What gives the region's cultures a meaningful coherence today is that they are interacting in the name of self-interest in a way that is quite different from the region's prior history, and most certainly different from the ways of that other geographical creation of convenience, the "West." When you consider that Cambodia and Thailand, not to mention Burma and India, are right next door to each other, what are "Asian Values"? Even though Italy and Yugoslavia, not to mention Surinam and Brazil, are located next door to each other, no one lumps them under the rubric "Western Values."

Even the most majuscule of these cultures—the Sinic, Indian, Malay, Arab, Persian, Mongol, and Aboriginal—break down quickly into niches of almost unencompassable individuality. Each has responded quite differently to history's epochal ideas—Buddhism or Christianity or democracy or socialism, for example—and they are certainly responding in their own way to the idea of capitalism. The Information Age, though we may disagree about the details of what the term means, nonetheless has served to speed up the pace of capitalism without materially changing it as an idea. This shift of pace is now about to energize Asia's capitalisms, and most likely, in much the same way.

Though it wasn't much discussed at the time, there was a powerful information gap playing itself out in the 1997 debacle, one that is likely to be narrowed substantively over the next decade. The gap was (and still is) between the decision elite at the highest levels of government and business, whose educations and mind-sets largely gelled in the 1960s when they began to make decisions instead of following them, and the young internationally educated MBA-conscious managers of today with their grasp of both economic and cultural interactivity. These young managers watched the devastating consequences of trying to manipulate world economies from the knowledge bases of the type exemplified by President Suharto and Prime Minister Mahathir. Both these men preferred the contentments of views they wanted to believe to the discomforts of fact, and they preferred the advice of good-old-boy chums as thoroughly unqualified to direct an economy as B. J. Habibie and Daim Zainuddin. Today's rising young business leaders are determined this sort of myopia will not happen again.

On the other hand, many of today's young business leaders are also the ones who dove blindly into the real estate and easy credit debacles that brought Asia's tiger economies to their knees. It remains to be seen whether these cocky young MBAs have learned that most get-rich-quick schemes are well-disguised get-poor-quicker schemes.

Today's generation of mid-managers and entrepreneurs tends to take as role models Singapore and Hong Kong and people like Stan Shih. A common thread among them is that they make their decisions from the springboard of information consciousness. The result is that these tiny city economies navigated relatively safely—and certainly with dignity—between the shoals and rocks of the gyrating giants around them. Singapore and Hong Kong are chief cases in point for the twin propositions that those societies which best inform themselves adapt most quickly, and that societies which learn to adapt develop the profoundest sense for cultural regeneration.

The quickest (and as it turned out, the most facile) interpretation of the 1997 Asian bubble bath was that it marked the beginning of a long-term regional economic decline. Many pointed to Japan and said, "Seven years after their real estate bubble and the finance ministry still hasn't got it right—so what do you expect out of troglodyte bureaucracies like Korea's and Indonesia's?"

Well, now we know. Those who prosper with Asia over the next decade or so will be those who make the transition to an economic strategy that aims at cultural vitality, not just business vitality. Cultural vitality is not expressed in tallests and biggests—which have long been considered the masks of insecurity—but a large, informed, inquisitive, and largely anonymous consumer class. The Information Age is not about transmission and distribution, it is about content. Content, as we see so clearly in the way the Internet has organized itself into myriad niches that markedly resemble Asia's historical culture organization into myriad niches, is about identity of locale.

BEYOND BUSINESS

If the word "cultural" shows up a good deal in these pages, it is because that word is often the most overlooked indicator of economic health. Economy, like markets or finance or commerce or production, does not exist for itself. We would be a very tedious world if all we did was produce and consume and tot up statistics about it all. While leaving the word "culture" up to each to define as he or she will, the fact is that what endures long into history is not money but the way we express ourselves using it. It is likewise true that we would be just as tedious if all we did was sing and dance. The word "*Uffizi*" from the famed art museum in Florence, Italy, originally meant "offices." That is indeed what the building used to be—one of the world's first bureaucrats' warrens. The point is, offices lead to bigger things.

So often the words "art" and "aesthetics" are primly drawn to mean tangible things devised to appeal. That is a rather simple view. Many Asian peoples have it that event is art. It is easy to see why so many take as much aesthetic pleasure in a well-constructed business deal or organizational structure as Westerners take in a ballet or a building. One thing the Information Age may help us do is learn the myriad ways we can broaden our definitions so as to include more of each other than we exclude.

The 1997 crisis may well turn out to be the healthiest thing that has happened to capitalism—and culture—in a long time. Many now grasp that economies go through growth cycles specific to the cultures from which they spring. There is no universal rule; there are many paths to progress. The Tigers and Dragons got quite a kick-start from cheap labor, cheap capital, and cheap land. Their motor engaged a noisy, quickly ascending, frantically revving first gear of low-end exports growth. The products might not have been all that great, but they sure turned over in a hurry. The noise we heard in '97 was the sound of an overrevved engine whining its way on down to a more manageable form of cruise control. This new gear may well be information-based trade expanding today's modest Asian consumer class into an economic engine of its own. It also may trigger the urge to reconfigure those fundamental values that impel a culture forward no matter which economic system provides for its subsistence. Consider the upside: If 1997 hadn't happened much of Asia would still be stuck at the conversation level of chipsets and golf courses.

NATURAL DESELECTION AND THE DECLINE OF SPECIES

What will the so-called Information Age do—or not do—within the framework of Asia's differing but adaptive economies? A consistent pattern throughout the region has been resistance to excesses from without and resilience to excesses from within. Another pattern is the ability to make rather quick and large changes to ideology in the name of self-interest. Many were fooled into thinking that Asia's great decade from 1987 through 1997 implied that breadth was depth. One look at the absence of any significant blossoming of the arts coinciding with the blossoming of the economy would have told a culture historian that this economic boom was an elitist transfer-of-wealth phenomenon, not a populist production-of-value one. It is similarly foolish to write the region off because, like a wave, it fell over onto itself when its top began moving faster than its bottom. The fact is, the bottom is still moving.

The clear lesson to this is that the greatest changes to come out of Asia in the Information Age are likely to come from directions wholly unexpected today. Those who prosper will be those who have learned litheness, perceptiveness, and non-judgment.

We can start this with ourselves. How many readers of this sentence feel they have clear ideas of what went wrong in Asia in 1997?

Good.

Now, what went right?

The 1997 crisis focused considerable negative attention on what went wrong. Much of the focus was accurate. A good number of financial, corporate, marketing, and management practices to be found in Asia still leave a lot to be desired. Some still persist in denial even though it is now well known that negative information—denial, opacity, churning, and sanctimony—is the most merciless betrayer known to a marketplace. Those with a sense for how great literature grows out of ordinary reality watched enough tragedy unfold from the politicians of Asia in 1997 to inspire a generation of Shakespeares. Impotent King Lears, Iagos whispering envies into hatreds, Lady Macbeths with blood on their hands, not to mention the marvelous comic relief of economic if-wishes-were-true thinking like "SMEs should build up the necessary capacities and capabilities to enhance the inter- and intra-industry linkages at domestic and regional levels and be able to competitively provide the required input to the larger industries in terms of parts and components as well as services" (Malaysia's International Trade and Industry Minister, Datuk Seri Rafidah Aziz).

But all the more tragic was that the criticism of Asia was brushed too broadly. What about the people who were doing it right but got caught in the middle, like Singapore? What about Stan Shih and the legion of young MBAs who realize he is far more important a role model for Asia than Bill Gates will ever be? What about the tiny SMEs quietly investing their profits in more modern equipment? What about those studious fingers jotting notes all through the management seminars who put their pens down at the beginning and end when the politicians dispense their self-flatteries? What about the invaluable market research being done at grassroots level by people who have never even been thought of by the mainstream press, like Singaporean fashion designer David Wang and Peter Teo who are showing how to restructure an entire industry on the basis of when people show up at the cash register?

Hence the better issue is what went right in '97 and what can be done to shift out of the mind-set of what went wrong. The physical world turned out to be more complex than Darwin's theory of blind selective forces; the economic world, too, is more complex than the blindness of the marketplace. We need to look at the market economy as operating software for the much more fundamental machine language of cultural economy. If any place in the world is prepared to address the issue of the cultureplace being greater than the marketplace, it is the myriad culture world of Asia.

DUE DILIGENCE

Certain economic sectors and their downstream consumer markets will benefit considerably from the lessons of '97. What are they?

The most immediate is likely to be the market for information as fact rather than information as pattern. One of the key faults of business practice in Asia was the failure to get the right information to the right people at the right time—the failure of fact recognition, in other words. An exacerbating factor was failure to respond to the reality of information when it did get there—pattern recognition, in other words.

The Asian information market in general, and the ways to which the Internet can be used to satisfy that market, are underappreciated by Asian businesses at large (though very much appreciated at the level of international research organizations like Forrester and IDG, and consulting firms like McKinsey and Arthur Andersen).

One example is the consumer information market. Asian businesses tend to ignore consumers and their needs: they are the last link in the food chain. Now it is becoming apparent to many Asian businesses that one of the more interesting things about Western economies is their emphasis on spending rather than saving as a wealth-accumulator. Marketing information to consumers, and learning how to respond to consumer intake of that information, are looming as very important business needs—needs with which Asians have little experience.

Other examples are culture-sensitive niche markets, information design and presentation, the high value Asians place on infotainment, and information targeting "Asian values" (the historical values of order, cleanliness, respect, responsibility, and emotional control; not the political ones of autocracy, denial, and cronyism). The markets for services associated with these historical values are poorly appreciated both in Asia and abroad.

On the other side of the world, most non-Asians don't how to deal with the Asian philosophy of information. What information is and what it is supposed to do are seen through the lenses of entirely different logical structures than deduction and induction. Some of these are additive reality (*vaisheshika*), conditioned origination (*paticca sammappada*), and fractional gradation (*'Ilm al-Balagha*). To newcomers accustomed to the West's logics of duality (right/wrong, good/bad, plus/minus, and so on), Asia's logics of gradation and coloration are like trying to make the conceptual transition from algebra to network theory. A neophyte information technology (IT) manager can fritter away a lot of time courting a non-decision-maker because he or she is dealing unwittingly with an organizational structure devoted to blockage rather than productivity. A few examples are:

- fear of fact
- face
- decision-trees and power mechanics in Chinese, Malay, and Indian-owned organizations
- the fault lines in Government, Inc., and family corporate structures
- the role played by eldest sons in family businesses

The 1997 crisis demonstrated that these blockages have to change if businesses are to prosper in the Internet era. But how to do that? The fact that foreigners don't completely understand the underlying cultural causes of these practices is not much help. Hence this book deals with several unfamiliar themes:

- Asia's information sociologies
- How information markets can be satisfied
- Restructuring delivery systems to fit value chains, not the other way around
- Building a business plan for an Asian informational enterprise

This not made very easy by the fact that the physical size of the information market is difficult to quantify. There are too few comprehensive books that deal with the subject and too many websites that are little more than gossip mills. In terms of institutions, Asia's information markets, in likely order of size, are:

- Large-enterprise businesses in Asia and abroad,
- SME business owners,
- Designers who need to package and market products and services,
- Government officials in IT-related bureaus,
- Organization and management functionaries,
- Universities and polytechs.

The key feature of the first three of these is that they largely think of fact in terms of design; and the key feature of the latter three is that they think of fact in terms of control.

Other issues include:

- Southeast Asia's response to a prosperous decade abruptly ending with an economic catastrophe is likely to shape economic and political thinking in the region for quite some time. One response is likely to be economic redefinition along cultural lines. People pay lip service to terms like "global economy" but in reality they think family. Information technology in the hands of future governments and businesses will either lay the seeds for repeat performances of '97 or devise preemptive solutions to them. This book adopts the view that information technology will provide a previously underutilized avenue for fact delivery that the region's people will respond to.
- The precise role the information marketplace is expected to play in economies, aside from generating investment income in hardware and software, is not particularly well un-

derstood. Business communities have responded well to IT as an infrastructural investment but have not much risen to the bait of constructive, original content. Most of the interest in content has come from Japan and the Western countries who see Asia's informational market largely in end-user terms—a market for consumer electronics and computer products or things like video games, electronic encyclopedias, and self-improvement syllabuses. The market for information is evident but unfocused. How information is to be produced, communicated, processed, and digested are all subjects many Asian business people have not thought through particularly well. The subject of Asia's niche cultures needs the same kind of analytic attention that is usually reserved for the demographics of middle-class markets. Many still think information is great for determining the faults of competitors but decisions are still best made by hunches and the gossip of contacts. There is relatively little consideration being given to replacing intuitive decision making with factual decision making.

- Despite all the theories attached to megaproject business development in this region, the plain practical fact is that the businesses in most need of relevant information technology are fairly ordinary SMEs. Only Singapore really seems to have a handle on this fact and this book will take a close look at its National Computer Board as an example of how public sector information technocracy can structure information systems of very high value for the private sector.

- Info-entrepreneurialism is likely to inspire financing and management vehicles—in particular entrepreneurial cluster enterprises of the Stan Shih and Cisco Systems type—which will have an important effect on the way business is done in the future. Much of the innovation in this area is emanating from unexpected quarters like the state government of Andhra Pradesh and the architecture of rural reform devised by the government of Sarawak in Malaysia. Readers need to know why these local method systems are so attractive to constituents and how they can be translated elsewhere.

- Many Western business people do not realize how important it is for informational services to take into account primordial imagery and symbolic relationships. A Western image package that uses Western image ideas comes across the way a software manual translated in Taiwan comes across to a Westerner: the words are correct, but the arrangement looks silly. Westerners don't know that Asian aesthetic systems differ considerably from Western. By translating the fundamental structures of the way Asians think into terms of visual content, aesthetics are in effect turned into thought. In Asia, thought often is aesthetics. Successful info content must appeal to Asians on the cultural as well as the fact level. Asian philosophies about natural harmony in the placement of things—*feng shui* (Chinese geomancy) and the use of empty space, for example—hint that design is as important as content. In Chinese, there is no clear distinction between a verb and a noun; you don't have a rock, you have a rocking. If this seems abstruse, consider it as object technology in which a fact and the instructions for what to do with the fact are contained in the same package.

- Another significant issue is what managerial, political, and financial pitfalls the private investor faces when learning to work with governments with a history of disinformation and denial on economically sensitive matters. Who will be held responsible if information a government considers socially undesirable gets out over a network by accident or design? The simplest case is an incompetent or disgruntled employee flooding a database for children with porn. The worst case is a company employee making on-line criticisms of a host government. More complex—and perilous—is the case of a small group of citizens disliking certain information and penalizing the deliverer rather than the originator. The Murray Hiebert case in Malaysia, discussed later in the book, is an example of what can happen when one person doesn't like what is disseminated over a public medium.

- Finally there is the issue of pricing. IT must become much cheaper and easier to use if Asia's Information Age is to realize its full potential. Universal Internet access isn't economically possible with current technology. Hardware costs that are modest by Western standards are all but insurmountable for vast portions of Asia's populaces. Personal computers are much too complicated for the mass market of middle-class Asia. Blandishments like "a fall in PC prices is spreading the market to new buyers" and "manufacturers could make the Net easier to use" have not translated into very much market research on what Asians actually want. The single great task for IT investors isn't how to make IT technically wondrous, it is how to make IT cheap.

Whatever the shortcomings of individual governments and privileged interests may have been in the past, this isn't the past any more. Asia's people share four common values at the grassroots level that are essential to long-term growth—work, saving, forbearance, and consumption based upon need. Ironically, it is these "Asian values" that were so completely turned inside out by some of the region's political leaders that they came out as indulgence, impatience, privilege, and waste. It is these same grassroots values that are likely to raise the quality of Asian productivity to more meaningful levels. More information, not more capital, is the best thing that could happen to Asia.

3
The Changing Nature of Asia's Capitalisms

A good deal of misunderstanding about the meaning of Asia's 1997 economic crisis derived from the fact that there is no one single form of capitalism in Asia but rather a broad sweep of enterprise-based economic structures that go by the name of "capitalism."

When most people speak about Asian capitalism they assume there is only one sort: that pioneered by Japan. Among its characteristics are heavy reliance on upwardly delegated decision making, economic direction from bureaucrats and banks, opacity, protective cross-holdings between corporations, a weak sense for entrepreneurialism, consensus management, the primacy of exports over consumers, and the value-added ladder system of regional development which exports lower-technology manufacturing to cheap-land, cheap-labor markets offshore.

Business people familiar with the region know there are considerable variations within this broad system. The strategies of China, for example, more resemble those followed in Southeast Asia than the Northeast Asian model of Japan and South Korea. Singapore and Taiwan vary considerably from the Japan model.

Indeed, there are three broad ways in which Asia's capitalisms differ.

- Some are much more open to foreign direct investment.
- Some are much less prone to try to second-guess the markets through government-directed industrial policies.
- Some have been much quicker to allow financial markets to develop.

The distinction is clearest over East and Southeast Asian attitudes toward foreign direct investment. The Japanese and the South Koreans were determined to build up national champions. They made it difficult for foreign-owned companies to set up shop. The Tigers of Southeast Asia, on the other hand, built their booms by welcoming foreigners. Singapore, which practically invented this strategy, now has an economy dominated by multinationals. The export industries of Thailand and Malaysia vary from the Singaporean approach by relying heavily on foreign firms but insisting on large equity holdings by local partners.

The distinction between East and Southeast Asia is more blurred when it comes to industrial policy. There is much admiration for the Japanese and South Korean governments' effective sponsorship of steel, shipbuilding, and other heavy industries. Both Indonesia and Malaysia have tried nurturing winners with protective tariffs, in aerospace and cars respectively. Yet Indonesia's determinedly orthodox group of economists who concentrated on macroeconomic stability and opposed subsidies did not prevail in the face of cultural rather than economic bases of action.

Asian countries approached the relationship between technology investment and development in quite different ways. Korea relied on its thirty-odd *chaebol* families to fund R&D via their corporations. Being disinclined to court foreign investment which would dilute their own holdings, their strategy was to invest in homegrown technology and improve on existing designs. The result was Korea's strength in heavy industry and industrial monopolies, shedding labor-intensive low-tech operations offshore and imposing tight import policies.

Hong Kong and Singapore avidly courted foreign technology by hosting foreign investment. Hong Kong tended to leave the mechanism to the free market while the Singapore government closely shepherded the process. The chief factor they have in common is that both encouraged businesses to value-add from outside sources. The fact that they encouraged in quite different ways appears to have made little difference.

Taiwan was the most liberal of all—on the one hand courting the wealth of knowledge in its expatriates working in places like Silicon Valley, and on the other by funding R&D parks like Hsin Chu to do research for anyone who commissioned it. Taiwan's development paradigm is a plethora of small and medium enterprises (SMEs) given a very free hand to value-add with little government oversight.

Until 1997 the general assumption was that if India and China were to manage the kind of economic miracles achieved in other parts of Asia, they seemed likely to do it the Southeast Asian way. Both countries set out to court foreign direct investment. India got into the game much later, yet even its nominally Communist politicians are now eagerly scouting the world for foreign investors. Both countries still have large state sectors. But both now see their nationalized industries primarily as a burden that must be reformed before there can be any fulcrum for economic strategy. Finally, both India and China, like the Southeast Asians, have encouraged companies to raise capital through their stock markets.

A factor common to all of these, despite their diverse manifestations, was reliance on home-market information sources. This led economies as diverse as South Korea and Singapore to build more computer chip plants ("fab labs") when it was obvious to others that the market was becoming glutted with them. Whether the problem was overcapacity, debt financing, sectorial bubbles, or top-down management thinking, lack of information was the thread that strangled Asia.

SOUTHEAST ASIA'S IMPLOSION

For more than a century Southeast Asia's economy was based on exporting primary products, mainly rubber, tin, palm oil, petroleum, and timber. These are still the single most reliable income foundation on which much of Southeast Asia's complex economic superstructure rests. From the 1960s onward, a processing economy came to overlie this primary economy. It was built using the value-added ladder model (VAL) in which each step further up the technological ladder resulted in shedding the technology levels of lower rungs to less developed regions. The so-called "Tiger" economies of Malaysia, Thailand, and Indonesia climbed four rungs on their VAL: import-substitution in the 1960s, labor pool for foreign-owned manufacturers in the 1970s, government-led industrial development in the 1980s, and in the 1990s, export-led growth.

Though growth rates varied from country to country and from sector to sector, and blipped up and down due to transient phenomena like the 1985 Plaza Accords[1] and the perennial boom-and-bust cycle of the semiconductor industry, the Southeast Asian economies as a whole were characterized from about 1980 through mid-1997 by high growth, high productivity, and high employment.

Southeast Asian businesses evolved a variety of corporate architectures in response to their differing types of broad economic development—family-owned conglomerates of opportunity, wholly owned offshore subsidiaries for capital transfers, privatized government enterprises, "build-operate-own/build-operate-transfer" (BOO-BOT) task-specific conduits for foreign direct investment, divested former subsidiaries, entrepreneur-driven single-service businesses, ethnic exceptionalism, Government, Inc., cronyocracies, and so on.

The common factors bridging these were: (a) they were averse to risk; (b) they relied on opacity; and (c) they were managed by authoritarian methods. Their success was based largely on carving out market share and cartels rather than creating new products and consumers.

One lesson Asians learned from 1997 was that focusing on security is no more reliable than focusing on risk. Another was that, while just about everybody makes mistakes, denial produces more severe mistakes. This has left them with a quandary: how can they shift from the present potpourri of systems that don't work to systems that do work but which make assumptions that impose a different decision culture?

SPURIOUS AND REAL CAUSES OF THE 1997 COLLAPSE

Between July and December 1997, Southeast Asia watched as speculative attacks pushed their currencies down by as much as 80 percent and their stock markets down 60 percent and more. Exports became more competitive, but the cost of energy, equipment, and components went up. Higher prices and weaker domestic demand forced Asian countries to cut their imports. The darlings of international investors were rocked by slow growth, plunging stock markets, and bankruptcies.

What shocked Asian government officials was that their economic predictions had been so rosy. For years, their high interest rates and cheap facilities were a magnet for foreign investors. Nobody worried much about foreign exchange fluctuations because Southeast Asian economies pegged their currencies to the dollar. They believed they were following proper economic rules—and to a degree, they were. Unfortunately, they were rewriting these rules to suit themselves as they went and not telling anyone.

The large currency inflows financed rapid growth. Many companies took on huge debt loads, believing the economy would keep growing perpetually. Too much money went to cronies of those in power and into unproductive real estate speculation (the so-called "conspicuous construction" phenomenon). It never dawned on people that golf courses—those icons of upper-crust contentment—could be as symbolically damaging to economies as they were factually damaging to environments.

Worse, like most people impressed with a unexpected success, they began to listen mainly to themselves. Taxi drivers in Jakarta and Kuala Lumpur were pointing out the five-star hotels with only a third or a quarter of the room lights on at 9 P.M. and were predicting a downturn two years before it happened. Bellboys and waitresses counting tips began to complain along the same lines a year later. But those were the likes of taxi drivers, not trained economists, even if they did know about all those dark hotel room lights at nine in the evening. Nobody paid much attention to what should have been raised as huge warning signs: China's devaluation of the yuan in 1994, which suddenly made China's exports much cheaper just as the country's economic czars were facing up to the reconstructing of their dismal state-owned sector by turning all those spare employees into producers of exportable products.

The region's growth began to slip on more formal economic charts sometime between the forecasts of the taxi drivers and those of the bellhops. Economists pointed to inefficient plants in Indonesia, the horrendous productivity figures and job hopping by Malaysia's labor force, the enormous amounts of money siphoned out of economies to finance politicians' luxury ranches in Australia and yachts in Europe, and Korea's plans to build many more fab labs just as international demand for electronics was weakening. Yet these dissemblings merely masked more fundamental systemic problems. Malaysia, for example, added just 15 percent of the value of the semiconductors it assembled to imported parts, while the cost of labor was rising three times faster than productivity. All the talk about the importance of SMEs produced excruciatingly little investment in them.

By mid-1996 articles in the international press were pointing out—complete with tables and statistics—that looming overinvestment in already clotted industries like steel, ships, fab labs, and television tubes would induce overproduction and underconsumption by 1998, just at the point when a glut of office space would arrive.

All this was raw information. Information is supposed to prevent, or at least help predict, disasters. This information was predicting an exports-market contraction in Thailand by mid-1996 and a crisis from South Korea's overborrowing sometime in 1997–1998.

The consequences of failing to heed information are almost as spectacular as failing to heed history. In Thailand, banks, speculators, and currency holders sold their holdings to buy the dollars needed to pay their debts. Thailand's central bank was forced to release its peg. The bhat promptly sank. Speculators attacked other Asian currencies, forcing them to depreciate as well. Despite Prime Minister Mahathir's anguished howls, the fact was that local business owners contributed more to the dollar-buying and stock-selling frenzy than internationals.

Most Asian economists couldn't believe this was happening. They had put their faith in the notion that unshakable growth was the inevitable result of high rates of investment, cheap natural resources and labor, absorbing the latest technologies, and government planning to insure against the turmoil of the marketplace.

What, they asked, went wrong?

The standard reply is that the larger their governments' presence in private investment, the more their economies became driven by rent-seeking, rewards from government privilege, and protection from competition. People found that success depended more and more on access to government than on efficient market behavior. This meant, in part, ignoring valuable markets such as consumer goods and education. Malaysia, Indonesia, and Thailand in particular were prime examples of what happens when governments confuse rent-seeking with capitalism. Singapore and Taiwan are example of what happens when they don't.

All this has been oft-said before, and indeed is quite true—as far as it goes. It just doesn't go very far. There were much deeper causes to the Asian bubble bath—the causes of the causes, as it were. Let us begin with the systemic cultural causes and work down the chain of economy to the day-to-day business causes.

ASIAN PATRICIATES

For thirty years Southeast Asia prospered under a patriciate model of social contract.

In business the patriciate took the agglomerative form, in which a small, sometimes family-based and other times colleague-based, nucleus of decision makers assembled many businesses under one umbrella held by a sole decision maker. The success potential of any particular venture was judged by the sole criterion of whether it was profitable. Although predominant all over Asia, this type of business was most extreme in the Korean *chaebols* and India's industrial empires, and endemic throughout Southeast Asia.

Politically, the patriciate took the exclusionary elitist form in which small groups of leaders called nearly all the economic shots, manipulating electoral processes and the media to remain in power. One marked quality among them was the low level of free information flow they tolerated among their peoples. This type of patriciate was the most extreme in Malaysia and Indonesia, and the least evident in Singapore.

Both forms relied on denial, secrecy, ignorance, intimidation, grandiosity, masks, and facades. The more freedoms and market economics they bypassed, the more successful they appeared.

This type of social contract linked small elites with modest middle classes. They rewarded each other with, respectively, unchallenged fealty in exchange for job-for-life contentments. The losers in the system were (a) workers, who were turned into nonentities by their illegal immigrant status or by co-opting unions allied with political parties, and (b) small and medium enterprise owners, who were squeezed out of the credit market by the agglomerates' business expansion on one hand and real estate developers on the other.

These systems had a common flaw: overextended economies could continue to grow only by further overextension. When that flaw cracked from an unforeseen stress in the international economy—a trivial thing, really, of computer demand dropping in the United States in late 1995—the weaknesses of the system were bundled into a basket and abandoned on the doorstep of the International Monetary Fund (IMF), leaving the patricians largely in place.

The 1997 crisis unmasked the myth that the Asian patriciate superseded the checks and balances that traditionally exist between governments and business. Top-down authoritarian businesses bought profits—and time—for themselves by keeping labor artificially cheap and, in the case of Malaysia and Thailand, by importing and exploiting it in massive quantities. The nature of the agglomerative patriciate was to rely on ever larger flows of capital to cover ever larger investments, ignoring the fact that too many of the investments were inefficient, were uncompetitive without artificial barriers, pursued declining markets, or faced tough competition from unexpected quarters, such as a suddenly competitive China. Cronycrat governments reinforced high growth rates by eliminating public needs like social spending, civil infrastructure like decent public transport, and environmental protection.

Today the global financial markets have all but shut off the money spigot to many Asian countries. People wonder if the patriciate decisional ideal—that dictum better promotes national development than debate—has had its day.

Information technology has major implications for the structures of Asian societies. To play the devil's advocate and address the most obvious flaw first: "If information is so useful, why didn't it work when Asians were told well ahead of time their system was about to founder?"

Westerners tend to equate freedom of information with foresight. Asians tend to equate freedom of information with uncertainty. The 1997 crisis has thus far only reinforced their respective attitudes. Southeast Asian government efforts to create an Asia-only financial bailout fund that avoided the strict accountability of the IMF only reinforced the Western investment world's conviction that many of the region's government leaders were still not listening to the global investment community. These leaders did not get the message that security comes from knowledge, not secrecy.

NOTE

1. An agreement reached at the Plaza Hotel in Bangkok in 1995 to devalue the yen led to Southeast Asian exports being more costly than Japanese, which in turn prompted a recession in Southeast Asia from 1967 to 1987.

4
Three Critiques of Asian Capitalism

The 1997 bubble bath was a long time coming and a long time forewarned. The complaints leveled at the state of Southeast Asian business practices in 1997 generally concede that while the region's success was admirable, using other methods to achieve it might have made the success more durable. Most of the criticisms about the events of 1997 were that these economies had tripped on themselves, not that they had been walking in the wrong direction. In particular, several aberrations evolved out of the 1987–1997 easy-money era:

- The best way to be successful is to make the same products that have been successful over the last five years.
- There is no difference between opportunity and opportunism.
- If you overinvest, more money is all you need to bail yourself out.
- Monopolies and racial-preference policies are secure because of their guaranteed market base.
- Government, Inc. is a brilliant new idea.
- Political leaders who pay attention to social unity don't need to pay attention to management skills.

THE YOSHIHARA THEORY

In *The Rise of Ersatz Capitalism in Southeast Asia*, published in Manila in 1988, Kunio Yoshihara put forward the first important critique of Asia's industrialization. Yoshihara called the systems of Thailand, Indonesia, Malaysia, and other nations "ersatz capitalism." They were being propelled, shaped, and changed in many ways by forces far beyond their control. As a result, they were growing but not developing. Cities were spreading, factories were producing, GNP figures were impressive. Yet these economies did not seem clearly to be "developing" in the sense of gaining new leverage and strength in the world. Modernization was not doing for them what it had done for the West—increase their ability to control or steer the economic activity going on around them. Yoshihara attributed this to three factors.

Dependence on Foreign Technology

The technology employed in Southeast Asian manufacturing, be it vehicles or consumer electronics, was provided almost wholly by foreign parent companies. Little or no industrial research took place locally.

Yoshihara attributed this to the trader origins of most of the region's industrial leaders, resulting in little interest at top corporate levels in technical training or technical research. The top-down nature of management implementation translated to very low levels of technical competence at the shop floor level. Technical illiteracy was reinforced by low levels of investment in science and technology training in schools. Southeast Asian economies were thus unable to devise their own forms of industrial technology, locally efficient manufacturing processes, or the creation of culturally relevant products. Japan had amply shown that all these were essential to a strong export identity in world markets.

This is still true. Industry in Southeast Asia depends almost entirely on foreign technology to initiate and to upgrade its processes and products. Prime Minister Mahathir inadvertently revealed the core problem in a July 1997 speech in which he said, "A few years ago we were building the housings for gearboxes. Today we are building what goes inside."

What Mahathir did not grasp is that it makes little difference what goes inside the gearbox. If you do not design it, you do not create the product that requires the gearbox, or you do not envision the market for such a product. Filling a gearbox with parts is impressive until you realize there is no end of R&D departments devising different means of power conversion than gears. Mahathir's proud observation is a vivid example of the destructive delusions in holding onto yesterday's mind-set.

Preference for Speculation

Yoshihara further pointed out that many Southeast Asian business leaders were more interested in speculative ventures promising quick and high returns than in creating well-managed industrial empires. They were not interested in money that takes time and requires hard work. Hence Southeast Asia blossomed with buildings—especially developments that could be made to look impressive. While the Japanese, Koreans, British, and Americans built factories for production, many Southeast Asians invested in five-star hotels, malls, office complexes, stock exchanges, and condominiums.

Government, Inc.

Most important, Southeast Asian capitalists focused on business ventures whose existence, and often profitability, rested on government intervention. Manufacturing got their attention when governments devised high tariffs or restrictive quotas. Business titans imitated the monopoly mentality of their hawker-stall forebears; they wanted their governments to bequeath to them exclusive distributorships, import monopolies, extraction concessions, sole licenses, low interest loans, and private variances on public regulations.

Business people were convinced that privilege guaranteed commercial security and protection against competition. The immediate result was more time spent building connections than building businesses. Politicians, bureaucrats, and generals were amply rewarded by the business people who prospered from their interventions. The result was a codependency relationship between business leaders and state managers. Among the well-known consequences of dependency relationships are denial, resentment, fear, exclusionism, withdrawal symptoms, and a pronounced desire for more of the same.

Yoshihara's term for security alliances between states and business interests was "rent-seekers." The term has been defined and redefined in several ways, but what it boils down to in reality is: "Rent is what's left after the payoffs." The less direct reality is that profits come to be delinked from production.

Why did rent-seeking become such a prominent feature in Southeast Asia? Why did the region's business leaders turn to monopoly alliances with the state rather than trying to build efficient industries? Compare the thinking of Malays, for example, with the Gujarati industrial titans of India. Both seek state protection. Yet in India nearly everyone wants to start a production enterprise; in Malaysia, few do. Why are so many Southeast Asian politicians, government officials, and military officers such eager devotees of skimming rather than making?

In contrast the region's Chinese, reflecting their strong thread to the Confucian ideal, placed high value on the moral image of being an official. Leadership and integrity were inseparable. The result is that Singapore is the most competitive and one of the least corrupt countries in the world.

Yoshihara noted the insecurity felt by many Southeast Asian capitalists, notably in Malaysia and Indonesia, in the face of Chinese dynamism. Often it more resembled fear of inadequacy than insecurity. The result was discriminatory policies founded on unanalyzed—and probably deeply sublimated—anxiety. The Chinese responded, ironically enough, with the same solution to the same fears. The result was that most of the economic attention in Southeast Asia's economies came to be focused on short-term or speculative ventures that promised quick, safe returns. Both shunned long-term commitments. Malays tended to seek their advantage by protective alliances with the state. The Chinese turned to family-based enterprises and *guanxi* (non-family networking based on ancient identity ties such as having originated from the same clan, village, or district). Malays who did well at it tended to expatriate their money to luxury lifestyle ranches in Australia and homes in Europe. The Chinese tended to expatriate it into investment ventures in Canada and the United States.

Singapore took exactly the opposite tack: long-term thinking has been part of the island-state's strategy from its earliest days. One example appeared in the seminal September 1994 Singapore Computer Society document, *Information Technology*. This master plan spelled out the most comprehensive theoretical model for a National Information Infrastructure (NII) that appears to have been inaugurated by any government anywhere. *Information Technology* was in essence the how-to manual on building a national multimedia network. It stood in sharp contrast to the multitude of other planning documents of its type produced all over the world in that a sizable portion of it was devoted to devising a system that would work just as well in the year 2025.

Yoshihara attributed the marked predominance of rent-seeking in Southeast Asia to political authoritarianism. In an authoritarian system there is little or no constraint on government allocations of national resources for private exploitation. Nor is there a limit to state intervention in the economy.

Southeast Asian governments had quite substantial resources at their disposal. Some of it was natural—petroleum, rubber, extractable minerals, timber, climate, sea lane confluences. The tycoons who built these into powerful industries are now the Old Guard. Much of their thinking dominates the attention of governments today.

But Southeast Asia's most important cheap resource was human—a massive and poorly educated rural labor force that could be shunted from project to project pretty much at will, yet could be relied on to return quietly home at the first whiff of economic adversity. Malaysia's infrastructural prowess was built not so much with Malaysian labor as with 1.7 million Indonesians, Bangladeshis, Burmese, and Thais—about half of whom were illegals working under conditions of extreme vulnerability.

Yoshihara's argument was that from the viewpoint of aspiring capitalists in authoritarian countries, rent-seeking was an appropriate strategy. He never explained why Singapore, undeniably authoritarian, turned to production and investment capitalism, and why, even back in 1988, Singapore was so corruption-free and competitive.

For the rest of Southeast Asia, much of what passes for economic achievement was, for Yoshihara, ersatz capitalism—a fake form of money manipulation that paid just enough lip service to capitalist phraseology to attract international investment. The reality was better articulated by an executive of a major oil company to this writer in late 1996: "Without cheap labor, Malaysia would cease to attract. There's no other reason to come here."

Because Southeast Asia's capitalists refused to independently develop the indigenous industrial technology essential for a strong export capability, they locked their economies into being client states for technologically advanced countries seeking cheap manufacturing bases. In practice this meant Japan. As rent-seekers they showed little interest in building efficient, internationally competitive industries, but rather hid their inefficiencies behind tariff barriers, preferential loans, and monopoly concessions, each secured through deals with state managers. The Japanese saw this system for what it was and responded by transferring as little competitive technology as possible and turning countries like Malaysia into client economies that economically resembled British Malaya. The Malaysians were so happy with Japanese investment capital that they turned a blind eye to the ironies of the relationship.

YOSHIHARA'S CRITICS

Anything as politically fulminous as the Yoshihara theory is sure to attract critics. Surprisingly, these did not come from Southeast Asia, which might have been expected to see some vested interest in attending to Yoshihara's views. The criticisms came largely from the West. They summarize to this: the behavior of a business person anywhere is determined as much by cultural conditions as economic ones. Business people will reflect the options and constraints within which they operate. Cultural conditions include class power, political history, psychological response, a sense of ancestor bonds, and the way men and women are permitted to interact with each other. Political and economic circumstances can mandate that capitalists indulge in rent-seeking and that state managers collude with them. This is a cultural fact not just of Southeast Asia but many parts of the world.

This criticism was largely directed at history; it asserts that the past has too much power over the present. As times change so do the ambitions and actions of businessmen, politicians, and bureaucrats. Yoshihara neglected the capacity for future change. In at least some parts of Southeast Asia, the region's industrial capitalism is clearly future-forward in its thinking. As Mr. Saw Ken Wye, Assistant Chief Executive (Industry) of Singapore's National Computer Board (NCB) puts it:

Silicon Valley evolved the way it did because it was located near an educational institution with a high number of brilliant innovators who did not think economically. In Singapore we see the same pattern, but it is not in close proximity to a freewheeling educational institution. What is achieving the critical mass here is not just the capital and the product and an economic mechanism, but the people. We cannot engineer the people, but we can engineer the environment.

The first and most fundamental is IT literacy—as close to 100 percent IT literacy as we can achieve. Well then, which level of the population will make the most impact? The young. Once the young become IT literate, there will be a crossover effect attracting the parents, grandparents, then the elder brothers and sisters. Indeed, after the young, we look next to the thirty-five-year-olds.

The second is making companies IT literate. How do you do that? One way is via the government interface—if government bureaus start demanding electronic in lieu of paper transactions with private companies. The second is to offer incentives which get businesses to see the benefits of investing in IT technology. The third is to maintain the fundamentals of free flow of capital, free flow of people, provide a good telecommunications infrastructure, make sure there is good business confidence on what the government is doing for them.

From this basis of confidence, the government can then encourage the building of truly innovative business applications without doing the job itself—that's business's traditional role. We believe that after some time, this will become a new model for economic development that will be just as effective as Silicon Valley was.

It is hard to imagine a more succinct antidote to the melancholy observations of Kunio Yoshihara. In all due regard, he was reporting what he saw, long before people like Saw Ken Wye were in their positions. Yoshihara's theory might not have arisen if there were more Saw Ken Wyes.

Ironically the most energetic response to Yoshihara's views came not from Southeast Asia (which studiously ignored him), but Massachusetts Institute of Technology (MIT) economics professor Paul Krugman.

KRUGMAN'S PERSPIRATION THEORY

Dr. Krugman drew somewhat different conclusions about Southeast Asia's clubby capitalism. He noted the differences between 1997 in Southeast Asia and Latin America's 1995 wave of financial jitters after the devaluation of the Mexican peso: higher interest costs because international markets feared further devaluations, lower export prices because the devaluations intensified competition between national economies, reduced capital inflows as foreign investors became wary, and growth slowdowns. Were these the end of the Asian miracle?

Krugman's reply was succinct: There wasn't much of a miracle in the first place.

Krugman cited some overlooked (but now widely quoted) research by Alwyn Young of Boston University and Larry Lau of Stanford which demonstrated that Asian growth, impressive though it appeared, was largely a mask. It was painted with high domestic savings and the movement of uneducated but hardworking rural peasants into the urban labor market. Young and Lau concluded that Asian growth was more perspiration than inspiration—like the horse in Orwell's *Animal Farm*, Southeast Asia worked hard, not smart.

Asia apologists often point to the way Asian governments direct their growth by selecting and promoting specific industries, technologies, and managers. Singapore is a good example of what can happen when this approach works well. But Singapore is a meritocracy, not a cronyocracy. Did government-directed rather than market-directed industrialization truly explain the Asian economies' soaring productivity?

Krugman pointed out that production efficiency didn't soar the same way production volume did. In fact, Malaysian and Indonesian factories had the most inefficient labor forces in the region. Job-hopping was common. Line-work output rates were dismal considering the number of hands involved. What made these two countries attractive was cheap land, cheap construction, cheap management, and cheap workers. Asian industrial policies seemed a lot less inspired when productivity was analyzed.

An important (and unwelcome) implication of Krugman's view was that the pace of Asia's growth would sooner or later slow. The two main measures introduced in the 1980s—increasing labor force participation and tripling the investment share of GDP—are changes you can't do twice. When their effects peak, what then?

Krugman suggested Asia's growth would slow down more quickly in places like Malaysia, which was investing 40 percent of its GDP, and Singapore, which was investing 50 percent. Slowdown would come later in low-wage China which still had huge amounts of underemployed rural labor to exploit.

Such a thesis was sure to draw fire. It did. Singed by academic and politico blasts but definitely not shot down in flames by business readers, Krugman's prediction of slowdowns held up under repeated challenges until, sure enough, two years later Asia sank before Krugman did.

However, the causes had less to do with poor labor productivity than poor capital productivity. In Thailand, the financial bubble revealed poorly invested real estate projects and a misdirected banking system. In South Korea, *chaebol* bankruptcies highlighted the runaway debts of family corporate empires and the shakiness of the banks that continued to loan despite their debts. Stand-up comedians joked that the first long-term investment an Association of South-East Asian Nations (ASEAN) business owner made was a new Mercedes and the second was a new putter. There was too much tart truth in this jape for it to not be funny. International capital markets finally tired of policies around the region that ran trade deficits bigger relative to their economies than Mexico's was just before the peso collapse.

However, Krugman's thesis had predicted a slow loss of momentum, not a crash. Why did a crash occur, then? Was it all a plot by perfidious internationalists, as Malaysia's Prime Minister Mahathir claimed?

Hardly: much of the ringgit and rupiah dumping was done right there in Kuala Lumpur and Jakarta by locals who had borrowed in dollars. Yet the disaster was so bad that it turned out to be good. The size of the slump revealed systemic defects that were much murkier than cozy currency pegs and current account snafus papered over by a boom.

Japan was the most obvious case. Japan's potential output (the output it could produce on average over the span of a periodic business cycle) began declining in the mid-1980s, at a time when many economists had become convinced Japan's work and savings ethic combined with its *kieretsu* system of interlocking corporate ownership was the answer to the bust part of business cycles. However, Japan's long-term slide was masked by the real estate bubble of the late 1980s, as runaway stock and land prices pumped money into seemingly unstoppable valuations. By 1993 Japan had learned the hard way that capital growth is not the same as economic growth.

At this juncture much of Southeast Asia indulged in a classic case of ignoring the messenger. It was hard to find any article in any of the regional business magazines pointing out why Japan's bubble had burst. It was quite easy, on the other hand, to find articles patting locals on the back for how astute they were for seeing all these great real estate deals and the timber to be cut in the Losing Highlands and Gabon. Didn't their growth rates prove it? From Thailand to Indonesia investors went on a stock and real estate binge that almost comically mimicked Japan's, only six years later.

Very few Southeast Asians paid attention to the fact that wages were rising much faster than productivity. Overheated infrastructure borrowing and domestic credit were creating current account deficits far above GDP. To Krugman and other "perspiration" theorists, these troubles confirmed the view that diminishing returns bring a slowdown in growth.

To others the issue was informational: Why did so many otherwise intelligent people choose to ignore the evidence that Southeast Asia was duplicating Japan's error? The overextension problems of South Korea and Thailand were known to Asia *Wall Street Journal* readers and devotees of David Roche for a long time before they crescendoed to a crash. But their government officials, like their Japanese counterparts, denied the problem by ignoring the evidence. Malaysia's response was to blame everybody else, despite the evidence from Brazil that grand but unproductive new capital and dealing with trade deficits via import restrictions are an almost guaranteed way to end an economic miracle. Indonesia's idea of a farsighted industrial strategy was to promote an inefficient auto industry with special tax and regulatory breaks, and then hope easy loans from neighbors would bail everyone out. When it became obvious that IMF bailouts would impose tough terms, many in the region clamored for a local bailout fund.

The question posed by Young and Lau and by Paul Krugman was the same as the question posed by Yoshihara: "Does the form of growth matter?" Asia's growth will probably continue, driven, as before, by education, savings, and growing labor force participation. It probably won't be as fast as it was, since Southeast Asian economies have by now pushed savings, education, and labor participation as far as they can. But there are still a lot of peasants in China, and the value-added theory of regional growth has it that every time you reach a technological plateau you shed it to a poorer country and go on to the next plateau in your own country.

Many of Asia's 1997 troubles were not about economics. They were about information. Information, supposedly, is the antidote to disinformation. Yet how welcome is an information business likely to be in a country whose leader, like Prime Minister Mahathir, when he was asked in August 1997 what the government would do to prevent further erosion in his country's currency value, replied, "We will do what is best for the country and we don't have to tell everybody what we will do. Foreign journalists are not interested in our country anyway." When asked why his country continued to import heavy machinery despite its high current account deficit, the reply was, "They keep importing because they like the design." Questions from investment analysts whether his economy was heading towards a slump brought the reply, "These are people who want to see our country go under."

Bizarre statements by Prime Minister Mahathir are not unusual. It is the spin controller's duty to rush in with clarifications when a leader speaks his mind and demonstrates it to be rather on the empty side at the moment. But when business magazines present as fact the exact opposite of what is being said by the world economic and investment community, it is worrisome. One has to shake one's head and read a second time to fully grasp the naiveté of the following editorial from the 16 November 1997 issue of *Malaysian Business*:

Unconditional Assistance

The move by the Group of 15 (G-15) developing countries to come up with a draft set of rules to regulate currency trading is indeed unprecedented. This will undoubtedly be welcomed by all countries which support fair and equitable trade.

The task is challenging and timely, given the recent turmoil in the world stock markets due to reckless manipulation of the currencies of Southeast Asian nations.

It has made the rest of the world wake up to reality. Markets do not operate in isolation, neither are they independent of each other. Indeed, the link between currency and equity markets of Asian and Western markets is not too distant.

Unfortunately, manipulators seldom realize the folly of their ways. They will never give up, but can be controlled. More importantly, it takes political will by all countries concerned to stamp out this menace.

Thankfully, something is being done. It is sad that it has taken a major shake-up in the world's stock markets to nudge the West into action.

It is noteworthy that the United States, Japan and the International Monetary Fund (IMF) have agreed in principle to set up a new mechanism to help stabilize Asian financial markets. Reports say the mechanism will incorporate a Japanese-mooted idea to create a fund for financial crisis in Asia.

But comments by the United States' Deputy Secretary of State Strobe Talbott reveal that the US is not convinced of the need for an Asia Fund as it feels the IMF is the proper body to tackle such crises.

Talbott's comments are strange given that the US supports the moves to stabilize Asian financial markets. Won't the setting up of an Asia Fund complement the efforts of the IMF? And will it not lead to greater financial stability?

The North, the US in particular, should be more sincere in its offers of assistance to the South. Attaching terms and conditions only serve to contradict and confuse.

It is hard to imagine that this editorial was written in this decade, so perfectly does it describe the economic thinking of the last one.

THE MICHAEL PORTER CRITIQUE

Harvard Professor Michael Porter's criticisms of Southeast Asia are aimed mainly at business practices, not government and economic policies. He is perceived as dismissive of Asia by many Southeast Asians. One reason is that he can be witheringly blunt to people who interrelate in the minuet-like spirit of Sun Tzu, "Be so subtle that you are invisible; be so mysterious that you are intangible." A more immediate reason is that Porter is often right in such a way that his rightness gives little room for people to maneuver. Asian critics feel that Porter opines like someone who has spent a lot more time in the classroom in front of students than the boardroom in front of bosses.

Still, some of his criticisms have merit. Basically, he says, for twenty-five years, while opportunities in Southeast Asia have been enormous the perceived need for a future strategy has been minimal. Most Asian companies do not have strategies. They respond to opportunities; they do deals. They diversify widely because their opportunistic mode of operation drives them to acquire anything and everything that is high-yield. The result today is enormous agglomerative empires, despite all the evidence that shows smaller, more responsive businesses enjoy better long-term profitability.

Up to now the agglomerative approach has been seemingly successful. But while Southeast Asia was embracing world opportunity, it was not embracing world competitiveness. Southeast Asia's politically shielded, opportunistic, exploitative, and authoritarian way of doing business was in reality less effective and less profitable. Asia's large, opaque conglomerates failed to become more worldly and innovative. They were not able to sustain their income and profit growth in the face of more focused and competitive companies emerging even in their own region. In two years China has made more progress creating an exports market than Southeast Asians did in ten.

Three-quarters of Asian businessmen flattered themselves that within the next ten years most of the competitive companies in their industries would be Asian. Yet they could not identify the reasons why, how their company would do it, or which companies would be the ones that turn out most competitive.

Nor did many business people examine the historical patterns in the rise and decline of institutions. Corporations are institutions just like bureaucracies and governments, and they exhibit many of the same patterns.

Most Asian business people failed to analyze the relationship between causes of success and causes of decline. There is a line of thinking in management journal articles that when businesses succeed, they face rapid rises in wages, costs, rent, congestion, and government regulation. Yet how many of Asia's strategic business plans had contingency items for these factors? Did any Asian business ever factor contingent liability into its business plans?

Instead of upgrading to the next level of competitive sophistication, Southeast Asian businesses prefer to duplicate what they've done at home in nearby countries that are lower down the ladder. This so-called value-added ladder model of development is not sustainable. It chases after cheap productivity instead of superior productivity. Southeast Asian companies have long shown the typical symptoms of cheap productivity: too many employees late in and early out, too many people administering instead of producing, too many people job-hopping and too many people hiring without thinking to offer employees longevity-based stock options. Businesses have to regenerate themselves from within as well as from without.

Overconfidence led to overdiversification. The result was the corporate acquisition equivalent of children in a candy store. A company that wants to genuinely develop has to do it through product development and marketing. That implies strategic planning and investment, not reading the business news for tips on finding good opportunities.

Enormity of scale turned out to be of little value. Companies ended up firing many arrows in many directions but ignored building long-term competitive advantage. They did not think in terms of building enduring brands, developing enduring technologies, establishing enduring distribution channels, creating enduring customer bases.

A company's ability to move up to more sophisticated strategies depends partly on the environment in which it is operating. Asian managers may very well read the latest management books and attend management seminars, but if they don't allow more and more skilled people into the decision and planning process, they won't move to higher levels of quality and service.

The rules of competition are no different in Southeast Asia. The way Southeast Asian companies approach competition, however, is very different. The biggest single advantage they have is their sense of a time horizon, their long-term view. Where the West has created an incentive system based on near-term performance, Asian governments and companies have controlling stakes that can ignore short-term fluctuations. This can make them complacent, not analytical. When there are many opportunities it is hard to decide which one to pursue.

Southeast Asian companies must become more strategic and analytical. The quick-buck opportunities in natural resources, infrastructure building, and real estate are dwindling just as their societies are becoming more complex. Businesses will face more complex problems and more discord among their various subsidiaries as these subsidiaries attain market share and have to innovate to keep it.

Intuition works well in an acquisitive market, but a sophisticated market demands innovation, not intuition. Presently innovation is a hallmark of very few Southeast Asian businesses, and most of them are in Singapore.

SINGAPORE'S ANSWER TO PORTER

Porter's main point is that Southeast Asia's companies will continue to decline in competitiveness until they alter their present strategies. Many Asian countries are, as the Americans were in the 1960s and 1970s, getting behind on a learning curve. When that happens it is very hard to jump back on.

However, Singapore is addressing these issues in a manner that, if adapted by other Southeast Asian countries, would hurry their jump back onto the international economics learning curve. Michael Yap, of the National Computer Board, described the Singaporean approach thus:

We are essentially working in new territory here. Management structures that work in the area of information provision are a topic not much encountered in the professional journals as yet. We have to discover our own solutions. We are doing it partly by listening and partly by experiment.

Policies about how you do things are inevitably affected when you change the structure of the way you do things. We have set up a group which is geared to process reengineering in an environment in which, by the time a system is introduced, the environment changes beneath the system. We are very aware that the way we manage, and our organization [the National Computer Board] must have an evolutionary management system. Our goal is an ever more responsive organization.

In the area of electronic commerce [EC], for example, we are quite aware of the fact that EC is not just a sophisticated replica of physical commerce. Starting several years ago we began working with "need visioning." We examined the fact that EC is much more than a method of securing payments in exchange for goods. We realized we needed to re-look at the way processes themselves are done. We inaugurated a series of one-day workshops with Arthur Andersen in which companies would come in and relook at their traditional way of doing business in light of what EC offers them and how they could adapt their processes accordingly. For example, when you introduce a system that can do in minutes what once took days, the whole support structure changes. A significant consideration is to get everyone in the structure to agree on a new process. Then there is the question of how they can adapt to the new markets EC makes possible. Understanding the nature of change is actually more important than building a system.

WHEN INFORMATION FAILS, MARKETS FAIL

Where were the lessons from these various critiques as the 1997 economic crisis deepened? Where was the resolve to act on this type of information, not to mention the information from the markets? What happens when you ignore information that goes against your wishes?

As the grim wheels of late 1997 turned, declines on currency and stock markets left traders wondering when governments would do something. But as the markets tumbled, many Asian leaders ignored the measures they were being told would bolster international confidence. Prime Minister Mahathir did little beyond blaming bogeys. The Seoul newspapers read as if nothing was happening. A vicious cycle began: noninformation was cycling to misinformation, and misinformation was cycling to disinformation. The theories of ersatz capitalism and perspiration economies might be faulted for technical reasons such as selective evidence, but they are correct on the practical matter that frightened minds prefer not to tune in to the news.

Information economies tend to be predictive, not reactive; responsive, not dismissive. The exact opposite happened in Southeast Asia in 1997. Political leaders needed to make difficult, sometimes discomfiting, decisions to show that they understood the punitive face of capitalism. The region's governments had staked their political identity on delivering economic growth founded on other people's investments and labor. In the fat years when the ersatz appeared to be genuine, governments grew ignorant, politicians self-satisfied, cronies indolent, authoritarians ruthless to questions. Without a sensitivity to information, leaders responded to misinformation—much of it generated by themselves. In 1997, the political leaders didn't take firm action because they didn't know how. Hence the scramble for scapegoats and bailouts from Japan and similar face-saving fixes.

Why did Asia's leaders fail to administer the right medicine? From all accounts it wasn't a case of no hands on the tiller, it was a case of too many of them.

5

Reconstructing Asian Values

Ideas have a tendency to overshoot. Shifts in the perception of Southeast Asia demonstrate this. In the 1960s when America and Europe enjoyed high growth and strong economies, Western economists viewed Asia as doomed to inefficiency and stagnation. Gunnar Myrdal's *Asian Dilemma* was twenty-two hundred pages of almost unremitting gloom.

When the East Asian "Tigers" began spitting out the fastest spurt of growth in economic history, opinions switched to excessive optimism. Giddily extrapolating present growth to future growth, the belief grew that Asia would dominate the global economy within a few decades. "Asian century" and "Asian values" replaced the "Asian dilemma," cheerled by Asian politicians who were not loathe to have everyone believe all this was due to their extraordinary prescience.

Now, one very tumultuous bubble bath later, doomsayers are again composing the headlines. The 1997 events marked "the end of the Asian economic miracle." A good part of this, of course, was wishful thinking. Bad news about Asia is welcomed by workers and firms outside the region who believe that Asian dynamism threatens their jobs. The theory that Asia's miracle was built on massive capital spending and not productivity gains was as exaggerated as were earlier reactions to its success.

Contrary to all the talk about Southeast Asia's growth being founded on superior cultural virtues, its varied economies are now seen as no more immune to the ups and downs of economic cycle than those of developed economies. The kernel of truth most everyone ignores is that Asia's economies are simply too various and complex for any one theory to encompass them all. They share a number of strengths but have individual weaknesses of their own. Just as there was no single cause of their late 1990s difficulties, there is no single solution to their problems.

One generalization is possible, however. The Asian bubble bath was in good part informational. Secrecy was the origin of many problems, disinformation made them worse, and denial turned the worst cases into catastrophes. While nearly everyone except Singapore and Taiwan underwent painful periods of denial, the economies that responded ably and nimbly to information were the ones that pulled out the quickest. South Korea is the case study in using unpleasant information to advantage; Indonesia is the case study in using it badly.

The Asian countries that will succeed in the information era are those that unhesitatingly correct the malignancies that were concealed by their rapid growth. One is the tendency for government intervention in matters like directing cheap credit or tax incentives to selected industries. Another is relying on import barriers to protect domestic industries. A third is keeping financial systems primitive and inefficient by tight regulation. Still others are corruption, autocracy, and inadequate infrastructure. Over-regulation, inadequate competition, and capital-market rigidities choked growth in Indonesia, while South Korea's industrial power concentrated too much wealth in the hands of a few giant firms, making it all but impossible for the SME sector to thrive. Yet Indonesia persisted in holding on to the idea that family values are government values, while South Korea turned to the higher authority of market forces.

To these the private sector contributed its own inefficiencies, some noted by Porter above, others ignored by him. The "big three" were reliance on contacts over competence, autocracy masquerading as consensus, and rigidly hierarchical management structures. Companies approaching the equity market sought to list only a small portion of their equity, intending to keep as much as possible under family control. Temporarily unused capital went into property and shares speculation rather than interest-bearing accounts. Short-term finance was easier than long-term finance. Borrowers paid less attention to the business intricacies demanded by their financial sources than the size of the cash pool they made available. Lenders paid less attention to a business plan than the political connections of the people presenting it. Many businesses enthusiastically courted export orders from overseas but failed to organize themselves financially to fulfill them. Most businesses focused on short-term goals and gave low priority to strategic planning. The environment was simply forgotten.

These weaknesses mattered less in the early stages of development when Asian governments were more market friendly than other developing regions. It is important to remember that on many basic structural issues the Tiger economies got a sizable number of macroeconomic essentials right—high savings, relative openness to trade, investment in education, secure investor climates, and, with the exception of Malaysia, a predictable legal system. The Krugman argument that growth was the result of heavy capital spending made a point but missed another: Asia's Tigers imported the same basic technology as other developing economies, but they used it less efficiently.

The fortunes of millions of Asians depend on how their governments now rise to the challenge for change. Japan demonstrates the dangers of delaying structural reform, just as Argentina demonstrated it earlier in the decade. Economic success and a financial market boom allowed Japan to put off change. It is now paying the price.

The biggest challenge to the Asian economic miracle is not economic but cultural and political. Because of lobbying by the heads of protected industries, or because of their own unwillingness to see growth falter, governments may be tempted to act shortsightedly. In 1997 Malaysia hinted that import controls would curb its current-account deficit. That would have tackled a symptom, not the disease, which in Malaysia's case is racially based preferences that create self-victimizing inadequacy.

In contrast, Hong Kong, Singapore, and Taiwan have flexible labor markets, less government intervention, and small, nimble firms. Taiwan pushed ahead with deregulation so swiftly that its industrial policy is now more suited to fast changing international business conditions than any other Asian economy. Hong Kong and Singapore are already as rich in GDP (Gross Domestic Product) per capita as many G7 countries. It is important to remember that, in terms of Asia's histories, inventing new technology may be less important to economic diversification than being quick at adopting available technology across a broad range of sectors. With information and judgment, the "miracle" is far from over.

ASIAN ECONOMIES AND ASIAN VALUES

The debate over "Asian values" versus "Western values" will likely go on for a long time, gratifying those who take one or the other side of the perennial debate between Asian cooperative values and Western self-reliance, disturbing those who don't. What matters most, however, is how businesses devise strategies that reinforce economic growth and social stability at high levels for a long time. What are some of these business ideas?

Asian values advocates tend to favor:

- hard work
- encouragement of learning
- openness to new ideas
- self-discipline
- harmony
- orderly society
- management clarity
- interest in new technology
- long-term planning
- desire to create and produce new products

On close look it is hard to distinguish these from what Westerners like to call their list of values. How have Southeast Asians in particular translated the above general themes into concrete progress? The following business practices became widespread in Southeast Asia during the late 1980s and early 1990s:

- identifying distinctive long-term competitive positions;
- taking a direct, active role in national economic upgrading;
- building strategy around family structure as industry structure;
- establishing long-term regional and global alliances;
- diversifying away from fading competencies in natural resource exploitation;
- moving from deal making to strategic planning;
- raising operational efficiency to global standards;
- widening regional advantage via the value-added chain;
- gaining control of international distribution channels;
- establishing direct contacts with foreign customers.

Yet even these did not necessarily arise from the unique social and political conditions of Southeast Asia over the last few decades. Save for the last point, every one of them can be said to describe equally well several other highly energetic business cultures—for example, the rise of the Gangetic nation-state economies from the Maghadha and Vesali kingdoms of the sixth century B.C. to the time of Asoka in the third century B.C. They would also describe the shift from maritime trade-base to manufacture-and-property development that characterized the Venetian republic in the fifteenth and sixteenth centuries.

Hence there must be factors even more specific to today's Southeast Asian success. What might they be? Here are a few of them:

- the basic business models that have emerged in response to value-added-ladder economic development in the region;
- the way Southeast Asian business leaders might deal with the unpredictable autonomy that certain provincial leaderships are allocating to themselves in China and India;
- the effectiveness of cluster strategies in penetrating consumer markets (the term "cluster" refers to alliances by cross-border government/business entities to accomplish specific tasks);
- management of the inverting roles of export-production and import-consumption in middle-class consumer economies;
- cross-reinforcement of cultural values via culture-site investment;
- demonstration by Southeast Asia's Chinese cluster-strategy enterprises to mainland Chinese that there exists a market-economics alternative to the traditional role of *guanxi*;
- the growing desire to reinterpret international commercial law in terms of indigenous legal forms rather than the legal traditions of the European Enlightenment;
- the significance of *muafakat* (consensus) and *mesyuarat* (group sensibility) in management thinking;
- the need for damage control foresight in Southeast Asian businesses and governments to forestall situations of the type that occurred in Japan's banking industry;
- the different assumptions of Southeast Asian advertising thinking being invented by that advancing army of recent design school graduates waving their diskettes;
- revaluing of traditional cultures within the wave of modernizing.

There are two fundamental qualities about the above examples:

- Family life is the origin of many ideas that end up influencing larger economic events.
- In Asia, ideas move from cultural importance to business importance, not the other way around as in the West.

The subject of Asian business as a manifestation of Asian culture has been largely ignored by the Western business press. Southeast Asian businesses are reinterpreting themes that have long existed in the region's three main cultures—Malay, Chinese, and Indian—in new idioms. Some of these idioms superficially resemble Western ones and are thus almost relievedly seized upon by Western interpreters as affirmations of their own culture, unaware that they are describing appearance and missing substance.

Asian cultures have manifested themselves over millennia in remarkably stable structural forms, among them economic pragmatism, caste mythologies, and ancestor bonds. Time and geography have mingled these considerably in Southeast Asia. Yet these respective primordial responses to life can today be traced in business culture as once they could be traced in palace and temple culture.

One reason Southeast Asia's historical traditions have blended so well, despite the diversity of their origins, is that they were largely propagated via a maritime culture. The fluidity, borderlessness, and market responsiveness of that economy is today being replicated in Internet and the borderless digital economy. Today's Southeast Asians are responding to opportunity mixed with the need for stability the same way they did to the arrival of the junk and the dhow.

OLD WINE IN NEW BOTTLES

The most farsighted Asian government insofar as e-commerce (electronic commerce) content is concerned is Singapore. While Taiwan may produce more hardware innovation and India has become synonymous with Asian software development, Singapore has thus far quietly assembled the most competent and comprehensive IT content anywhere in Asia. As this book is concerned with the market for information rather than hardware and software, we will be taking a long look at Southeast Asia's two major e-commerce content flow-through sites, SingaporeONE and Malaysia's Multimedia Super Corridor.

For the moment, it is sufficient to briefly mention, in light of the point at issue here, that Asia's long record of reevaluating old ideas in light of modern economic developments (the "old wine in new bottles" phenomenon) has seen Singapore jump unexpectedly into the lead as the region's foremost IT content creation and e-commerce marketing innovator. That Singapore has done such a remarkable job with so little hype and self-aggrandizement is largely because the island-state's achievements are largely an effort to stimulate homegrown innovation rather than an attempt to lure overseas investment capital as a pump-primer, which was Malaysia's approach. It is also clear that Singapore has been so low key because they accomplished their goals before starting to chat their accomplishments up on the world media circuit, whereas Malaysia made quite a stir about something that did not yet exist.

As far back as 1995 Singapore's Prime Minister Goh Chok Tong was warning Singaporeans that they must adapt quickly to rapid technological change or risk holding back the island's competitiveness in the long term. "Getting ready for the future is not a choice," he has said. "Getting used to technological changes is a must. Only then will we maintain our relevance and value in this fast-changing world. We must turn the whole of Singapore into an Intelligent Island, a multimedia-intelligent island." Goh also has said, "If the public fails to adjust to technological change, our whole country will be held back and not be able to move to a higher level of productivity quickly."

Singapore's progress has been just as remarkable since then. The island's economy has long relied on advanced manufacturing industries and financial services. Now the entire island is being wired up to a cable network that by the end of 1998 will see video and computer services available via modem and Net TV in every home (although a February 1998 government statement indicated that installing higher-speed fiber-optic cable into every household was not yet in the cards).

All Singaporean public schools are being equipped with computers under a program costing over US$1 billion.[1] Government agencies maintain websites on the Internet allowing them to conduct paperless business with citizens. All these efforts are far in advance of any other Asian country.

Prime Minister Goh has summed up the psychological drive for the country's e-commerce push this way: "The largely unregulated Internet is overflowing with information for all kinds of purposes and audiences. Our children need guidance in navigating the Internet. We must teach them to choose and use information wisely. If adult Singaporeans don't embrace this change, we will be left behind by the continuous improvements in technology that are taking place. We will also be holding the next generation back."

THE PLACE OF CHINA AND JAPAN IN ASIA'S E-COMMERCE THINKING

One reason why Singapore is so concerned with building up a highly IT- and Internet-informed citizenry is that its economic authorities have a broader view of the 1997 debacle's causes than the Soros-bashing of Malaysia's Prime Minister Mahathir. Singaporeans are not much given to self-flagellation, but they are honest enough to admit their own shortcomings. One shortcoming that showed up in 1997 was the widespread Asian belief that China and Japan are economically benign simply because they have no special ideological ax to grind in Asia. Singaporeans did not believe for one minute the idea that 1997's currency and stock market upheavals originated from speculators in New York and London.

Singaporean politicians saw the role of technocrats in Beijing and Tokyo as among the hidden causes of the 1997 mess. Singaporeans have been almost alone in foreseeing that Asia's small economies are being squeezed not so much by the financiers of the world as they are by the competing economic agendas of China and Japan. Both countries have significant economic problems and relatively few means and little time to solve them. China's factories are churning out everything from garments to watches and toys at rock-bottom prices. These products are quickly eroding the ability of Southeast Asian cheap-exports economies to compete in low-end manufacturing. In Japan, the surge of exports engineered by a depreciation of the yen is intensifying the squeeze at the level of high-tech consumer exports like electronics, which countries like Malaysia had seen as their next step up the value-added ladder. Malaysians have watched their prime minister's starry-eyed faith in "Japan, Inc." betrayed by Mitsubishi's foot-dragging on the transfer of meaningful technology to Proton in their joint venture and the reluctance of other Japanese firms like Hitachi to regard Malaysia as anything more than a cheap-land, cheap-labor manufactory. The result was the tart irony of Malaysia buying out the fading Lotus automotive works in much vilified former "colonizer" Britain to get automotive technology that Japan won't give. It may not have dawned on the Malaysian government that perhaps the Japanese had noted the ubiquitous photocopy shops in Kuala Lumpur churning out hundreds of copies of university textbooks and technical manuals without bothering with niceties like royalties.

The 1997 crisis also resulted in China and Japan being ever poorer markets for Southeast Asia's exports. Unless China and Japan loosen their markets for their neighbors in the south, the fragile cohesiveness of the region based on "Asian values" could become very shaky. China is the central player in the open markets crisis. China analysts calculate that $18 billion worth of merchandise was sold by China to the world in 1997, a volume that makes Southeast Asia's export volumes seem anemic. China is rapidly upscaling itself into a huge, competitive manufacturing base for electronics, telecom equipment, and household appliances—precisely the sectors countries like Malaysia had earmarked as their own next rung upward on the value-added ladder. It salves no one's wounds that Beijing needs this export growth to burn off its bulging capacities and to offset the tight credit policies at home that were implemented to keep China's volatile inflation in single digits. China also needs to buy time to overhaul its unprofitable state-owned enterprises and find new employment for millions of laid-off workers.

Singapore's emphasis on high IT literacy derives in part because the country realizes Southeast Asia did not come to grips with its problem of failing to train enough skilled workers when economic times were good. The region's surplus capital and good credit went into playgrounds for the wealthy instead of training for the laborer. China's huge population base and its relatively strong school system bequeath the country's economy as many as three hundred thousand new technicians and engineers per year.

Today's Japanese multinationals are increasingly unlikely to cede any ground to established rivals, let alone newcomers. The upshot of all this is that Beijing and Tokyo have sufficient vested interest in making sure the financial turmoil in

Southeast Asia doesn't push these economies into the abyss, but neither are they inclined to making life easier for the Malaysias and Indonesias in the middle of the value-added ladder who squandered their opportunity when it was there.

NOTE

1. Throughout this book the "$" sign will refer to U.S. dollars unless otherwise specified.

6

Information in a
Time of Great Change

Southeast Asia is changing. Rapidly, dramatically, and possibly problematically. The 1997 economic crisis simply brought to the surface deep and long-term inadequacies that were brought about as much by the failure to respond to information as they were by economics or politics. Some countries like Indonesia are dithering away what few chances they have left to escape economic collapse. Others like Malaysia are taking steps so regressive it is hard to imagine their ever becoming competitive again in an age based on the power of information rather than the power of privilege. Others like Singapore have a clarity of vision (and the drive to match it) that is almost too good. They are so far ahead of their neighbors that there is a real chance of alienating them.

Substantial issues, these. How will Southeast Asia's future be communicated, understood, and managed? Two major topics need to be addressed:

- the quite different information transfer models being built by Malaysia and Singapore;
- the way information technology can substantially improve the efficiency and profitability of Asian business practices.

INFORMATION INFRASTRUCTURE

The transformation of the Asian economies to a multimedia-services base began in Singapore in 1994 with the vision of a physical infrastructure named IT2000 and an information product named SingaporeONE (quickly shortened to the nicely euphonic "SingONE"—the "ONE" standing for "One Network for Everybody"). The basic concept was to massively transform Singapore into an information-adept society, and the basic tool used to accomplish this was supply-side or "push" services in which every imaginable kind of database was laid at the public's door to see which kinds of information were the most demanded and

fruitful. There was no real motive of profit involved—this was a purely governmental initiative—although it was clear to everyone that once the market for information demand became defined, there would be substantial opportunities for
private enterprise.

The next year Malaysia took up the idea of a multimedia-based information hub
but turned it in quite a different direction. The exact chain of decision has never
been made clear, but it appears that in 1994 the Malaysian government realized
that the goals of its Vision 2020 plan to achieve fully developed status within
twenty-five years would not be reached if the economy was based solely on value-
added exports. The U.S. consultancy firm McKinsey & Co. was contacted, and
one of their recommendations was that an information infrastructure could stream-
line Malaysia's existing production base. The management visionary Kenichi
Ohmae added that IT could better inform the rural sectors of the populace on matters the government deemed fit. These views were conveyed to Prime Minister Dr.
Mahathir Mohamad, who immediately seized on information technology as the
next step up on Malaysia's economic climb.

What happened next was a fateful decision. In 1995 Malaysia was enjoying a
strong record of success with government-stimulated infrastructure building. The
experience gathered during years of using the infrastructure-building approach to
investment was applied to Malaysia's information era. The proposed centerpiece
of Malaysia's IT revolution, a physical plant that came to be called the Multimedia
Super Corridor (MSC), was conceived as the IT version of an industrial R&D
park. It would attract sizable overseas R&D investment to the country, much the
same way Malaysia had attracted investment capital while building its manufacturing sector.

However, information can produce economic and political volatility in ways
that products do not. Hence the decision was made to sharply limit the amount of
information that would be allowed to penetrate into Malaysian society beyond
government-approved channels. Unlike SingONE, Malaysia's IT planners did not
envision the MSC as a nationwide, populace-penetrating, information flow-
through channel. Instead, they saw the MSC as an industrial investment magnet
that would attract international companies to those virtues that had originally attracted Japanese manufacturers to Malaysia: cheap land, cheap labor, and tax incentives. The size of Malaysia's internal market for IT was never particularly
attractive to begin with, and now it was sequestered to all but favored IT developments such as telemedicine, smart cards, smart schools, and the like. Malaysia saw
the MSC as an infrastructure tool not a social-development tool—almost exactly
the opposite direction taken by Singapore. This decision virtually guaranteed that
Malaysia would fall behind the rest of Asia as the region embraces open-ended information and its technology.

In sum, Singapore sees its looming information era as a massive opportunity to
prepare its citizenry for a future quite different than the world of today. Malaysia appears to see its MSC as a force for controlling what its citizenry can know in order
to preserve its long-standing political structure and ethnic preferences system.

Their divergent approaches have significant implications. The conduct and flow of international finance into the region, political models in Asia, improvements in management, the investing and spending patterns of an increasingly educated populace, and the kinds of social change that result from economic development in new directions—these will evolve largely on the way Asia's Information Age is assimilated and managed. The two basic issues likely to arise are: (a) the degree to which a significant increase in the quantity of information will change the nature of economies, and (b) the direction economic change will steer political change.

It seems safe to say that as the world advances into the next millennium, the world economy will continue its present highly turbulent and highly competitive character, prone to abrupt shifts as both the nature and the content of knowledge continually change. Singapore and Malaysia represent two very different models for the role of information in society. Malaysia is very good at marketing itself but considerably less adept at technical achievement. Singapore is very good at achievement but terrible at marketing itself.

Singapore sees itself as a proving ground for an Asian society based on the most fruitful use of information. A detailed look at the way Singapore has configured its SingONE as a public-education site demonstrates how useful IT can be in improving nearly all aspects of a society without also laying the seeds of disruption. Of chief interest to investors is that Singapore clearly is setting itself up to be a future flow-through site for information between all of Asia and the rest of the world. Singapore's long-standing investment links with China, plus its recent investments in the e-commerce market of India, make Singapore the likeliest candidate to be the preeminent informational hub linking Asia with the rest of the world.

These physical-plant facts mask underlying philosophies that will prove themselves in the economic marketplace in the years 1997–2006. The philosophy that underlies Singaporean thinking is that information is more important to future society than technology. The philosophy underlying Malaysia's Multimedia Super Corridor is that technology is more important than information.

As Asia advances into the e-commerce era, it has at least these two models to draw upon. Others will no doubt emerge before long. We might call them, until a better term comes along, the information productivity model of Singapore, and the information investment model of Malaysia. China and India are even now evolving models of their own.

Whichever information models eventually prove the most useful, their success will have profound consequences on both Asian values and the future of the Asian way of life. When one door of happiness closes, another opens; but often we look so long at the closed door that we do not see the one that is now open.

INVESTMENT MARKETPLACE

Asia's business organizations and management styles will change dramatically as information products and services are sent into their marketplaces. Up till now the Asian infoplace—the fact-driven equivalent of the product-driven marketplace—has been thought of largely in terms of improving content. SingONE's databases, for example, are multimedia-enhanced versions of previous print-delivered data. At present, information delivery occurs almost exclusively inside business and government organizations. Moreover, approximately 90 percent or more of the information any organization collects is about events inside that organization—accounting, distribution, sales, ordering, internal e-mails, and so on. One effect of this is that, in this early stage of Asia's information era, corporate intranets represent a much larger source of investment opportunity than the Internet.

Yet the chief opportunity presented by SingONE and the MSC is not their rather small local markets—3.5 million and 20 million respectively—but their role as information flow-through sites serving the rest of Asia. Singapore sees what Malaysia does not: information is not just another rung on the value-added ladder, it is an entirely different kind of market. Hence the term "infoplace."

In basic concept, the MSC and SingONE apply Internet-like capability to advance their governmental interests at home and the interests of their business communities abroad. While there are differences in technical sophistication between their ventures, basically they rely on high-bandwidth T3, ADSL (asymmetrical digital subscriber lines), and ATM (asynchronous transfer mode) connections to ferry around multimedia graphics and sound with the same facility an office network ferries around letter-and-number databases. What gives the databases of both their appeal is that the general public responds better to—and learns more from—complex visual/sound presentations than from letters and numbers. The analogy is the difference between a video and a newspaper.

The technical and cost issues associated with broadband delivery—the high-speed, high-volume transmission system that multimedia requires—are fairly well known to investors. They are expensive systems at both the sending and receiving ends, fussy about things like "clean" electrical current, and very little is presently known about the public's taste for what their governments want them to see.

Even less well known is the size of the ultimate market the MSC and SingONE are trying to court. Neither delivery system has existed long enough to address some important economic questions:

- Where is the market (or rather, the infoplace)?
- *Who* is the infoplace?
- What level of discretionary income can people be induced to part with in order to access the information the MSC and SingONE have to offer?
- How difficult and costly will it be to penetrate this market compared with trying to serve it via the existing means of television and print?
- What cultural and economic obstacles lie in the way?
- What are the respective strengths and weaknesses of the MSC and SingONE?
- Given that the MSC and SingONE are largely funded by government initiative, once they are up and running, will private ventures then steal away their market share with more attractive—and perhaps socially adventurous—offerings?

- What are the comparative advantages and restrictions that Singapore and Malaysia present to offshore investors?

- What social and political repercussions are likely to occur as a result of a large influx of non-native, and many Western, techno-workers into these countries—especially Malaysia, which has ambivalent attitudes about the West to start with?

- What managerial, political, and financial pitfalls does the multinational investor face when learning to work with governments with a history of disinformation and repression on politically sensitive matters?

None of these questions has a simple answer. Broadly speaking, they break down into issues related to technology and investment, and issues related to social consequences.

There is also a not inconsiderable political dimension. SingONE, the delivery machine for the broad array of information services that Singapore's IT2000 project plans to deliver, is roughly three to four years ahead of the MSC in terms of operating hardware and much further than that in quality of its information. SingONE has been soft-pedaled by a government that doesn't want to see egg on its face if the offerings or the technology don't deliver what the visionaries promise.

The MSC has entered the information technology arena with a razzamatazz publicity blitz that comes perilously close to the pomp-before-performance phenomenon that afflicts so many Malaysian ventures. Many wonder if Malaysian technical capabilities are anywhere near as competent as the country's politicians claim. The consistent comment one hears from international consulting firms is, "Can Malaysia really deliver on its promises or are they just more big talk from a political leadership with a record of overclaiming and underperforming?" Japanese and Korean plant managers interviewed for this book were quite explicit with their complaints about the Malaysian work force's very low levels of productivity, high rates of job-hopping, and lack of interest in competency.

Also important is the fact that in both the MSC and SingONE there exists governmental unease that this new technology will bypass the tightly controlled television market and enable people to roam freely through facts and ideas their governments may not like them to know. The year 1997 saw a credibility bubble burst with too many we-know-it-all governments running into economic disasters attributed to cronyism, the Government, Inc., attitude about business, and cozy transfers from bureaucracy to boardroom. Singapore, Hong Kong, and Taiwan largely escaped the Asian bubble bath, presumably because their information sectors are fairly open. In Malaysia, Indonesia, Thailand, and the Philippines, while the local popular media presented Asia's economic woes as a combination of a dip in exports demand and the duplicity of investment speculators, people saw on CNN and read in the Western press that the real problems were incompetent politicians, incompetent business leaders, too much secrecy, and too much greed.

It is very doubtful that the Malaysian and Singaporean governments will allow international investors to influence the content of their multimedia programming.

The biggest unanswered question in Southeast Asia's information era is: "Where is the market?" For foreign investors, the multimedia market has some clear pitfalls:

- Assumptions made about middle-class buying power have yet to be proved in a case when expensive high-tech equipment is required compared with the cost of delivery via television.
- Unlike the case with present consumer brands, with information services local appeal is likely to command more customer loyalty than imported appeal.
- The infoplace is the most underresearched market in Asia, in part because the networks either are not operating at all (as in Malaysia) or in so few homes that no consumer base can be said to meaningfully exist.
- There are significant differences in organizational and profit management styles throughout Asia that will inevitably affect marketing decisions.

Overseas investors realize their contribution is likely to be confined to hardware and software technology. There are fewer prospects for profits based on content. For example, there is a fairly clear market for inventory and reorder software for the retail industry that can substantially improve profit margins. One consultancy firm believes an astonishing $1 billion in software services can be sold in this market alone. This is undoubtedly a rosy prediction considering the floundering state of retail stores all over Asia. Predictions like these point up the faults of prediction from an unknown database more than the prospects for big profits to be made by improving a specific industry.

There are also issues posed by the conflict potential of Asian exclusionism and Western interventionism:

- It is unclear who will be held responsible if information that governments deem socially undesirable gets into a delivery system by either accident or design. One example is a small group of citizens disliking a certain kind of information and attacking the deliverer rather than the originator. Another example is a drunk or malicious employee sending socially corrosive information—for example, pornography—into public access channels.
- Where, exactly, will authorities draw the judicial line on exactly who is responsible for information content? The Murray Hiebert case in Malaysia is an example of what can happen when one individual doesn't like what is disseminated over a public medium. Hiebert, a journalist for the *Far Eastern Economic Review*, was jailed like a common criminal after the mother of a student he wrote about decided that his article showed contempt for Malaysia's judicial system. It so happened she was married to a figure within that judicial system. Until the mother complained, the Malaysia court system had no opinion on the matter. Once she did, the court discovered that it had indeed been impugned. The much vaunted Malaysian cyberlaws have a glaring loophole: there are no protections once information considered free within the MSC firewall is disseminated into the community at large.

Information economies represent a dramatic shift in the relationship between information and government. The social engineering consequences of the MSC and SingONE projects have received very little attention. From the international investment point of view there are several key issues that need closer scrutiny:

- International business people need clearer facts about the long-term markets the MSC and SingONE aim to serve.
- Investors who see the infoplace of Southeast Asia as a testbed for introducing multimedia information to all Asia need more complete facts about the role they will be allowed to play.
- Investors need clearer guidelines on their degree of legal culpability in the event of unforeseen social or economic effects. No one wants to invest into a milieu that includes denial, blaming the messenger, and scapegoating of the type Prime Minister Mahathir indulged in—blaming George Soros for the ringgit's drop in value when in fact Malaysia's own financial community was frantically buying dollars to service its dollar-denominated loans.
- Southeast Asia's blame-everybody-else response to a prosperous decade abruptly ending with economic difficulties is likely to shape economic and political thinking in the region for quite some time. A contributing failure was willful governmental blindness to impending problems. Multimedia technology in the hands of future governments can either exacerbate similar situations or enable their preemptive solutions. The fact that truth solves more problems than denial encourages the view that multimedia technology can provide a venue of fact outside government channels that the Asian populace much needs. The problem is: will information providers be turned into scapegoats when anything goes wrong?
- The precise role the MSC and SingONE are expected to play as investment sites—aside from hardware and real estate purchases—has not been spelled out well by their governments. Malaysia's business communities have not much risen to the multimedia opportunity with constructive, original content. The primary interest from Western countries and Japan is in the MSC and SingONE as funnels for their own e-commerce products into Asia. None of these attitudes points to a particularly innovative use of a technology whose principal promise is innovation.
- Despite all the theories attached to megaproject business development in this region, the plain practical fact is that the businesses in most need of improvement are fairly ordinary SMEs. Except for the lead Singapore is taking in this direction, interest in SMEs as engines of an e-commerce economy has been disturbingly small.
- Asia's information era is likely to inspire financing and management vehicles that may have as much or more effect on the way business is done in the region's future than any specific technological advances.

IDEA MANAGEMENT

Management as it is presently understood originated some 125 years ago to systematize the production of physical objects—pieces of hardware combined with a distribution that makes them useful.

Today we are beginning to produce information objects—pieces of data combined with software that makes them useful. Economically the two have many similarities. Managerially, however, they require very different systems. The chief of these is replacing hierarchy with hyperarchy.

Hierarchy is a tree of decision that organizes the effects produced from causes. Hyperarchies are networks of independent modules that are interlinked with each other by a common function such as money transfer, management authority, product distribution, and the like. They produce effects, but in nonsequential ways in which randomness and nonrelatedness are as important as sequence. "Surfing" the Internet and computer games achieved such quick and high popularity because they tapped into a deep-seated mental proclivity for responding to the unexpected. This mental trait has always been thought of as "the gambling instinct." In fact it is a deeply embedded, perhaps primal, response to the excitement of discovery and the wealth of opportunities that lie in chance. The world is, after all, a random place. As a philosophical attitude, opting for the formless is as old as the Tao. More recently, article after article in management and philosophy journals has pointed to the conclusion that randomness is as important as order. And of course, what is important to someone is profitable to someone else.

This has significant implications for Asian management style in the information era. Previously unthinkable ideas turn out to yield useful results if given a try. One of these is source-shifting, which occurs when you reverse a traditional assumption and then look for profit potential in what you find. Another is the entrepreneurial cluster model of business structure, which is managed by hyperarchical means rather than hierarchical ones. Still another is the modular marketing of modular information—adapting to a single purpose information about events and conditions from noncustomers, grafting technology from outside those currently being used, perfecting products in niche markets before tackling main markets, allocating knowledge resources to produce the highest knowledge mobility, and so on. None of these is new; they just haven't been applied to Asia's Information Age.

Knowledge workers, unlike manufacturing workers, are their own means of production. Their productiveness is literally in their heads. They can move anytime. Presently most Asian businesses have little idea how to deal with knowledge mobility, any more than they know how to deal with market mobility. As the knowledge needs of organizations change, organizations must rely increasingly on a workforce that cannot be "managed" using traditional incentives like job security. The obvious alternative retention tool—stock options—is little used. Organizations must change their structures to include growing portions of a workforce made of contractors, experts, consultants, part-timers, telecommuters, joint-venture partners, and so on.

For more than a century Asians have been searching for the "right" organization for companies. They adopted the family model because that is what they know. The father is assumed to be not just the authority, but the most informed. The infoplace makes it clear that there isn't any such thing as a sole authority who is always informed. Organizations must turn to plug-ins, each devised for a specific task, market, culture, and economic niche. Instead of the perfect organization, we have to evolve a shopping list of them, which, like modular employees, modular markets, and modular opportunities, are part of the modular hyperarchy called economy. Economies have always been hyperarchies; it is only recently that we have discovered this.

This raises the most politically volatile issue implied by Asia's Information Age: the notion passed down to us from mythology that leaders are heroes.

Today we know they are not. To give everyone the benefit of the doubt, no one is perfect. All a hyperarchy does is make the maximum amount of information available for decisions.

The village consensus model that was so well suited to agricultural production proved not to work well in complex interrelated economies. The lesson of Japan's prolonged economic misfortune has shown just how unfortunate holding on to a consensus ideal can be. Overreliance on hierarchy—or more properly, the too zealous encouragement of delegating upwards—runs an economy up against the limits of what it knows. The result is loss of opportunity, and it emanates from one of three oversights:

- failure to pursue discovery;
- linking personal charisma to professional competence;
- ignoring the pursuit of practical everyday products.

Many Asians look wistfully at Silicon Valley's success as a money-making machine. It is most certainly that. Yet it is more. Silicon Valley's entrepreneurial cluster style of business organization assembles into a single purpose bits and pieces of organization that don't normally coexist. They are the ivory tower, the shop floor, and the cash register. In most businesses these three activities are conducted by unrelated functionaries—consulting firms, manufactories, distribution/retail businesses. Too often, what results is management as fire fighting and enterprises bouncing from unforeseen problem to unforeseen problem.

Silicon Valley sees these (and other bits and pieces of the business enterprise) as modules to be plugged in when and where necessary—each vital to a particular stage in the functioning of an enterprise but not in charge of it. Yet isn't this view reminiscent of what the Asian family enterprise would be if there were no family? They, too, plug in business modules as needed and unplug them when not. The problem is, they also impose no restraint on the family. Stan Shih created Acer Computers after he watched a self-interested family bleed the profitable parts of a company dry so they could pursue unprofitable hobbies. When the heroic leader listens to the flattery of the people who see success for themselves in the leader's aura, the result is all too often a self-important fool.

Asians tend to think of "We" as "I" and Westerners tend to think of "I" as "We." Hierarchies seek order by limiting the lines of relationships and maximizing internal coherence. Their chief defect is poorly explored opportunity. Hyperarchies seek order by maximizing the lines of relationships and minimizing internal coherence. Their chief defect is opportunity overload. One helps you make a living; the other helps you make a life.

Southeast Asian businesses face two management challenges posed by the e-commerce era:

- how to address problems for which hierarchical leadership is insufficient;
- how to harness the intelligence and spirit of people at all levels of an organization.

Much needs to be done. But Asians—and those who invest in the region's looming Information Age—shouldn't think of it as negating the past. Rather, the issue is how to advance to the next level of complexity via the route of competency.

Never doubt that a small group of thoughtful people can change situations for the better. They are the only energy that ever has.

PART II
Delivery Systems: SingaporeONE

7

Meet Your New Market—II

More than Net-to-Newspaper Time

Dinner was ready, but Mat was too tired and worried to even think about it. He asked Cik to bring him some tea instead. Said it would stimulate his appetite. In fact, he was exhausted and just needed to be by himself.

It had been a long day in a series of job-hunting days—ghastly days of enduring life rather than pursuing the middle-class ideal of making the most of it. Doors opening, then closing. Many people in the waiting rooms, many who were a lot like him. Who would ever have expected so secure a time to become so insecure? What was he going to do?

He loosened his tie and began to pore—yet again—over the classified ads in the business section of the newspaper. There were far fewer now than two or three short months ago.

"Looking for a job is a hundred times harder than O-levels," he sighed to himself. "But if I can find a job where I can do something important with my computer training, it'll be worth all my years of school, and then some!"

Then his eyes stopped abruptly and narrowed as he spied a tiny four-by-six-inch "tombstone" with no fancy graphics or typefaces that read:

DATA COMMUNICATIONS MANAGER—recent graduates and data communications specialists invited to interview. The successful candidate will be responsible for developing and maintaining a worldwide data communications network headquartered in Penang, Malaysia. Branches in Vancouver and Sydney, with affiliates in the Philippines, India, Singapore, and Jamaica. Knowledge of the configuration and economics of networks essential. Must be willing to travel. Ideal opportunity to grow with a young, dynamic company. Nth offers a very competitive compensation and benefit package which includes holidays, vacations, medical/dental benefits, supplemented with performance-based stock options. Qualified candidates should forward their CV with particulars to: Mr. Liu, Nth Sdn Bhd, Pilau Pinang, Malaysia.

Mat reread the ad three times before he took another breath. He went into the future baby's room, where presently his computer resided. He turned it on and opened up a file, "CV.job."

"Wonder if it'll get me very far," he sighed. Then he stopped abruptly. "Wait! How can I apply for a job with a company I don't know anything about!?"

Suddenly no longer quite so tired, he typed http://www.yahoo.com and started in.

Half an hour later he knew what he wanted. "Ayooohh," he breathed softly to himself. "Nth is international, all right. Sales offices in Amsterdam and Sydney. Data entry subcontractors in Manila, Hyderabad, and Jamaica. Programmers subcontracting out of Toronto and Bangalore. Management staff of 25, but 2,300 subcontract employees." He stopped and looked again. Two-thousand-three-hundred!? "What do these people *do*?"

In another ten minutes he had that answer, too: "They acquire and convert databases in Unix and convert them to JAVA, then sell them to businesses and governments over the Net. They also sell to corporations using workstations."

Mat went on to read that Nth distributed its databases online, yet also via FAX, tape, disk, laser disk, and print, using satellites, common carrier land lines, overseas cable, fiber optics, and microwave. "How did they organize this business?" He thought, "Its organization chart looks like a plate of noodles fell on the floor."

"Interesting sounding people, too," he mused. "Started by a Hong Kong entrepreneur who formed a partnership with a retired Indian army officer who got interested in data communications in the service."

Mat also found that Nth's revenues rose from $123,000 in their second year of operation in 1992 to $114.5 million in 1995. "They did that in three years!?" he exclaimed. Their stock traded over the counter from HK$2.23 when they first went public in 1995, rose to HK$9.97, but now hovered around HK$7.75 on the Hang Seng. The archives of one of the financial newspapers yielded up a story stating that Nth needed to upgrade its hardware if it was to continue being competitive through 1998, but most of all needed to reorganize itself to keep up with the fast pace of global data demand.

"What a job!" Mat sighed. "How do I get it?"

Cik called from the kitchen, "Ku, dinner's getting cold!"

"I'm starved," he called back.

Electronic commerce is a port. Throughout history, ports have developed their own culture. Mingling with visible features like the tos and fros of ships or camels or elephants (and sometime all of these at once), a sense for cosmopolitanism and desire for the new and the unusual, they also embodied a less visible feature. Yet this was the most important one.

It was the fact that a port's culture gradient was steeper and peaked more quickly than in the more settled hinterlands. New and unusual goods appeared first in the port's markets and often had become passé in the port by the time they began to appear in the villages as the latest thing. Other times they never penetrated beyond the port at all—goods transshipped their way through, noted by a few uncomprehending officials but largely gone before they made much of an impact.

People with different skins, hair, noses, languages, cooking, and deities slept at night in their own enclaves but by day mixed freely with shippers, wholesalers, and the organizers of trade. Their ways, too, sometimes stayed and sometimes transshipped

The economies of ports differed from the simple barter base of hinterland villages. The most notable difference was the notion that the abstract can have value. Cargo came to be valued more than its means of transport; ships, after all, weren't that hard or costly to build. Hence came the joint-venture company. When it was first conceived, it had originated as a means to protect against the fear of the loss of cargo. The significance was that a value could be assigned to risk.

Ports devised banks, periodic resetting of far-flung accounts to zero by physical transfers of gold, and factoring or the lending against accounts receivable at a discount. Ports, too, devised the courier system—first runners and then horses—so men of means could be the first to know of momentous events inland.

The port helped transform the coastal fishers of Southeast Asia into one of the world's most sophisticated trading cultures for eight centuries, between the time of Islam's great fervent first spread in the Western calendar's eighth century until the advent of European colonialism and transoceanic navigation in the fifteenth. During those eight centuries, names like Funan-Khmer, Srivjaya, Palembang, Nanyang, and Temasek came and went. What was left behind was Asia's first Golden Age. Though it was an age of commerce, we still call it the time of the Silk Sea.

The receptionist was soft-spoken and gracious enough, but Mat was still more than a little intimidated by the variety of equipment in Nth's office building. It was located in a tree-lined business park of two- and three-story buildings on the southern shores of Pilau Pinang. The logo on the sign in front simply said "Nth" and gave no hint of the company's operations. When the taxi had dropped him off he spotted immediately the three 3.7-meter satellite dishes on the roof, one aimed near the eastern horizon, another almost overhead, and the last somewhere out over Africa, to judge by its elevation of nearly thirty degrees. Mat realized Nth was up- and downlinking a tremendous amount of data for a building its size.

Now, as Ms. Chan, the personnel director, gave him a brief tour of the company's operations center, Mat began to feel uneasy. There weren't that many people in the production area—thirty at most, each in a partitioned area with its own personality. Photos with the kids on vacations, notes to not forget to bring home *nasi* (rice) after work, meeting schedules, a potted plant on a shelf instead of books, CDs playing soft saxophone jazz and ghazals and Dadawa and Colonial Cousins. It might as well have been an ad agency.

But these people weren't facing PCs with letters and numbers onscreen, they were facing Sun and Silicon Graphics workstations running multimedia and graphics applications. Mat had a feeling that whatever Nth did now, it certainly wasn't the simple data comm outfit he'd read about three nights ago while waiting for dinner. What he was seeing was almost entirely based on image comm. "It's mostly PhotoShop and Director in here," he thought as he looked over the menu bars on the screens. He realized he had to throw out his assumption that the job interview would involve phrases like "stop bits," "parity bits," "bits per second," and "ASCII"—all that archaic communications stuff.

He suddenly felt at sea, uncertain. His experience was with data. He didn't have a clue how to handle a job interview for a business that was so heavily graphics based.

Then they stopped as Ms. Chan opened a door into an office cluttered with technical trade journals and equipment specs sheets and said, "Mat, this is Mr. Singh, our managing director."

Tolerance was among Nanyang's greatest assets. With tolerance came more communication, and with that came more trade. Southeast Asia came into possession of a fundamental thought process that was little known elsewhere. Unlike Western countries that created a rigid boundary between secular progress and religious tradition, Southeast Asia's early leaders came to see the future of the region as a long-term integration of spiritual and material values to be accomplished over decades, even generations. They felt the most important quality in any long-lived society was that quality which could reconcile social change and social harmony with business development and the culture gradient of the port. The quality was integrity.

Integrity can't be readily defined, yet everyone knows deep inside what it is. They know integrity will endure despite the challenges of new technology, shifts in the international business and political climates, even globalized finance. The information superhighway, genetic engineering, and borderless equity/money markets are only three examples of technological change imposing unexpected social challenges, and with them come the fears of people who are getting too far behind the wave of the future.

The media—especially television—is a poor problem solver. It induces overreliance on emotion at the expense of thought, preoccupation with personalities at the expense of principles, short-half-life trendiness, attraction by excess, and the reduction of complexities to the lowest common denominator.

Popular feeling is not much better. Its worst defect is that it responds so well to peer forces and not much else. Its second-worst defect is that it works almost always on the downside of a culture gradient.

The most important insight needed in Asia's information age is how to turn rapid change to positive effect. What response is there to change that comes so quickly it outstrips management models based on existing institutions? How is information to be managed in such a way that it enhances the making of progress?

"Now that you've had a bit of a look at our operation," Mr. Singh addressed Mat, "what do you think?"

Mat thought a moment, looked out the windows of Mr. Singh's office. "Where to begin," he wondered. He returned his gaze to Mr. Singh. "The first thing, of course, is those three dishes on your roof. Or more exactly, where they are pointed. One is aimed west about thirty degrees above the horizon. That one I haven't figured out yet. Penang is about a hundred degrees east longitude, so a dish pointed upwards thirty degrees would downlink from a satellite pretty near the Greenwich meridian, and I didn't know there was one up there. The other two are easier. Our part of the sky has satellites just about every four degrees apart, so your middle dish could be uplinking to Amik B at 109 degrees west, Amik 2&3, Satcom 2, Westar 5, or Comstar 4 at 127 degrees. Maybe even Satcom 3R, at 131 degrees west. My guess is Satcom 2 because from what I read about you, you've got a lot of data going to India."

He looked at Mr. Singh to see how he was swallowing what he had said. There was no expression on his face.

Mr. Singh noticed his sudden silence. "Go on," he said, "I'm wondering where you're going with all this. Everybody sends data to India."

"The fact that you've got your own $200,000 dishes means you're running too much data to be buying dish time from vendors like Tymnet or AT&T."

"We decided from the beginning to not rent our time," Mr. Singh interrupted. "It wasn't an economic decision as much as a reliability one."

"In that case my guess was right, that you run all hours of the day, every day of the year, and more important, to fixed stations, not mobile ones," Mat replied. "The advantage of using a 3.7-meter dish is that you can uplink using your Ku-band big dishes but downlink using four-foot very small aperture terminal—VSATs—that only cost a few thousand dollars. The fact that you're not doing that tells me that you're either using C-band or you need unrestricted antenna access, and that means data coming in from anywhere in the hemisphere at any hour of the day or night. I noticed from your management-to-employee ratio you run a lot of subcontractor operations who probably set their own schedules. The only kind of operation that would do that regularly is one that moves data by deadline, not by volume. Might I ask what kind of transponder time are you leasing?"

"Twenty-two 128 Kbps's. And by the way, you guessed right: we do indeed use Satcom 2, but not because it's a workhorse. We can just reach Portugal."

"I didn't know you dealt with Portugal. There wasn't anything about that when I looked you up on idc.com."

"It's a new operation. I'll tell you more about it later."

Mat heart jumped, and he smiled inwardly. "He wouldn't say that," Mat thought, "if this interview was going nowhere."

Mat began again, using the kind of analysis he would have used in his old job writing software. "128 kb is about two thousand bits a second. Twenty times that is forty thousand bits a second, divided by eight is about 5000 characters a second. So you're downlinking roughly 720 words a second. That's 431,200 words a minute or 2.6 million words an hour. How many hours do you run at a stretch?"

"We don't stop. But tell me, why are you talking about character transmission rates? We don't do alphanumeric, we do multimedia."

Mat's heart fluttered, and he suddenly couldn't find anything meaningful to say.

Mr. Singh sensed his moment of awkwardness and changed the subject. "No matter. What we are doing, nobody is doing. You wouldn't have guessed it anyway. But tell me, what kind of experience do you have solving interface problems affected by propagation delay?"

"Propagation delay?" Mat said quizzically, "Back-and-forth between earth to bird to earth again? It takes almost a second, hence the term 'propagation delay.' But the only people affected by that are people working applications simultaneously from different parts of the world."

Mr. Singh slapped the desk and laughed. "Most people have to worry about Net-to-newspaper time," he laughed. "The time it takes between when ideas start showing up on the Net and the time they start appearing in newspapers. That's the window-of-opportunity time, the available time they have between when they see an idea, realize it is marketable, then devise and get a product into the market by the time the trade mags and newspapers create a demand for it. Right now it takes about nine months to a year between the time someone starts a chat group devoted to some new app and the time the app turns up in a pretty box being reviewed in *PC World*. But that's not our problem. Nth's problem is errors that can get introduced in nine-tenths of a second."

"So you are doing simultaneous applications around the world."

"What do you think they might be?" Mr. Singh asked. He leaned forward on his desk with his hands folded in front of him and looked at Mat straight in the eyes.

Today's cultural gradient lies in foreseeing how process will change product and how product in turn will change culture. Information technology can impact product volatility the same way it impacted financial volatility in 1997. The rapidity of external movement in an economic sector, which shocked editorialists and politicians when it occurred in the financial sector in 1997, is likely to affect the production, export, and consumption sectors—and all three at once—in first decade of the next century.

There is no reason why rapid movement in a given economic sector should shock people. Almost invariably its precursors are there all along, but people fail to read them. Anyone paying attention to wsj.com, dowjones.com, or asiaecon.com could have seen the 1997 bubble-burst coming—not with the bellwether decline in electronics exports in mid-1995 but when the Chinese yuan was devalued a year earlier, thereby altering fundamentally the direction of energy flow in the cheap exports sector.

Southeast Asia is still a port. Beyond its busy activity is a vast region that will take varying amounts of time to acculturate to what happens as the ships come and go. Those changes will turn up first not in the physical marketplaces of the media but in the infoplaces of the chat rooms.

Let us take an example.

When a clothing designer like Donna Karan in New York designs clothing, she tosses off a few core ideas. Assistant designers take these and sketch eighty or more variations from them. These are refined down to perhaps eight. These eight then go back to Ms. Karan, who will zero in on two or three that have possibilities—price point, the "Karan look," fabric availability, and so on. The assistant designers redevelop these more fully, cut patterns, then sew sample garments (called maquettes) in raw muslin. They put the maquettes on a model, change the drape, and alter them in lesser or greater detail until they get the fit right. Only then is the actual garment cut from the fabric chosen for retail stores. This is then sewn, put on models, modified, and redraped for the catwalk shows. By the time the catwalk shows for the trade are over the orders are already off to Sri Lanka and China, where legions of juki-machine workers crank the garments out by the thousands. The process is long, arduous, expensive.

Most people who look at this production cycle see room for efficiency only at the design stage. Ms. Karan sits down at a screen, chooses the two or three designs that are particularly good. These are mixed and merged using graphics software, using the best from each sketch. The pattern is then generated by the computer. The muslin stage is eliminated altogether since the computer can take the sketch and "drape" a particular fabric, color it, then show what the garment will look like in full-motion video. If Ms. Karan wants to change to a different fabric, say, change from a seven-ounce wool to a three-ounce silk, the computer can simulate that, too. It can also simulate changes in pattern, weave, color, drape, and do in seconds what used to take hours or even days.

None of this is news. It is basic CAD, computer aided design. It merely speeds clothing design. It does not change the process fundamentally.

Where computers will change the garment industry fundamentally is not at the designer level but at the retail level. You go to a store and there are videos of different suits that you can call up onscreen by style or wearing occasion. You pick the style you want, then a fabric. You go not into a fitting room but a 3-D scanner that determines your exact measurements. After the scan, the machine combines your body information with your style information, any modifications you wanted, and the fabric you chose. It then shows you a video image of what you will look like walking down one or several streets in your city, entering and leaving buildings, working, dining, or making a presentation, all dressed in that outfit, and all so well done even you think that's you in the video, even though what you see is only a graphic.

If you like what you see, the computer sends the complete specifications not to a tailor but to a loom, which creates the garment without sewing. Instead of being tailored from pieces your garment is instead woven to order. It comes to your door by courier as fast or faster than the alterations department of a traditional store could deliver you something modified off the rack.

The next time you want a new suit, you don't even go to the store. You go to a website. What you are buying is now not a product, it is a process in which everything has been eliminated but you and the product.

This is the garment industry equivalent of the devaluation of the yuan in 1995. A similar scenario can be drawn for a great many retail consumer products that presently exist only on the web pages of market analysts.

The overall impact will be the elimination of almost every person and piece of real estate lying between the consumer and the product. What are you going to do about this?

Mr. Singh asked Mat what problems he could think of that might affect Nth's product mix, based as it was almost entirely on image processing.

Mat thought a moment, then replied, "As we become more globalized, the assumption is that we have to compete in globalizing terms. Yet already there is unhappiness about the loss of the old cultural values. I see it myself, when I go *balik kampung*. The old crafts people in the *kampungs* live in houses with TV aerials. They are no longer producing the fine weavings, kites, and batiks of the past. They let commercial establishments do that and while their days away watching the soaps."

Mr. Singh eased back in his chair and looked out the window. He was Punjabi. He wore the turban. His wrist had the iron ring. He addressed his friends as *khalsa*, his wife as *kaur*. He got dewy-eyed with them over the old ghazals sung at the *gurudwara*. But he'd never been to Punjab. What was he holding on to?

"Ahead-of-the-art imagery has always flown quickly past the icons of the old ways," he said. "It is the way of history that things change. Why should we not be ahead of it instead of behind it?"

Mat paused to gather his thoughts, knowing what he said now meant either a job or no job. He needed this job. The baby's room wasn't going to be empty forever.

"There have been recent situations in other countries similar to what Southeast Asia is experiencing. In Japan during the 1980s it was hard to tell there was a Japan. Everything was so modern, so somewhere-else. Yet the old ideas were hiding inside the modern goods. Japanese designs still reflected *heihaku tansho*—the ideal of light-slim-short-small. The reality of the space crunch in Japan's cities and homes simply reraised the opportunity to express the old feeling for simplicity in smallness. You see it in cassette players, calculators, cameras, cellular phones, laptops. All you have to do is look beyond their surface, and there they are, the old ways, still as strong."

"Nth's product isn't design, it is information," Mr. Singh replied. "I don't quite see your point."

"My point is that information requires us to throw out all our ideas about being governed by the marketplace."

Mr. Singh blinked several times at Mat, then leaned forward in his chair, put his arms back on the desk, as though he was not quite right in his ears with what he had just heard.

"Could you say that again?" His voice sounded like what Queen Victoria's must have been upon the news of an unwanted pregnancy down in the maid's quarters.

"Information isn't a marketplace," Mat rephrased his answer. "It never has been. We can't manage it using marketplace rules."

"I see," Mr. Singh said slowly. He moved forward in his chair and shifted the fulcrum of his weight to his arms as if about to rise. "Well, it's been very nice of you to come by. I'll be sure to let you know if something turns up."

Mat made no motion to rise. "Information has always been associated with the word 'courtyard,'" he said. "A courtyard is a meeting place, much as to most people the term 'market' designates such a place. If Nth's three satellite dishes up on the roof mean anything, it is that they are our great courtyard of the Alhambra, Caliph al-Mamun's Bayt-al-Hikmah 'House of Wisdom' in Baghdad, and the imperial palace where Xuanzang related The Record of the Western Lands. Our ultimate purpose isn't selling things, it is meeting minds. Information is just a dictionary of deeds. We don't need to update it, we need to rethink it."

Mr. Singh leaned forward with his hands on top of each other on the desk. "Very well," he said. "Where do you suggest that we begin?"

"It will cost quite a bit."

"Everyone's got a price. My job is to see if they're worth it."

"That's not what I meant. I was going to suggest you take another look at the cost of those sat dishes for what you are getting in terms of downstreaming, and think about ISDN."

8
Malaysia's MSC and SingaporeONE

Opportunity and Pitfalls

The marketplace of Asia's e-commerce era is likely to be defined in good part by the success or failure of the region's two major delivery systems, Malaysia's Multimedia Super Corridor and SingaporeONE (SingONE). It is difficult to imagine two information technology services conceived and implemented from such entirely different ideas of what information is for.

The public relations flurry generated by Malaysia's Multimedia Super Corridor has obscured the similar but far more advanced public information network venture in SingONE. SingONE is three to five years ahead of the MSC in sophistication and implementation. The Singaporean government has been far more reserved about its progress than Malaysia, which has made a great deal of clamor about a service that doesn't yet exist. As of early 1998 the MSC was a large number of earth movers converting palm plantations into dirt roads on one end and a sizable public relations office on the other.

Technically, both projects offer sophisticated, eye-catching information services via a single very high bandwidth site that the governments as primary investors feel will better inform their own populaces than either television or print can do. The main question is when they will be up and running. Malaysia's current Concept Request for Proposals suggests completion dates in 1999–2000. SingaporeONE, on the other hand, has been in actual operation since mid-1997 and is presently being tested in some two thousand residences on a beta-phase test. The fully installed system will connect some eight hundred thousand homes and businesses by the end of 1998. Despite the early stage of their development, both governments have the potential to extend their services to all of Asia, penetrating the Asia market with information and services that will be of great profit to their own business communities.

To hear the Malaysians tell it, providing multimedia medical, social, and educational information will leapfrog Malaysia out of the low-tech cheap-labor manufacturing economy where it presently seems stuck and into what would be tantamount to Asia's high-tech information technology conduit linking the production empires of the West with the consuming empires of the East. The Singaporeans are producing a system that looks and informs a lot like America Online, albeit lighter in fees to the consumer but heavier in government control. The chief distinction is that while AOL embodies the sometimes banal and sometimes enlightening character of private enterprise information and news, IT2000 as delivered by SingaporeONE tends to reflect mainly the virtues of Singapore.

Both systems embody a philosophy that the West very poorly grasps: supply-side information. Both the MSC and SingONE are information delivery systems based on attention-getting mixes of image and sound. What they deliver is another matter. Where the Western private enterprise system tends to go in for mental diversion, SingONE focuses on infotainment: information their respective governments feel the people need, presented in a way that looks a lot like TV but conveys content more like a government agency. Singapore's approach simply ladles out a copious bowl of information soup (including video on demand, or VOD) and lets each viewer pick and choose the morsels he or she likes most. Malaysia's MSC is geared to a much simpler database, consisting of health-related services under the rubric of "telemedicine," education under the aegis of "smart" schools, chip-coded identity cards, stored-value technology, and so on.

It is very doubtful that the Malaysian and Singaporean governments will allow international advertisers to influence the content of their multimedia programming. Public taste also imposes a fairly hard investment reality. In matters such as health care, why use an imported database when a local one is more culturally relevant? In entertainment matters, why deliver content via an expensive multimedia system when ordinary TV does almost as well and is in almost all homes?

Business investors need more—and more accurate—information from the Malaysian and Singaporean authorities before committing themselves to investment beyond the simple provision of hardware and software. The absence of candor by Malaysia as to the real state of the MSC's progress (or rather the lack of it) is a significant warning sign that the country is playing fast and loose with the real facts of the country's ability to perform as promised.

Malaysia has serious and unacknowledged problems with productivity rates in its manufacturing industry occasioned by the use of cheap immigrant labor and the entitlements mentality of many of its *bumiputra* (native Malay) citizens. The result is a *tak lah* ("So what?") work ethic that keeps Malaysia near the bottom end of productivity figures among Asian manufacturing industries. Moreover, Malaysia's inattention to basic civic matters like decent public transport and clean streets demonstrates the sharp distinction between what top government leaders say they will do and what low-level bureaucrats and managers actually do in practice. All the promise of the MSC will turn into very little result if the indiscipline of the country's society precludes its use.

Singapore, on the opposite end of the scale, is far more advanced than they let on. They are planning the export of SingONE and its management philosophy to

China and India. Singapore has worked out an arrangement for providing high-tech information services with the government of Andhra Pradesh that has the air of turning Hyderabad into a multimedia version of Bangalore. Singapore's regardful relations with China and its underutilized SuZhou industrial park outside of Shanghai make Singapore a natural penetration point for IT services into the China market.

The bottom line at this point is that Malaysia initially oversold itself and then ruined its efforts with a histrionic display of pique that unmasked the hostility with which the Malaysian government has long viewed the West. Malaysia wants lots of Western money but none of its culture. The country's "Malaysia, Inc." approach is likely to result in one economic swerve after another as the country continues to deny the consequences of its favoritist business practices.

Singapore on the other hand is better positioned in terms of its state of the technology and its probity in remaining low-key until its system is proven. There are doubts about how much information the country is willing to let loose despite its growing sophistication at delivering it. The real advantage in SingaporeONE is that it has been conceived and designed by people who habitually think in fifteen- to twenty-year time frames.

9

SingaporeONE

Singapore's goal is to provide Asia's first operating and most sophisticated and comprehensive IT site by mid-1998. Its system is composed of two basic parts: (a) a public information superstructure, IT2000, and (b) a high-bandwidth multimedia delivery system, SingaporeONE (SingONE).

Although Singapore's IT plans were kept low-key in public announcements, IT2000 and SingONE moved very quickly, reaching the beta-testing phase with sixty-six consumer-oriented databases installed in five hundred homes and offices on 31 July 1997 and two thousand installations providing one hundred plus databases six months later. The commercial launch in 1998 targets eight hundred thousand installations in homes, businesses, and schools by early 1999.

This in effect made Singapore the first, and thus far the only, provider of a broadband multimedia IT network of any significance in Asia. By direct screen-to-screen comparison, SingONE is more content-appropriate and approximately as user friendly as AOL, given their different kinds of content. (Whether it breaks down as often as AOL remains to be seen.) In short, for the first time an Asian multimedia services network is being seen not as merely the servant of a government but as a flow-through channel for IT and e-commerce services to the mass markets of Asia. SingONE also is the first Asian service that has the look and feel one expects of an international e-commerce extranet, and although SingONE is not intended for e-commerce the way international services are, it is Asia's best homegrown role model.

HOW SINGONE DEVELOPED

As far back as 1975, an initiative mooted by the chairman of Telecommunication Authority of Singapore (TAS) and the CEOs of the National Computer Board (NCB) and National Science and Technology Board (NSTB) foresaw the need for the government to jump-start IT via setting applications and standards that—at the time—did not yet exist. The only real models were U.S. database vendors like Lexis and CompuServe. As there was no specific commercial case in mind at the time, no one could forecast market demand. In other words, Singaporean officials saw IT as a speculative jump-start venture that could, if it turned out to be successful, play a significant infrastructural role in Singapore's business growth.

Singapore's plans had reached such a state by September 1994 that the journal of the Singapore Computer Society, *Information Technology*, spelled out the most comprehensive theoretical model for a national information infrastructure (NII) that appears to have been published anywhere. This document was in essence a how-to manual on building a national multimedia network.

The recommended approach was to leverage on the private sector so the government would not become involved in a capital investment role. This in effect cast the government in the role of oversight participant rather than systems manager.

Singaporean communications and computer people planned on a major infrastructure project from the very beginning. This implied an organization devoted solely to the project. The government brought together representatives from the NCB, TAS, the Economic Development Board (EDB), the Singapore Broadcasting Authority (SBA), and National Science & Technology Board (NSTB) into a new unit named the Multimedia Broadband Network (MBN).

TAS proposed that the future service should embody several features that found their way into today's SingONE:

- open platforms for technology and communications,
- open architecture and high capacity (now called bandwidth),
- flexibility and market response,
- no digital coexisting alongside cable.

Three additional parameters subsequently evolved in practice:

- No impediment should be placed in the way consumers choose their own delivery vehicle; they should have as many options as available.
- System operators should have a great deal of individual choice between competing vendors.
- Singapore should make the best use of the facilities and equipment already on tap, but quickly adapt to new technologies as they arise.

Singapore has a history of planning carefully rather than seizing on an idea because it sounds good or somebody important has it. SingONE in fact is being planned using a fifteen-year strategic cycle rather than the typical five-year corporate cycle. The NCB advocated a "supply-push" approach to the market rather than "demand-pull." This means devising products and putting them out there for the market to sample. In an investment environment as hard to forecast as a networked consumer/business/schools community, the Singaporean approach of providing services on a supply rather than demand basis has enabled them to create demand rather than guess it. This is an innovative approach and may rewrite the rules of the most efficient way to determine long-term capital investment in the culturally and linguistically complex Asian market.

Given this framework, the decision to first build the high-speed core broadband network came naturally: without a working system no one could assess the then-unquantified cost-effectiveness issue. No cost answers meant no pricing answers. The only way to discover competitiveness was to build the system. From the strategy point of view, the approach was to fuse competition with cooperation.

As everyone wanted to see success occur from mutual cooperation, the NCB's National IT Forum (NITF) avoided a heavy hand in choosing independent service providers. It was then unclear which industries and ISPs might become interested. The solution became codified in the motto, "Let nobody be the driving force." Amorphous as it may sound, this management philosophy proved the best for a project of this type.

On the hardware side, TAS designed custom telecommunications equipment in conjunction with Sumitomo, Siemens, and NEC. They also visited many other systems in the world. The conclusion was that the most effective system for Singapore was a semi-turnkey approach in which a supplier builds the system and the NITF refines it based on the patterns of long-term use.

The NITF approved SingONE's master plan in January 1996. A working mock-up to test how the system would work was in operation by May 1997. The participating multinationals include the likes of IBM, Microsoft, Oracle, Sun, Reuters, Bloomberg, Hewlett-Packard, Andersen Consulting, Yahoo, Motorola Multimedia, and what can only be called a glittering array of others.

DELIVERY

The National Information Technology Centre's business case had to be based on what they would be selling. Should these be value-added or specialized services?

Two delivery options were available: cable or video on demand. Singapore Telecom's research found ADSL would give customers the highest-speed access, but many customers would see little need for services faster than the traditional modem. Hence the choice of communications infrastructure was based on the highest-bandwidth ATM for core delivery and local access networks using cable modems and ADSL subscriber lines. This gave customers a delivery choice of copper, cable, or modem. These have several features in common:

- They are not interactive.
- They can source from a common pool of services.
- They are customizable.

NITF believed that the ultimate size of the market should not be provider-limited. That is one reason why so many multinationals invested so quickly. The NITF approach was to assume the simplest of parameters—high capacity and high delivery—and let market demand determine the fees. Since demand scale was very hard to predict back in early 1996 when this system was being shaped, NITF tacked broadband onto basic telephone flow based on a 20 percent to 80 percent line allocation formula. The technological investment for SingONE thus far is S$150 million. Of this, S$100 million went into the development effort. Considering the value received as demonstrated in the actual working system today, this was a remarkably efficient use of the investment dollar.

IF YOU BUILD IT THEY WILL VIEW IT

Singapore's ultimate goal is an "Intelligent Island" whose SingONE access point provides IT2000's content faster and more reliably than the Internet. The overall scheme includes:

- news on demand
- entertainment
- distance learning
- teleshopping and e-commerce
- video-conferencing capability
- online government services
- high-speed (128kb) Internet

Adapting the terminology originally devised to translate office terms to computer screens, the concept of "desktop" became "webtop." Accordingly, "SingaporeONE Webtop" is the first menu users see:

- Event Announcements
- Directory of Services
- Video Help Desk
- SingaporeOne Online Magazine
- System Messages
- Links to Popular Sites
- Promotional Games
- Online Software Downloads
- Classified Ads
- Personalized Homepage
- Video Digitizing Service

The second item on this list is the gateway into SingONE's five major databases. (Their individual offerings are listed below.) Navigating SingONE is a snappy affair: screen-build time is as quick as the 128kb feeds one finds in a cybercafe (and without the expensive coffee!). The graphics are direct and without the blimpy overweight clutter one finds in screens designed by people with more HTML literacy than graphics literacy. With the exception of a few duds for the international viewer such as what to expect in one's first one hundred days in the Singaporean army, the databases themselves have been very well thought out.

This is particularly true of the "Learning" database set, some twenty items long, which appears determined that no possible chink in a Singaporean child's education should go unarmored. A quick glance at the original information providers (OIPs) of this database set demonstrates just how seriously the Singaporean Ministry of Education takes quality information: they include Global Knowledge Network, Pacific Internet, MacroMedia, Inc., Temasek Polytechnic, Oracle Systems, Systems Education Center, Information Technology Institute, Times Learning Systems, Arthur Andersen, Singapore Science Centre, and so on.

Another feature of SingONE's educational databases is how strongly they are weighted toward thinking and reasoning skills, not blind memorization. This should dispel the view that Singapore neglects creativity in the learning process. Indeed, the single most striking feature of SingONE's offerings is the high degree of intelligence it expects in its users. Whether by intent or simply the high caliber of SingONE's OIPs, there is a strong emphasis on assuming the highest common denominator in its viewership rather than network TV's long-standing tradition of pandering to the lowest. A bright, young graduate student searching for a Ph.D. topic these days could do no better than to document what happens to Singapore's children after a decade of SingONE fare compared with children who average seven hours a day in front of commercial television.

All this sums up to the fact that SingONE is the world's first, finest, and fastest operational multimedia network invented by a government to stimulate the intelligence of its own populace. It is a truly remarkable achievement. SingONE should be studied carefully by those who feel that the mid-1990s idealization of the market economy may have gone too far, to the point of ignoring some models that demonstrate what positive effects a good government can have on its society.

IT2000 and SingONE have brought to Asia's e-commerce era several innovations that should receive more of the world's scrutiny:

- The supply-push approach of offering the public information for its own sake may be the first economic alternative to the market-driven approach of servicing the largest common denominator.

- SingONE provides a testable model for the theory that people prefer challenge to mediocrity. What SingONE is really doing is switching the direction of cathode communication from nodding heads to thinking heads.

- Twenty-year vision builds better media than Arbitron and better economies than quarterly reports.

SingONE is a remarkable achievement—one made all the more remarkable because it has progressed so far in relative obscurity. The Singaporean government wanted to make certain its system worked as advertised before making a substantive public relations push unveiling it.

SingONE is perhaps the most original and well-planned venture of its kind anywhere, a history-making credit to everyone involved in its making.

10
SingONE's Public Access Databases

SingONE's street kiosk application for the visitor or casual passerby is *PET+ONE*. This database is the traditional video-in-a-box on the street corner or public facility. It gives public access to SingONE not just to visitors but also people who don't own a PC or Web TV but who need to access SingONE's databases. *PET+ONE* kiosks also provide useful streetside services such as movie previews and reservations for cinema and other performances.

At home or in the office, the Me to You database set encourages interaction among SingaporeONE users. Active World enables many on-line users to simultaneously interact and communicate with each another in a 3D virtual environment. This is what chat rooms should have been from the beginning. Enhanced CU See Me Reflector, ICQ, and NetMeeting respectively provide on-line text-only chat, a virtual 3D community, and on-line multiple-player gaming.

SHOP & FUN

ABACUS Interactive is a premier website for travel information and reservations services. It allows travelers to book air tickets, hotel rooms, tour and cruise packages. It also offers invaluable sightseeing, dining, and shopping tips.

Asia Cuisine contains segments from the publication, *The New Asia Cuisine Scene*, plus the recently launched *Resort Kitchen*. Users can download recipes plus obtain tips on domestic and commercial kitchen designs. Doesn't do the dishes, though.

Cold Storage Virtual Mall offers a home delivery service so users can order items from Singapore's Cold Storage supermarket chain. The mall promises quick deliveries (though there are no guarantees with the ice cream). This is an invaluable service for the ill or disabled.

Cyberwalk Thru Philatelic Museum offers a virtual tour of the Singapore Philatelic Museum. The museum has an impressive collection of first-day covers, stamp art, printing media, printing proofs, progressive sheets, stamps from around the world that have been exchanged with other postal authorities since the early 1960s—in fact, everything but the envelope.

etc Magazine Online is targeted at youths and late teens, offering entertainment content based on the best-selling Singaporean publication.

Focal Point is an interactive optical mall. Users can try on virtual frames and sunglasses to see how they look before ordering online.

Hotels and Restaurants carries hotel perusal to new heights of ease. Users can "walk through" hotels, then make reservations. (Hotels currently accessible are Hotel New Otani and Pan Pacific.) At the on-line restaurants, the famished can inspect menus, pre-order their desired dishes, then make reservations.

InfoLand Online Store offers customers a searchable database of more than two hundred current-release CD-ROM titles. Shoppers search by product category, target age group, or platform. Hot titles can be previewed via video clips.

Kali with Death Rally and *Descent* allow multiple users, mostly teens, to play the same game simultaneously.

Metro Online is a virtual theme park. Users can immerse themselves in a 3D virtual world to experience a whole new way of shopping at Metro.

Paradise for Birds features high resolution images, videos, and information on the many species of birds that can be found at the Jurong BirdPark. Users can generate a customized itinerary at the BirdPark using its Interactive Tourguide Planner.

Plaza One offers merchandise categorized under Digital Domain, Arts and Books, Kids Station, Wine and Music, Sports Arena, and Gift Gallery. Plaza One also offers on-line games, on-line chats, and other interactive services.

RadioWave gives users access to PlayList music charts, from which they can save their favorite songs. A big attraction to PlayList is its background music function: selections can be retrieved and played while surfing the Net or working on the computer. RadioWave includes the Top Twenty charts from RCS stations, a CD showcase, and an on-line forum—all in high-quality stereo.

S1 Collectibles is the place for SingaporeONE memorabilia. Visitors can explore the premises before picking up items such as SingaporeONE mugs, caps, and pins. Sure to become the bane of future knick-knack shelves all over the island.

Self-Serve Electronic Commerce Bureau provides software, content publishers, and web merchants a cost-effective service for their high-volume transactions. This service ensures the secure distribution of content while protecting confidential consumer data. As part of the Global Electronic Commerce Processing Infrastructure, the bureau provides Internet commerce solutions that can process multiple currencies for transactions. It can also add country-specific sales tax.

Sentosa: The Singaporean Playground provides—surprise!—an on-line interactive tour of Sentosa. Users can explore places of interest such as Fort Siloso and the Image of Singapore museum to learn more about the history of Singapore.

Singapore Shopping Village offers cyber gift shops, shopping events, sales, and bargains. From 9 June through 9 July each year, more than fifty merchants offer over one hundred Red Hot Items for sale in a Shop on the Net.

SingTel MAGIX is a content aggregator that allows users to watch their favorite movies, catch the latest news, learn new things, play exciting games, or shop on-line, all in the comfort of their homes.

The Night Safari and *The Open Zoo* simulate a wander around multimedia virtual enclosures where viewers can watch fascinating videos of animals from all over the world and test their knowledge by playing "Did You Know?"

GOVERNMENT

Asian Civilization Museum is an on-line multimedia version of the Asian Civilization Museum in Singapore. Users can explore and delve in depth in Chinese ceramics and Chinese history. Beautifully illustrated interactive screens, videos, and animated stories hallmark this application.

First 100 Days is a multimedia web-based application that provides information on all aspects of basic military training (BMT) in the Singapore army. New recruits (and more likely, their parents) can experience BMT through videos and 3D walk-throughs. Just the thing for the nostalgic corporal.

Government Video Online Library provides government videos on demand. Users can access one hundred sixty videos from forty government ministries and statutory boards. Featuring a wide range of themes, the service includes videos on public information (e.g., health care), national education (e.g., footages on Singapore history), training (e.g., Speak Mandarin videos), recruitment, advertisements, and promotion.

Healthy Life Style Information is an attractive multimedia website featuring sharp images and full-motion video.

OphthWeb delivers eye patients their e-mail records securely via the Internet. Multimedia data such as photographs of parts of the eye and visual fields can be sent to patients and their doctors at their convenience no matter where they are in the world.

Singapore InfoMap is Singapore's national homepage. It provides a comprehensive directory of Singapore's public-sector and private-sector websites. Other useful information found in the site includes Singapore's history, up-to-date facts on Singapore, calendar of events, and postcard service.

Speak Mandarin Campaign Homepage contains practice conversations, vocabulary lists, a directory of Mandarin courses, and videos that teach Chinese proverbs.

URA Online offers a host of useful information and services pertaining to the physical planning of Singapore. URA's policy guides, estate information, and other corporate information are also available.

LEARNING

Curriculum ALIVE is a multimedia learning software for primary students. Based on the latest Ministry of Education teaching syllabus, it uses theme-based stories to facilitate language learning. It integrates eighteen hundred interactive learning activities per subject per level with animated stories and educational games to make learning fun.

Education—The Fun Learning Programme for Primary Four students covers English, Mother Tongue (Chinese and Malay), mathematics, and science following a Ministry of Education syllabus. The program is localized, which makes the contents relevant to a child growing up in Singapore.

HistoryCity is a virtual community for children, modeled on 1870 Singapore. Full of historical buildings, costumes, objects, news, and stories, it encourages children to explore and play with history while learning about Singapore's cultural heritage.

I-Dia uses MusicPen's "Clicktoons On-line" technology. I-Dia provides users with "cool tools" to create, play, and interact with others in a way that is intuitive, imaginative, and entertaining. Spontaneity, interactivity, and multi-player game action meet the high-speed communication capabilities of broadband technology.

Internet Tuition Centre is targeted at Primary One through Primary Six students, the pure Internet-based tuition center comprises biweekly tutorials, assessments, quizzes, and spelling tests. The site also contains a large database of vocabulary and links to the web. Qualified teachers will be on hand to mark and design the web content.

Learn@Home is part of the Singapore Polytechnic's Virtual College project. It conducts tele-seminars and tele-tutorials over SingONE. Education providers can use it to conduct sessions with multiple students at home. Multiple media is also provided for interaction and courseware development.

Learnet is an interactive broadband network environment for secondary and junior college teachers and students. It is designed to impart to students real-world skills such as creativity and higher-order thinking skills. Real-world information is provided by historical events around the world as provided by Reuters.

Mentys allows users to receive training at their own convenience and pace at the office or at home. A unique feature is its ability to integrate a variety of tools, such as "Competency Management Services" and "Learning Warehousing" under a single umbrella. Mentys also has an assessment tool that allows users to define the best training curriculum according to their specific needs.

MirrorS offers carefully selected educational resources on the web, mirrored locally in Singapore to allow faster access. It is a one-stop location for quick educational information.

Multimedia Jukebox is targeted at young audiences between six and twelve years old. It showcases a library of CD-ROM contents from Octogram Design and Double Click. Its most interesting feature is that Jukebox allows high-bandwidth Internet users to access the same interactive features in today's CD-ROM titles without having to buy the actual CD-ROMS.

Online Learning Environment offers short enrichment and structured format courses for the public. All learning activities, such as interactive discussions and tutorials with instructors, are carried over high-speed (128kb) Internet. Through OLE, Temasek Polytechnic hopes to extend educational programs to people who can't attend regular courses because of varied working hours or distance.

Oracle Learning Architecture is a comprehensive education service that provides multimedia educational content on demand. It will help companies lower their cost of training per user, yet ensure flexible and consistent training programs for a bigger pool of employees (fast Internet).

SEC-Multimedia Gallery showcases titles on ShockWave and QuickTime Videos that allow users to browse before purchasing.

Skytutor Online is an educational service for "O"-level students in English, physics, chemistry, and mathematics. It uses progressive teaching methods to help students prepare and review for their exams.

SpaceALIVE! is a virtual environment on the Internet for education, entertainment, shopping, and tourism. It makes possible real-time collaboration among an unlimited number of simultaneous users. It can be used for distance learning, arbitration in a virtual courtroom, and electronic commerce in a virtual mall.

STW@Home delivers lesson packages and courseware for Singapore schools. Its resources are available to teachers and students in six pilot secondary schools.

Times Learning Tree enables users to access interactive multimedia education. It comes with tutorials, assessments, stories, and fun activities to help children learn the fun way. "Taro and His Grandmother" imparts language skills to children, and "Zarc's Maths Adventure" is a mathematics series.

Training Infocosm is a one-stop website with a comprehensive list of training courses, resources, and services for human resource managers, training coordinators, and individuals. These can search for courses, seminars, and training resources relevant to their needs.

Virtual College emulates many aspects of an educational institution without requiring physical attendance. VC makes it possible to learn regardless of space and time barriers by using remote access and network communications. Advanced diploma and shorter courses offered by Singapore Polytechnic enable students to attend an experimental VC from home, participate in group discussions, attend lectures and tutorials, browse relevant Internet sites, and prepare and submit preformatted assignments.

Virtual Science Centre is a computer-based science education, research, and technology outreach project delivered via the Internet. It promotes activities in science education, encourages information exchange and resource sharing among students, teachers, and the public.

INFORMATION SERVICES

AsiaONE Video Wall is an interactive news review from the major Singaporean newspapers, plus multimedia business news from *Business Times* and *UTV International*. Its multimedia magazine *Wiz* lets users watch movie trailers and read music reviews with short sound clips. Cyberzone brings games demos and updates of the latest computer games.

Calendar ONE offers a quick reference guide on food promotions, product launches, sales, entertainment events, training courses, and conferences. Users can access private organizations' calendars.

Central Chinese Content Service is a directory of Internet resources supported by multilingual technologies.

Click Diz is a complete online environment for CD-ROM titles. Users can search and review the titles, check out demonstrations, obtain technical help, and purchase on-line.

CNET Briefs is a leading publisher of computing and technology content on the Internet. CNET provides authoritative information on computers, the Internet, and future technology in an easy-to-understand magazine format on the web. Users can access numerous multimedia tutorials and guides to using the computer and Internet more effectively.

Discovery Alta Vista has two components: "Search Engine" and "Forum." The search engine searches only for local and regional sites enabling users to locate these sites faster and more accurately. The "Community Forum" in Discovery is dedicated to topics that add content value and social awareness. An attractive "Forum" feature is that users can post documents, URLs, and graphic images to supplement their discussions.

Health ONE is a health information resource for the public as well as health professionals. This resource can be accessed by nearly one hundred twenty countries worldwide.

Help@Home is a video help desk in which users can access a database of subscribers whenever a subscriber dials into the help desk.

Intelligent Web Travel Guide is an electronic version of the print-media Singapore Street Directory. It allows users to find locations and route information on-line. Other functions are navigating maps, finding the shortest route between two locations, and finding places within a vicinity. Unfortunately, it does not find a readily available taxi.

MediaCity offers users the ability to watch TV programs at the viewer's own convenience. MediaCity includes programs such as news bulletins, business and financial news, entertainment, tabloid news, drama serials, sitcoms, telefeatures, and music.

NCIS Directory brings you contact information of people and organizations in Singapore. Its search capability helps locate contacts by searching multiple on-line directories in one simple operation. Other information such as product descriptions and company business interests are also accessible from the service.

Personal iAgent (Pi) fits every user's unique personality. Pi modifies bits entering the browser to give users a truly personalized web experience. Pi can automatically locate interesting web pages, newsgroups, and highlight interesting passages from a long web page.

SingaporeONE Community Directory contains the names, contact information, and homepage URLs of all SingaporeONE users. The directory also contains the complete list of application owners and service providers who contribute to the SingaporeONE initiative.

TIARA (Timely Information for All, Relevant, and Affordable) is a comprehensive one-stop information source that allows users to access information found in three hundred databases and eight library catalogues.

Voices.net (Internet Voiceover Database Program) allows local and overseas advertising and casting agencies to search and locate suitable voiceover talents. Voices.net can provide instant access to a wide and current range of voiceover talents, saving users the tedium of sifting through cassette tapes.

Yahoo! Singapore is a mirror site for Yahoo! in Asia (www.yahoo.com.sg). It provides users throughout Southeast Asia with faster and more efficient service. Yahoo! in Asia has the same content of the original Yahoo!

11
SingONE in Government

The 1996 World Competitiveness Report placed Singapore second in the world in exploiting IT for business competitiveness. With 207 computers for every 1,000 citizens, Singapore ranked twelfth in the world, and first in Asia. Singapore's Internet connection of 7.74 for every 1,000 population is the highest in Asia. Singapore was ranked by the 1997 Global Competitiveness Report as the second most computer-literate country in the world.

The island-state's IT industry is, to say the least, briskly businesslike. Total sales of hardware, software, and IT services grew by 34.3 percent to a record $6.7 billion in 1996. Export sales accounted for 51 percent of this total while domestic sales accounted for the remaining 49 percent.

Starting in April 1996, the National Computer Board divested its system-development role in the Civil Service Computerisation Programme (CSCP) to National Computer Systems Pte Ltd. (NCS), in order to focus primarily on its IT architect and catalyst roles. A new Government Chief Information Office (GCIO) was set up within the NCB to drive the next phase of computerization in the Civil Service, focusing on developing and establishing Civil Service-wide IT standards and practices.

The NCB took the cluster organization approach, each mirroring a key economic and user sector in Singapore. As of early 1998, each cluster adopts a holistic approach, addressing technology, business, and IT policy matters as a single issue. The clusters (a) identify and spawn flagship applications in their sectors, (b) promote the development and investment of IT-related activities, and (c) guide the IT industry as a whole to collectively drive IT2000 projects. New incentive schemes, such as the Innovation Development Scheme (IDS) initiated by the Economic Development Board (EDB), were devised to encourage Singaporean companies to innovate and be more competitive. Promising local enterprises are identified and nurtured into homegrown multinational corporations, typically within a five-year cycle.

Extending the reach of IT to the man in the street was the next priority. Promotional and educational programs were organized for the general population to make them better aware of IT and its applications and to increase their IT literacy.

IMPROVING GOVERNMENT

The Singapore Civil Service is one of the most highly computerized in the world. Two out of three civil servants have a computer and all government ministries have implemented Internet websites. Over S$1 billion has been invested since the early 1980s to install more than 900 computer-based systems. Each year, an average of S$200 million is spent on upgrading and acquiring new systems.

The NCB has drawn up IT plans to take the Civil Service into the next phase of computerization that will help realize the plan for a first-class public service for the twenty-first century (PS21). The Internet and information kiosks are being exploited to improve government efficiency and effectiveness and to offer even greater convenience for the public to do business with the government.

> *Government Intranet*, launched in June 1996, links some 16,000 computers in a secure network that allows multimedia information to be shared across government departments and statutory boards. Civil servants have on-line access to government directories, instruction manuals, details of Civil Service Sports Council facilities, and PS21 information services such as newsletters and updates on WITS projects. The Government Intranet also provides a news alert service, where a user can specify selected topics of interest from major information sources, such as AsiaOne, to be sent automatically to him.
>
> *Common Software Pool* distributes generic applications across the Civil Service. This saves individual ministries and statutory boards from having to redevelop the same applications. Software available from the pool include XtraS (a staff suggestion scheme), Word Macros, and Electronic Leave Applications.
>
> *Public Sector Smart Card* (PS Card), inaugurated in 1996, is a common identification document for civil servants. Depending on the holder's security and privilege levels, the card allows entry to selected government buildings and access to computer systems. As the PS Card is compatible with the NETS Cashcard system, it can also be used as an electronic purse to pay for goods at canteens or retail outlets, for public telephone calls, and for purchases at vending machines.
>
> *Computerised Investigation Management System* links police headquarters to all police units and the Criminal Investigation Department (CID). Police investigators using notebook computers at the scene of crime will

have immediate electronic access to case files, police reports, and record statements more efficiently.

Electronic Filing System. A total of S$30 million was invested in the development of an Electronic Filing System for the Judiciary of Singapore. With the implementation of the Electronic Filing System, law firms no longer need to make physical trips to the courts for filing or extraction of documents. The filing service can be made available twenty-four hours a day so that documents can be submitted at the law firms' convenience. Legal documents are stored in the system, and up-to-date information can be viewed by more than one person at the same time. Improvement in productivity is expected with the streamlined automated workflow and the automatic case tracking and monitoring features of the system.

IMPROVING GOVERNMENT SERVICES TO THE PUBLIC

Singapore Government Home Page was set up on the Internet in April 1995 to provide on-line access to information on government services, policies, and procedures. By June 1996, all ministries and twenty-five statutory boards had implemented their own websites with links to this home page. A few transaction-based applications were also developed. At the Ministry of Community Development website, the public can now look up information on child-care centers as well as register their children on-line at the desired child-care center. The Ministry of Labour website has an application that allows the public to apply for work permits for foreign maids electronically.

Civil Service Recruitment has been conducted on the Internet since the August 1995 and February 1996 mass recruitment exercises. This was the first application in the Civil Service to make use of the Internet for transaction processing. It demonstrated the convenience with which job applicants could send in their applications or make enquiries, and the ease with which job applications are channeled automatically to the relevant ministries for short-listing.

Electronic Procurement System (EPS) automates procurement workflow and establishes electronic links with government suppliers via fax and electronic data interchange (EDI). EPS was implemented by the Ministry of Finance's Budget Division and the Ministry of Health's Pharmaceutical Department, then deployed to other government departments and statutory boards.

BizCore was implemented in May 1995, as part of the Registry of Companies and Businesses' (RCB) $4.5 million information systems planning project. The Registry has introduced more services to its customers. These include the electronic filing of RCB documents, provision of information on Teleview, and the retrieval of information via an interactive kiosk or a telephone.

Singapore Titles Automated Registration System (STARS) enables the Land Titles Registry to capture transactions on private property titles. Anyone, especially lawyers and real estate agents, now make on-line enquiries from their own offices, shortening the turnaround time to process the registration of titles.

Business Process Re-engineering improves services to the public. The NCB proposed an electronic link-up of immigration checkpoints, companies, employers, and insurance agencies. Only one visit to the Worker Immigration Department is required, with not more than thirty minutes of waiting time. Applications are processed in one day. Indirect savings from these improvements are estimated at S$3 million a year for employers.

Pupil Registration has streamlined and computerized Primary One school child registration. Launched in July 1995, the new system allows registration to be done on-line at schools, with updates on vacancies made easily available after each phase of the registration. The system also helps the school authorities to detect parents who reserve places for their children in several schools.

Information Kiosks have been installed at the Subordinate Courts, the Traffic Police, and the Land Transport Authority for the Automated Traffic Offence Management System (ATOMS). ATOMS will result in tremendous personnel savings, since traffic offenders who fail to pay their fines within the stipulated period can now do so using the kiosks without having to attend court. Another kiosk application makes it possible for the public as well as lawyers to obtain information pertaining to court schedules, processes, and procedures of the law. In 1997, there are three such information kiosks available for public access, two in the City Hall Building and one in the Supreme Court Building.

LEARNING AND EDUCATION

In 1995, the Singaporean government began to emphasize developing technology-based learning and teaching in schools and making information more accessible electronically at schools, libraries, and the home. As of early 1998 the following components had resulted from that effort:

Digital Library is a network of borderless libraries and electronic databases, with information readily accessible from the desktop. Some twenty libraries and two hundred information databases have been linked, allowing all segments of the user population—children, adults, professionals, researchers, and the business community—to enjoy more convenient access to information. Other services include electric searching and requests for books and information, and an alert service that notifies users of new information related to their fields of interest.

Student's and Teacher's Workbench (STW) is a multimedia software environment for secondary schools. Teachers make use of STW to prepare lesson packages and deliver these lessons in class with participation from students. Students can access the lesson packages later for review or if they have missed the lessons in class. The STW was begun in six secondary schools in January 1996 to deliver science lessons to Secondary One students.

Accelerating the Use of IT in Primary Schools (AITP) was launched in June 1995. AITP aims to equip students with critical information and higher order skills necessary for the knowledge-based economy of the future. The six pilot schools were equipped with about one hundred stand-alone personal computers and a wide range of educational courseware. Teachers were trained in using computers and pedagogy involving IT. Pupils were able to access computers for different learning activities including project work, enrichment, and remedial lessons.

Internet for Schools was introduced in the Ministry of Education (MOE), fourteen junior colleges, twenty-four schools, and four institutes. A number of seminars and workshops were organized by the NCB to acquaint students, teachers, principals, and parents with the use of the Internet. A newsgroup, coordinated by specialist inspectors from the Curriculum Planning Division of MOE, was set up to allow mathematics teachers in junior colleges to share their experiences.

Local area networks (LANs) were set up in schools starting in mid-1997. In addition to streamlining nonteaching tasks such as records management, the LAN infrastructure will enable teachers to prepare multimedia lesson materials through the sharing of common resources, such as data, software, printers, optical mark readers, CD-ROMS, and video on demand.

12

SingONE and Economic Competitiveness

MANUFACTURING AND DISTRIBUTION

The NCB's efforts in this sector have largely been focused on setting up data exchange standards and information networks for electronic transactions and information sharing and exploiting IT to upgrade the skills of the manufacturing sector.

Electronic Data Interchange for Manufacturing (EDIMAN) was first launched in March 1994. It enables suppliers to carry out transactions with multiple buyers without having to implement proprietary procurement systems for different ones. Thirty-two multinational companies from the electronic sector have implemented EDIMAN. A Chemical EDIMAN Working Group (CIWG) has also been formed by the NCB to promote the use of the EDI standard within the petrochemical sector. An *EDIMAN Implementation Guide* covering procedures, tips, and business models for EDI implementation was published in May 1996. Four multinational corporations began to implement EDIMAN starting in June 1996, with a goal of reaching an average of one hundred to one hundred fifty suppliers each.

Furniture Manufacturing Information System (FMIS) was launched in January 1996 to help furniture manufacturers upgrade their manufacturing, administrative, financial, and logistics operations. It allows local furniture manufacturers to communicate electronically with their manufacturing and distribution facilities throughout the region. The FMIS is one of the cornerstones of the council's master plan to turn Singapore into a major Asia-Pacific furniture center. The NCB also provided technical assistance to the Singapore Furniture Industry Council (SFIC) to launch its Internet website. This was the first of its kind in the region, and helps promote the

270 SFIC members and their export activities to potential customers worldwide.

SME First-Stop Centre Web Site. The NCB is working with the Singapore Productivity and Standards Board (PSB) to set up the First-Stop Centre for SMEs website on the Internet to provide first-stop information and advisory services. This site will be linked to the G7 and APEC-proposed Global Information Network for SMEs.

Mechatronics Design Centre. In July 1996, a memorandum of understanding (MOU) was signed among the NCB, Autodesk Inc., and Temasek Polytechnic to set up the first Mechatronics Design Centre (MDC) in Singapore. Located at Temasek Polytechnic, the MDC will eventually reach out to more than eighteen hundred manufacturing workers to upgrade their 3-D design skills. The NCB and Autodesk will cofund the infrastructure; Temasek Polytechnic will provide teaching staff and facilities.

THE CONSTRUCTION INDUSTRY

The Construction and Real Estate Network (CORENET) is an industry-wide network that streamlines information flow within the construction industry. CORENET automates building and development approval processes and procurement of contracting and maintenance services. It also provides one-stop access to information ranging from property prices to land development.

The first CORENET application, BP-Expert, inaugurated in 1997, automates the checking of building plans. The user requirements for the feature-based CAD interface for the BP-Expert have been accepted by the six pilot sites.

Another system under CORENET is the Automatic Quantities Take-off System (AQTS). This system, which reads directly from CAD drawings and automatically calculates the amount of building materials required, was prototyped with the Public Works Department (PWD).

TOURISM AND LEISURE SERVICES

One emphasis of the NCB has been to exploit IT to provide convenience for tourists and locals alike in gaining access to tourist attractions and leisure activities. It also looks into setting up information networks for the exchange of information within the travel and tourism industry.

The Singapore Tourist Card (STC) is a smart card issued to tourists to make it convenient for them to gain entry to tourist attractions, travel on public transport, and make purchases.

Singapore Events & Arts Ticketing System (SEATS) enables ticket purchases to be made from the home, through information kiosks, and even from overseas. Since the conclusion of a pilot study in October 1995, the NCB has been working to facilitate joint ventures between local and international ticketing operators.

Travel Exchange on the Internet. Approval has been obtained to set up two travel exchanges on the Internet—a Singapore Travel Exchange to support the local industry and a Virtual Travel Exchange for the region. The exchange will incorporate an electronic travel mart, trading services, travel and tourism project exchanges, on-line information services, and classified advertisements. It will serve as a focal point for networking between potential travel and tourism partners in Singapore and the region and allow license applications and renewals to be submitted and approved electronically.

HEALTH CARE SERVICES

The main focus of the NCB in this sector has been new IT capabilities for hospitals and health care providers, specifically in the areas of electronic medical records and telemedicine.

Electronic Medical Record System (EMR) allows patients' medical data to be easily retrieved and shared among healthcare providers. An EMR Selection Task Force has reviewed several EMR solutions for consideration by Tan Tock Seng Hospital (TTSH) and Singapore General Hospital (SGH).

Telemedicine. A joint technical working group develops the nationwide network infrastructure to support Singapore's telemedicine needs. The telemedicine programming will position Singapore as a provider of domestic and regional telemedicine services. The first application would be a teleradiology network for transmitting X-ray images electronically between SGH as the image reading center and a polyclinic as the data acquisition site.

Healthcare Information on Internet. The NCB promotes the development of healthcare information services on the Internet to bring greater awareness of healthcare matters to the public. The MOH has since implemented such a service on the Internet. Sembawang Media has launched a pilot service called *Doctors' On-line* for the healthcare community.

13

Evolving a National Information Infrastructure

The NCB's plan for a National Information Infrastructure focuses on designing an NII backbone and a multimedia broadband network. Projects also explore new media technologies such as cable networks and wireless networks.

LIVEwire is an experimental network infrastructure developed by the NCB. It will help the IT Industry and government agencies to better understand the technical challenges, implementation hurdles, and policy issues related to putting up an NII in Singapore. It contains some forty subsystems and development tools built upon the Internet technology and has been released to about one thousand pilot users. To date, the number of registered users has more than doubled. LIVEwire has produced a strong multiplier effect, spurring industry partners such as Singapore Network Services (SNS), National Computer Systems (NCS), iMedia, and Sembawang Media to license it. SNS licensed thirty-six subsystems of LIVEwire starting as far back as 1995. Other commercial applications that were developed together with various partners using LIVEwire technology include INtv-Online (Television Corporation of Singapore), StockWatch (Stock Exchange of Singapore), NL.line, Library Phone-in (National Library), URA-Online (Urban Redevelopment Authority), and Online Street Directory and Record Plans (Ministry of Law Land Systems Support Unit).

On-line Technologies Consortium (OTC). The momentum generated by LIVEwire has led to the establishment of the On-line Technologies Consortium (OTC). There are eight founding sponsors for this consortium, an industry-led effort that will pool resources to acquire more enabling technologies and solutions to nurture the local on-line services industry. It focuses on technologies and solutions central to the on-line service industry, such as secure transactions, information agents, broadband services, and information search engines.

NII Backbone. Approval to lay the foundations for the NII Backbone was granted by the National IT Committee (NITC) in January 1996. The first implementation phase of this high-speed network infrastructure was to link up network providers, data hubs, and government networks by the end of that year. The NII Backbone went on to provide e-mail, universal directory, and information exchange to the public. At the same time, the infrastructure for electronic identification (public key) was implemented for secure transactions in electronic commerce (SET).

Innovation Development Scheme. A number of industry development programs have been put in place to help nurture the Singaporean IT industry. The NCB was granted approval-in-principle agency status by the EDB to administer the Innovation Development Scheme (IDS). Since the scheme was introduced in January 1996, some nineteen IT-related companies have received IDS grants of between 50 and 70 percent of their proposed projected costs.

Promising Local IT Companies. A program to help nurture promising local IT companies was launched in March 1996. Eleven companies have been identified. For a start, total business planning studies will be conducted for their operations.

LECP, SDAS, and LIUP. The Local Enterprise Computerisation Programme (LECP) supported a total of eighty-one projects. As of 1997 more than six hundred small and medium enterprises have benefited from the LECP. Another fifteen projects were supported under the Software Development Assistance Scheme (SDAS). The NCB took over the management of all IT-related Local Industry Upgrading Programme (LIUP) projects from EDB, with effect from January 1996. Projects initiated included applications from the process industry, the manufacturing sector, the shipbuilding industry, and the construction industry.

Shopnet, a pilot project aimed at upgrading small retail stores through computerization, was launched in May 1996. By July of that same year, more than thirty suppliers and ten retail stores had joined the Shopnet program, which provides IT capabilities for automated checkout using bar code readers and automatic update of inventory levels.

IT Manpower and Skills Inventory Survey was launched to ascertain the number and type of skills required to support the IT industry. With a current pool of about 21,000 IT professionals, the demand for manpower in the IT industry is expected to grow by 13 to 15 percent per year. The skills in demand were networking, client-server technologies, object-oriented development, and multimedia and project management. A $6 million fund has been allocated for the Critical IT Resource Programme to subsidize the training of five hundred IT professionals each in these five critical skills.

Multimedia Diploma Programs. Two new multimedia diploma programs were launched by Nanyang Polytechnic and the Singapore Polytechnic's Japan-Singapore Institute of Software Technology. The programs received an overwhelming response. A grant of nearly $1 million was given to Lasalle-SIA College of Arts to train more IT-literate creative talents for the multimedia industry.

THE NATIONAL COMPUTER BOARD AND A SINGAPOREAN IT CULTURE

The NCB's vision is to create an IT culture in which people from all walks of life are comfortable with and adept at using computers at home, school, work, and play. Singapore has been working closely with industry partners to promote the benefits of IT to everyone and to accelerate the adoption of IT in homes, libraries, and community centers.

IT Roadshow is the NCB's effort to reach out to the public, to show how IT can enhance their quality of life. Four roadshows were organized last year in close partnership with the People's Association. They provided many people their first opportunity to see, touch, and play with computers. Activities at these roadshows included talks on multimedia in education, ranging from how to select the right educational software for children to how to select a PC for the family. More than five thousand residents attended these roadshows, which were held at community centers. The show was extended for four days at the Singapore IT Exposition '95.

Edutainment Centers. The concept of computer playgrounds or edutainment centers was initiated to promote IT literacy and fluency among the young and to create a pervasive IT culture in Singapore. Designed for children between the ages of five and twelve, the playground will provide an affordable, fun-filled, and stimulating learning environment to help children become fluent in IT. Quest IT, the first computer playground with sixty computers, was launched in May 1996 at Suntec City Shopping Mall. A second computer playground was opened in Toa Payoh in August 1996 and is targeted at HDB residents.

Hall of IT. An exhibition hall showcasing how IT services can improve the quality of life at home was opened in November 1997 at the Singapore Science Centre. This permanent Hall of IT, initiated by the NCB, will help create awareness of the benefits of IT. It will also encourage the public to use IT to make their work more efficient, their daily chores less time-consuming, and their personal and social lives more rewarding.

Creating and Deploying IT Innovations. The NCB continues to experiment earnestly with new and emerging technologies to offer state-of-the-art IT innovations and solutions to help it realize the IT2000 vision. The Information Technology Institute (ITI), the NCB's applied R&D arm, plays a leading role in developing new and innovative products. Some of these have been commercialized.

Autocell, a system that automates frequency allocation for cellular networks, received the "1995 Innovative Application of AI" award from the American Association for Artificial Intelligence. (This was the third AAAI award won by ITI.)

InfoShip is a multimedia authoring tool jointly developed by ITI and iMedia. It is used to produce *New Media Interactive CD-ROM*, one of the world's most popular multimedia magazines. Among the key features of InfoShip are its ease of use, efficient design, and page layout features.

Live CD is a technology that enables a developer to combine the static contents of CD-ROMs with live, up-to-date information from the Internet. It was made available to the industry in May 1996 in the form of software development kits. Licensing agreements for Live CD have been signed with iMedia, Times Information Systems, and Sky Media.

WAVEVISIONS is a virtual reality software jointly developed by ITI and the ATS group. Launched in June 1995, the software enables architects, designers, and manufacturers to present their ideas in a realistic interactive three-dimensional environment. The software enables interior designers and homeowners or renovators to see, evaluate, and alter designs as they "walk" from room to room or move around a room. Mistakes in choosing the wrong paint colors, tile patterns, and wall surface textures can be avoided, saving customers thousands of dollars and ensuring customer satisfaction. WAVEVISIONS is the first locally developed virtual reality software and is one of the few in the world that are available on the PC Windows platform.

The Financial Interactive Service Hub (FISH) is the first locally developed on-line financial information service that can be accessed worldwide via the Internet. Launched in September 1995, FISH enables the public to access real-time information from the Staff Exchange of Singapore and provides instantaneous information on Singapore financial news, share prices, stock transaction details, and other finance-related data. FISH won the Gold Tiger Award for Global Business News Sites in December 1995.

The Student Multimedia Integrated Learning Environment (SMILE) is a student testing system developed for Informatics Computer School. It allows users to create and retrieve multimedia questions from a question bank for online assessment or for constructing tests. It can also be used to assess or analyze students' test results.

Pictoria is a picture bank system for the digital archiving of high resolution pictures, photographs, and vector graphics. The system supports simultaneous selection and retrieval by a large number of users. It was developed and deployed for Singapore Press Holdings (owners of Singapore's largest newspaper publishing group) and is being used by *The Straits Times* and other major local newspapers.

IAgent, a search engine that can search across databases according to user-specified criteria and automatically generate summaries, has been applied to systems for the National Library Board, the National Heritage Board, and the Government Intranet.

OneView is a multimedia messaging system integrating voice, fax, and e-mail on a PC. OneView is the result of a collaboration between Centigram, a major United States voice mail company, and ITI. The collaboration began in August 1993, and the product was launched in the United States, Hong Kong, and Singapore in May 1995.

Hansard Verbatim Retrieval System is an application built using RightOn, ITI's document management system, which features a powerful concept-based search capability. The Hansard system enables users to search and retrieve free-text information on parliamentary sittings from their home and office, and allows Parliament reporters to create, update, sort, and print indices.

POLICY AND LEGAL FRAMEWORKS

The NCB works with the Telecommunication Authority of Singapore (TAS), Singapore Broadcasting Authority (SBA), Monetary Authority of Singapore (MAS), and the Attorney-General Chambers on policy and legal issues that will impact the implementation of the National Information Infrastructure and IT2000 flagship projects. The main areas of emphasis have been copyright and intellectual property rights in a multimedia environment, security and privacy of information in a highly networked environment, secured payment over Internet, and admissibility of computer-imaged documents as evidence in court.

NII Scan, produced by the NCB, is an electronic web publication of major NII policy trends around the world. NII Scan reports progress of information superhighway policies in the United States, Canada, the European Union, Japan, Korea, Singapore, Australia, and other countries. From last year, the NII Scan made its presence felt on the World Wide Web and attracted contributions from individuals and other NII agencies from all over the world.

Scenario Planning. Translating the IT2000 vision into reality is a massive undertaking that requires good planning at the outset. There is also a fair amount of risk and uncertainty involved as Singaporeans are looking a considerable number of years into the future and at technologies that are changing rapidly. In order to harness collective intelligence and strategic thinking at various levels of the organization, Singaporeans have begun to incorporate scenario planning into its strategic planning process. Scenario planning enables its developers to think of the future in terms of several contingency scenarios and how Singapore should shape its strategies to respond to these should any one of them happen.

Environment Scanning. The NCB has stepped up its environment scanning efforts to monitor and track IT and market trends around the world. This is to anticipate what is coming ahead, to identify the opportunities and threats. The easy accessibility to vast amounts of information worldwide through the Internet has made the job of environment scanning much easier. The challenge Singapore faces is how to interpret the trends and use them intelligently to reshape its strategies for added competitive advantage. The reorganization of the NCB into clusters has enabled it to focus better on the sector a specific cluster is supporting and to have regular dialogues with the key people to understand their concerns better. Singaporeans thus have greater confidence that their IT strategies will be aligned more closely with the business strategies of the city-state's various economic sectors.

14

Information Technology and Practical Applications

INTERVIEW WITH SAW KEN WYE, ASSISTANT CHIEF EXECUTIVE (INDUSTRY) OF THE NATIONAL COMPUTER BOARD, SINGAPORE, JULY 1997

What are the goals of IT2000 and SingaporeONE?

As the Singaporean population matures—especially the younger people—it will continue to demand more. Singapore is laying down the foundations for a full information society right now. We are doing this with much due haste because this is the one time in our history where our size is an advantage. Because of the compactness of our urban areas and the smallness of our land mass, we can accomplish things a lot faster.

The question of how hardware will develop under the impetus of SingaporeONE is really the question of how IT will evolve in the lives of every Singaporean five to twenty-five years from now. Our goal is the universal availability of interactive media services to every person in Singapore.

IT2000 is the overriding blueprint for IT development in Singapore. Hence SingONE is one of the projects under the IT2000 umbrella. How do we see SingONE developing technologically?

Presently we are going in two platform directions for SingONE: hybrid fiber coaxial cable and ADSL. We are not sure which will emerge the clear winner. It does appear that in five years, and perhaps beyond, there will be at least two global broadband delivery systems in Singapore. We foresee that with broadband certain characteristics will change over time. One is that interactivity between computers with multiple interfaces will improve tremendously.

With today's on-line services and Internet we are accustomed to what some people call a 2D paradigm. Broadband will enable a more 3D or what we call an "immersive" paradigm. It will be more vivid and more experiential than what we get on the best CD-ROMs today.

We are not sure what kind of clientele for these services will emerge from the Singaporean market. Some will evolve around network computers and processing applications. In other instances rendering and 3-D imaging will be important. Since delivery will be accomplished by two broadband technologies, people can decide which to use depending on the application. Whether the final delivery speed will be ten megabits or one hundred megabits, we don't yet say. Delivery will certainly be greater than MPEG today [at least three megabits per second]. In fact, this bandwidth is already being delivered in Singapore through ADSL and the hybrid coax network.

What this means is that people will have the ability to do on-line real-time video streaming. This in turn implies that we will have to start to work on building more compelling applications.

As technology gets more sophisticated, it also should get easier to use. As we add a more intuitive, interactive use interface, there must be more and more intelligent features built in. The only way to do that is to use more technology.

How will Singapore's IT push affect its school system?

Our Master Plan for IT Education will be in place by the year 2002. Every child who leaves school after 2000 should be IT-trained. By 2002 these youngsters will be fairly sophisticated from their practical experience in the job market. They are curious, hungry for more, eager to explore more, willing to push the boundaries. They will not be satisfied with older technology.

Today all home computers are more powerful and have more features than most computers in offices. In Singaporean offices these days, people are generally satisfied with a Pentium 166 and a 2GB hard disk. But if I go buy a computer for the home, I need a 166 MMX or Pentium 200 with 4GB. This is not just because of the kids growing up, but that many kinds of homes are creating an insatiable demand.

This implies that, these days, the home, not the office, is driving the kind of computer that manufacturers should be making. In the United States, shipments to the home exceed shipments to business. In Singapore, the home market is growing much faster than the office market.

Computer makers come to us to see what applications we use. From applications comes functionality and from the functionality come the specifications. I sit on an informal advisory group for Microsoft. They come to us and show us their plans for products and invite our comments. Leading multinationals like Sun and IBM similarly bring their latest products here. When Sun wants to introduce their Net PCs here their first question is how these would fit into our schools market.

Our response is that we feel that a Net PC is fine for information surfing, but if the consumer wants to do transactions over the Internet or via SingONE, he must use a smart card. The conclusion Sun takes away from this interaction is that a Net PC should have a smart card reader incorporated to be appropriate for the future of Singapore.

We realize the twenty-first century mind-set will be shaped by the inquisitive minds of today. That's why we call it "The Knowledge Century." Exploration, information seeking, playing with fact and image—all these are what will shape such minds. The reason for Singapore's high focus on computers in schools is that we believe that one of the hidden virtues of the computer is the way it can break down the limitations of the classroom. The Internet opens the world to a child in a way a book or CD-ROM cannot. We want to develop our youngsters fully, so we want to give them the tools. We could have spent millions of dollars on social-impact studies about the rise of IT in the lives of children. Instead we just went ahead and put computers in classrooms. The assumption was, "You can't avoid it, so do it." We addressed the task of coaxing kids into using interactivity to learn rather than just play with it.

We have to make learning interesting. This is why we went into IT with such a big bang—allocating S$2 billion for IT in education over five years [1996–2000]. At the end of this period we plan on spending another S$600 million a year on upgrading and expansion.

A continuous stream of investment of this magnitude certainly gets the attention of all the leading hardware and software developers in the world. We want them to give serious thought not to just the size of the market in Singapore, but what we want to do with it through our educational system.

Is Singapore getting too far ahead of the rest of Asia?

Because of Singapore's historical and strong investment ties today with China, many of the things that Singapore brings to the Asian table will be consumed in China.

Many people have plans and ideas and visions. The difficulty is turning those visions from rhetoric into implementable projects, and implementable projects into demonstrable showcases. We have learned lessons about what can and cannot be done, what sounds good versus what makes sense, and what is vision and what is practical. I believe it is practicality more than visions that people will pay money for. It is the realm of the practical application where Singapore can best extend its influence.

India is another area in which we see mutual IT interests. In July 1997 we signed a memorandum of understanding with the government of Andhra Pradesh to provide consultancy services to help them devise applications for government services. Andhra Pradesh, having looked around the world, decided they liked what was being done in Singapore. They asked the National Computer Board to help them. Our MOU provides for our helping them transform the government of Andhra Pradesh using IT technology. Andhra Pradesh can then position itself as the model to help the rest of India.

While this example relates specifically to India, what it tells us is that the Singaporean IT management model can apply to widely diverse localities. We have also been approached in a somewhat similar context by Mauritius, the Philippines, and Indonesia.

This is not to say that we know it all. What it does say is that Singapore has gone through a considerable thinking process which we are willing to share.

There is of course payback for Singapore and Singaporean companies, because of commercial relations and technology transfer. When there is talk of Singapore being too far in front of the rest of Asia—an island of wealth in a sea of poverty, that sort of thing—it is our desire that everyone who wishes can rise at his own best pace.

A good analogy for technological push here is the head and the tail. Although the head may be pushing out somewhere, the whole body will come along behind. "Intelligent Island" is a metaphor for "Automated Island." You can automate Singapore, but it is still an island. The real Intelligent Island occurs when we become a strategic node in the whole connected world.

How do you view the market for flow-through information services?

Although SingONE is high-bandwidth, it is likely to be high-bandwidth only in Singapore. All products we develop here must have two versions: one for the Internet at 33.6 or 56 kilobits per second, and another for Singapore at two or three megabits per second. Hence our stipulation that the architecture must be TCP/IP-based for Internet.

How will IT improve the competitiveness of Singaporean SMEs?

We try to wear two hats when we look at a technology. One is the application hat—the technology itself as a product that can generate wealth. The other is using a technology to improve productivity within sectors.

SingONE will introduce new paradigms of working, delivering products and services, fulfilling needs. In the case of SMEs, let us take the example of the lowest probable level in the chain of technology: a neighborhood "Mom & Pop" provision shop. How does one envision using IT technology in such a business?

We approached this setting using a project called ShopNet. Our assumption was introducing technology to improve things like inventory control, sales ordering, and more effective use of assets and resources.

This was Step One. Step Two was using this link to technology to link further up with other business potentialities—home delivery device, Internet shopping, and the like. But the potential flaw we foresaw with this idea was that three or four small companies would give Mom & Pop money for computers, some minister would get his picture taken switching it on, there would be articles in the press, and three months later the computer would be gathering dust.

Why does this happen? "Let's help the little guys" rhetoric too often ends up this way. The reason is often that not enough consideration is given to the carry-through factors that keep the system up (like maintenance) and business-specific issues (like who decides inventory ordering as products change, or who inputs the stock levels). You can't expect Mom & Pop to do this, they don't have the time. They didn't have the time before the computer, how can they be expected to have it now?

Hence it is not the technology that fails, it is failure to address the behavioral processes of the business.

One solution is to minimize the computer-training stage so that as much as possible happens at the point of sale terminal. Every piece of goods sold is bar-coded, so stock levels are automatically deducted. Goods received from suppliers are put into a closed loop so the shopkeeper doesn't have to key in that information. The goal is to put the entire process of stocking, sales recording, and reordering into that closed loop.

Since we started this project in March 1996, we have implemented this system in one hundred sixty shops and have another two hundred in the queue. This latter group of two hundred has organized themselves into a publicly listed company whose aim is to target the home shopping/home delivery market. Aside from the convenience factor for the average consumer, this type of service can be invaluable to the elderly, the ill, and the handicapped.

The true lesson in all this is that the technology has to be not just available but to be made meaningful. Entrepreneurs will then think of new ways to use it.

You have described a service situation. Does new technology help stimulate new products?

Let us take the example of parcel delivery. This kind of business requires the development of new equipment—for example, the hand-held tracking device. We feel the demand-push model best satisfies this type of situation. If we were to require that all items be bar-coded, the first result is that all hand-held recognition devices would adopt a common language. The second would be messaging standards for the bar code to be used throughout the supply chain from manufacturer to distributor to retailer. Once such a basic infrastructure is in place, the large suppliers—Nestlé, for example—tend to rather quickly fall into place by the simple and cheap add-to of printing bar codes on their products.

However, at the lower end of the economic scale—the nearer you get to the consumer—the matter of add-on is different. In the provision shop we foresaw that there would be resistance to the costs involved for hand-held scanners, computers, software, and so on. Therefore we devised a subsidy scheme to help them with some of the costs of purchasing the system. We limited the subsidy to the first one hundred shops (which we might expand to two hundred). Our idea was instilling a sense of urgency in the minds of the shop owners that they should embrace the system now, not later. Our goal was to more quickly achieve critical mass.

The next retail shop sector we plan to tackle will be the book shops. Note that the applications we devise this way are largely Singaporean in origin. While Microsoft and others have small business applications of one kind or another, we noted these tend to be geared to the U.S. small businesses, which tend to be a lot larger than Singaporean ones. Hence rather than meddle with an existing system we decided to build our own.

One consequence is that Microsoft and Hewlett-Packard took a look at our specific needs and came to us. Now they are working directly with us to devise the best ways to bring IT to SMEs. In fact, we've rewritten the acronym SME to mean "Solutions Made Easy."

Your description could apply anywhere provided there are marked differences between traditional technology and computer technologies. Is there really a difference between the Western way of doing business and the Asian way?

The Asian SME market has become a testbed for developing further applications. One reason is that the business applications market in the United States is close to saturated. In Asia the SME community is far larger and more diverse than in the U.S. Software firms realize there is a gold mine in Asian SMEs.

The Western information model tends toward large solutions developed by large corporations for large customer bases. These are then scaled down or up depending on the specific market, but using the same basic rules of the business game. This works well when the end-users are businesses using the same sets of rules— what is called a horizontal application base. The universal appeal of Quicken in accounting is an example.

The Asian milieu is mainly small corporations with small customer bases. Applications for financials, inventory, and the like are not uniform. Specific markets are not large. Business in Asia often involves interaction with a large number of parties. Sometimes these are rival parties. Who will set the standards for complex transactions involving complex partner relationships? Hence we are accustomed to bringing together quite diverse parties with diverse attitudes.

To return to the example of the Mom & Pop shop, we saw the need to simultaneously involve the manufacturers, the suppliers, the distributors, and the retailers. Quite different levels were sitting together at one table with the intent to iron out efficiency questions. This took not only convincing, but more important, someone to make sure all this would come about. If a private sector company were to try to do that, it would take much more time to reach agreement.

Isn't this a variant of the "Government, Inc." approach which dominates business dealings in Southeast Asia?

The Singapore business model is a blending of business and consumer interests with government consultation. Individuals in the Singaporean government are not involved in the actual business ventures that result from the government's guidance or inspiration. They do not realize a sizable business for themselves arising out of their influence. We at the NCB see our role as making sure whatever is done has a holistic impact. When we act as "consultants," this doesn't mean we are acting as a consulting firm. We see our role as putting together elements that will result in a critical mass for a specific business sector. We draw on the academic community, our own experts, and the international consulting community. The advisory mix depends on the study we want to make.

We find that sometimes even the established consulting companies don't have the type of experience we require. For example, when we did the IT2000 study, the natural thing would have been to get a consulting firm to help us. However, when we went to them we found that they were taking old models with which they were familiar and assuming, "If we tweak this a little here and there, this will work for national development the way it worked for corporate development."

We realized that when you work from a government perspective, business models don't always apply. In business or a business-based consultancy, the starting point is always, "How do you maximize revenues and profits?" For us the starting point is, "What will be the social impact? How do we deliver better services to our clients, the people?" We are forming the architecture for an information society, not just an information economy.

We now believe that the kinds of processes we have discovered work well enough in practice that we can share our experience and knowledge with other Asia-Pacific countries.

What are your thoughts on the cluster model versus hierarchical model of business organization?

Asian business has always been hierarchical. But Asian business has also always been networked. While academics might spend hours and hours debating whether to use this model or that model, in Asia we tend to take the pragmatic approach of getting it done.

One pragmatic approach has long been the coexistence of the hierarchy and the network. At certain times it looks as though Asians are using a hierarchical model and at other times a network model. Yet on close examination both are in fact operating simultaneously. There really isn't a name yet for this model.

The question arises, where and how does this alignment take place today? Personally I feel it is along the lines of paradigmatic thinking. If you look at all the Internet people, the older Asian pecking order of where one graduated or whose grandfathers came from which village doesn't matter. In Singapore today it is what you know, not who you know. Our business style is to share resources.

What are some of the differences between the Singaporean and the Malaysian business styles?

Singapore has always been a technocrat-driven rather than a politician-driven society. Politicians have some say, but business people do the deciding. When the MSC was launched in November 1995, several of us from Singapore were there. We shared our vision of IT2000, what we had done wrong, what we had done right. We welcomed the whole idea of the Multimedia Super Corridor as attracting more attention to the region as a whole. It can only benefit all of us. We don't have the attitude of the Kung Fu master who teaches a pupil only 90 percent of what he knows. When that happens, the pupil teaches somebody else 90 percent and that person teaches somebody 90 percent, and at the end, hardly anybody knows anything. Malaysia and Singapore are small and the IT pie is big. It is not a zero-sum game.

Can IT be an economic stimulus for Asia over the long term?

In the mid-1990s Singapore became overly dependent on the electronics sector. Electronics comprised some 60 percent of our manufacturing output and manufacturing was 75 percent of our total GDP. Any shock to the electronics sector could not help but have a knock-down effect on the transportation sector, logistics sector, banking, and so on. A tough lesson, but we have learned it.

Now we have to be careful thinking of IT2000 as a panacea the way we fell into thinking of electronics as a panacea. The things we do with IT2000 will not provide a forever-smooth ride. The world is never going to be a permanently smooth ride. Hence with IT2000 we have to lay down certain fundamentals for competitiveness, for the development of innovative products, and thus growth. If the fundamentals are right new industries will grow and old ones will rejuvenate based on the ideas of the new. In the end the whole basket of sectors which comprises our economy will balance. In that basket, not all sectors will go up or down at the same time. If one sector—for example, electronics—goes through the hiccoughs, it will not seriously endanger us, provided that other sectors—notably the services—have been made more efficient through IT. The by-product of IT is smoothness lubricated by efficiency.

Do you feel you are even now overlooking certain things as you develop your IT prowess?

One problem is that we haven't found a way to meaningfully quantify our results. For example, how do we quantify all the work we have done building IT2000? What is the demonstrable benefit to the GDP and the country? We simply don't know.

We also don't know how to distinguish the real benefits of IT versus the immediate, the surface, benefits. For example, when the World Bank did a study of the effect of road building on national economies, they found the principle beneficiaries were not the construction companies but the telecommunications and power companies. The houses opened up by the roads wanted power and phones. About ten years ago India and China had roughly the same proportions of fixed phone lines within economies that were roughly at the same stage. Today there are fairly sound predictions that China's economy will overtake the U.S.'s in something like 2030. One certainly cannot say that of India. A significant reason for the change is the massive road building and industrial park development that China undertook while India neglected it.

Is "Build It and They Will Come" Asia's post-Silicon-Valley model of economic development?

IT2000 has brought us to reexamine some fairly old assumptions. One is that we don't try to measure the effects of computerization by return on investment (ROI). In fact, we don't even *try* to determine ROI in computerization. Trying to calculate ROI for a desktop PC doesn't make sense. Is there that much difference in the total productivity, in ROI terms, between the slowest and the fastest machine in the office? It's a fairly well-known fact that the CEO is often the most computer illiterate person in the organization. How do you compare the ROI of his or her cost with that of the PC?

When we presented the SingONE concept to the Cabinet, only one person asked the typical corporate board ROI type of question, "How do you know whether it will work, and what's the payback?" Another member of the Cabinet replied, "Look, this is experimentation. How do you know when you build a road that you're going to get traffic there?"

Silicon Valley evolved the way it did because it was located near an educational institution with a high number of brilliant innovators who did not think economically. In Singapore we see the same pattern, but it is not in close proximity to a freewheeling educational institution. In fact, it appears the Singaporean government is assuming that role.

We have discovered that what achieves critical mass is not capital or product or economic mechanism. It is the people.

We cannot engineer the people, but we can engineer the environment. Hence we are looking at which fundamentals are most important for IT, and therefore an IT industry, to flourish.

The first and most important is IT literacy—as close to 100 percent IT literacy as we can achieve. Which level of the population will make the most impact? The young. Once the young become IT literate, there will be a "trickle-up" effect affecting the parents, grandparents, elder brothers and sisters. After the young, we look next to the thirty-five-year-olds.

The second fundamental is making companies IT literate. How do we do that? One way is via their interaction with the government. If government bureaus start demanding electronic transactions in lieu of paper ones, private companies will soon follow, much the same way that companies responded to our requirement for bar coding.

The third fundamental is incentives which help businesses see the benefits of investing in IT technology.

The fourth is to maintain the free flow of capital, free flow of people, provide a good telecommunications infrastructure, and make sure there is good business confidence on what the government is doing for them.

This is how the Singaporean government encourages innovative business applications without either mandating them or doing the job itself. The doing is business's traditional role. We believe that after some time, this will become a new model for economic development that will be just as effective as Silicon Valley was. In the Silicon Valley model, you get parties together by lobbying through a network. In Singapore we invite three or four critical agencies to talk about it. This gets things moving a lot faster.

In Silicon Valley the payoff is ROI, taking an idea public, the glory of having devised "the incredibly neat idea." In Singapore it is pride in what we are doing with our society, the way everybody advances along with a few farsighted individuals. In brainstorming sessions here you tend to hear a lot of terms such as "interconnectivity" and "cross-sector applications." Then, once the idea is generated, the talk shifts to attracting the entrepreneurs or companies who can see the business in the idea and put their money on the table.

15

Beta Testing for Asia

Singapore's "Intelligent Island" Concept

INTERVIEW WITH MICHAEL YAP, ASSISTANT CHIEF
EXECUTIVE, INFRASTRUCTURE AND SYSTEMS, NATIONAL
COMPUTER BOARD, SINGAPORE, JULY 1997

Singapore is the beta test site of the idea that Asia can become an
Internetted society. How did Singapore's "Intelligent Island" concept
evolve?

The National Computer Board (NCB) has gone through three distinct phases of IT planning. In 1981 we began to see advantages of computerizing entire service sectors. The PC had only been on the market about five years and was just beginning to show up on desktops. At the time they were slow, memory was moderate at best, and there wasn't all that much software available. However, we had seen the sizable efficiencies brought to office productivity by the photocopier. We realized the computer would make possible much greater efficiencies and that it would be able to do so across all the typical functions in an office, not just duplicating copies.

The idea of computerizing an entire government service in the form of in-house MIS's for each ministry under a ministry chief information officer was just then coming out of the realm of the futuristic into the realm of the achievable. We planned, consulted, and set standards. The NCB's role was unique in that from the very beginning we realized we had to coordinate the MIS programs for all Singapore's ministries. In 1981 our efforts took the form of computerizing the civil service, acquiring MIS technical manpower, and establishing standards for IT manpower.

We devised a national IT plan in the mid-1980s. It encompassed seven building blocks we felt necessary to Singapore's future—administration, R&D, culture, and so on. We quickly realized what we were really attempting was to rationalize the sizable databases within each ministry into what amounted to islands of data—we came to calling them MediNet, TradeNet, and so on. From that perception it was a very quick step to the concept of "Intelligent Island." This was the culmination of what we now call our "mixed stage" of IT development.

In the late 1980s we determined to produce a coherent plan which would bring together every fragment of IT planning that we had worked with. The result was IT2000, the master plan for Singapore's IT future.

IT2000 prescinded on our view that all Singapore's sectors had to be involved—education, economy, health care, and so on. The economic sector was easiest to define since it broke down naturally by relative contribution to GNP—manufacturing, services, construction, and the like. In each of these we wanted IT to make not just a quantifiable but rather a significant improvement. We knew certain sectors such as petrochemicals would not respond particularly well to the IT2000 system because it was largely controlled by multinational companies. But other sectors—eventually there were ten in all—were considered key sectors for IT transformation. In each of these we approached one of the leading captains of the industry—for example, banking—to chair an IT study group to determine how IT could best improve that industry. The NCB's role was to act as the equivalent of secretary, providing the study group with all the necessary technical and capabilities information they needed to address the question, "What can IT do for you in the 1990s?" In six months they came back with sector recommendations. We collated these together into our IT2000 Report, which was a summary of each of their IT infrastructural needs.

The most immediate realization was that there was a significant degree of interconnection between their application and their communication needs. Thus what we really were addressing was Singapore's need for a national information infrastructure.

We assembled this information into a single document called *NII Telecommunications*. We assumed that an information infrastructure would one day be a given. The difficult thing was making assumptions about software and applications. The NII was always considered a layer of common services. From early on we had the idea that beyond the common services lay the need for an object-oriented approach to services—objects being metaservices that could be used and reused by an entire sector without reference to application.

Thus from the very beginning the NII was to be composed of the physical layer, the common services layer, and the framework or architecture layer. The common services comprise stored-value payments, business-to-business payments, a postal system like the Giro systems that are used around the world, and other kinds of services such as security, communications, video conferencing. We identified these as our basic set of common system-consumer services. Today we are spreading this infrastructure throughout Singapore. In short, the NII is a model for a city-state type of situation.

It took some time for these pilot projects to build their momentum up. Today [1997] common services are being put into place fairly coherently. Now we are working on the "large objects" control functions which operate at the national level—for example, the framework for a national construction and real estate network in which we can put all the meaningful players onto the network.

What do you foresee as important niche markets for IT?

One of the principal features of Asian life is diversity of languages and dialects. Chinese language character recognition is one of our main focuses. Our Central Chinese Content (C3) project is a directory in Chinese of Internet resources designed to link all local Chinese websites together, with the goal of creating a Chinese-content database. It is supported by multilingual technologies such as WinMass and Chinese handwriting recognition.

In the teaching realm we are bridging the English-Chinese gap by using culture-awareness devices such as teaching Chinese proverbs, using Mandarin as the Chinese language.

Your SingaporeONE databases appear to consider information as a supply side issue rather than demand side.

Our approach is indeed based on stimulating the supply side of the supply-demand curve—pushing supply and only later assessing demand. This is essentially commercial-application thinking conditioned by the fact that it is easier to create an application than it is to maintain and run it. It used to be in the text-only days that creating content was easy. Now with multimedia, while creating content is fairly easy, updating and maintaining it is very expensive compared with text. It is unlikely that private companies would risk the capital and ongoing costs trying to operate a database like C3. We do it because C3 (and many other of our informational databases) is part of what the Singaporean government feels to be a necessary public service.

What are some IT solutions to management problems?

We are working in new territory here. Management structures for information provision are not much encountered in the professional journals as yet. Policies about *how* you do things are inevitably affected when you change the *way* you do things. We have set up a working group to address the implications of process reengineering in a situation in which by the time a system is introduced, the environment has changed beneath the system. We are quite aware that our organization and the way we manage it must be an evolutionary system. Our working group deals with the process reengineering required to create an ever more responsive organization.

In the area of electronic commerce (EC), for example, we know that EC is not simply a replication of physical commerce in on-line form. Starting several years ago we began working with Arthur Anderson Co. here in setting up something called "need visioning." For example, EC requires a much more intricate method for securing payments in exchange for goods. We needed to reexamine the way processes are done. One way was to inaugurate a series of one-day workshops with Arthur Andersen in which companies would come in and relook at their traditional way of doing business in light of what EC offers them, and how they can adapt their processes accordingly. For example, when you introduce a system that can do in minutes what once took days, the whole support structure changes. A significant consideration is to get everyone in the structure to agree on a new process. Then there is the question of how they can adapt to the new markets EC makes possible.

Understanding change is actually more important than building a system. A lot of countries, for example, decide they want to introduce IT into education. The result is putting computers and software into a schoolroom. All too often the result is a computer used less and less until it finally ends up gathering dust.

Our approach was more cautious. We wanted to understand the pedagogical impact of the way the *teacher* effects learning. In 1995 we introduced a project called Student-Teacher Workbench (STW) in six pilot schools, focusing on one course, one class size, and one grade. We used these six as a test model for one year. We learned quite a number of things; for example, how to provide meaningful teacher support. A teacher does not want to end up a system administrator to a technology. A teacher wants to teach.

We ended up with a system in which we started with making the teacher comfortable with the IT system. We're also learning from the teachers—or rather, their responses. After a year we had the teachers audit the system themselves. The working group consisted of the teachers who would run the system and the principals who would buy it, all under the chairmanship of the Ministry of Education. We learned some quite unexpected things. For example, many schools did not have enough power points to supply the power a multicomputer IT system needs. Others needed air-conditioning. Another discovery was how many students sharing a computer was the ideal situation [two], how to support students at home doing their homework or teachers at home making up lesson plans, how to organize a school so each school can customize its curriculum and yet conform to its charter. Today the refined system has been introduced into mixed-level schools.

However, the NCB's role did not finish there. We believe that a central point of process reengineering is how people react to the system. Hence we originated a project in which we installed computers and a lot of software, again in different six classrooms. We watched how the classrooms evolved when working in free-form, using both teachers and independent auditors to do the evaluations. This helped us foresee problems like how two teachers with different curricula can use the same computer.

Hence our approach is not only macro, conceiving a system on the large scale, but also micro, examining at a fine level of detail the specifics of how the system works in daily practice. We suspect that the reason most IT learning systems look good at the beginning but end up poorly used in comparison with their potential is that not enough attention is paid to the detail work at the beginning.

How do you think IT will affect old-line industries with entrenched ways of doing business?

We did a time analysis of construction in Singapore. An inordinate amount of time was taken up in the planning and approval process—a third or more of the total time from conceiving a building to opening the doors.

Our approach was, again, getting as many principals as possible into a group problem-solving session. (In fact, one of our core practices is to get everyone involved together, not just a particular segment of an industry.) In Singapore the construction industry is highly complex and highly structured. It comprises architects and blue-collar workers, civil engineers and inspectors, financiers and suppliers. Each of these, within the context of their own profession, has a body of standards to adhere to.

We found that the amendment process was a big time-consumer. A change of any kind in the plans involved a cascade of people and organizations, each of whom had their existing schedules to maneuver within. We realized that if a single agency received and distributed both original plans and amendments electronically to all parties—approvals agency, engineers, suppliers, environment people, public works people, and so on—the entire process would be rationalized.

We discovered that the plans checking stage could be converted to artificial intelligence (AI) based. We devised software which systematically checks item-by-item to see whether doors, for example, are large enough so the largest object that will go into the room can fit through it, that the windows will open in areas where necessary, and so on. The next stage was to check on an AI basis the details that quantity surveyors have to assess—the amounts of concrete to order, ree-bar, wiring, electrical wall plates, and so on.

It soon became obvious that the government didn't have to do this, the contractor could. If the contractor was supplied with the proper software—on a CD-ROM, for example—the plans could be prechecked for conformity to every rule imposed by every organization likely to be involved in the project. This would enable the government to approve the project details much faster.

Like many of our IT projects, our basic assumption was that an IT service should be driven largely by serving the needs of the user—in this case the PWD (Public Works Department). Because we saw we would eventually be working with multiple agencies with multiple rules, we prototyped the concept (by now named Plan Checker) and showed it to the PWD for comment.

Any IT application that benefits the construction industry financially also benefits Singapore financially. For one, factories that can be built faster are more responsive to market forces than to economic cycle forces. Getting a factory up in eighteen months instead of thirty-six months can mean the difference between coming on-line at a peak of a cycle or in a trough. In an era when the life cycle of a logic chip is nine months, factories associated in any way with the rapidity of computer technology have to be up and running in the shortest time possible. And, too, raising productivity and improving timelines in the construction area frees up the time architects have to work on the design phase of a project compared with the time they have to spend on the checking phase.

How are you preparing your work force to deal with a world of rapid change?

We watch very closely the quality of our manpower; fine-tuning is a constant process. Presently we are working with the polytechnics on a new concept which we call "just-in-time training." One part of this is a quick-response curriculum in which highly focused courses lasting, say, a few weeks or a month are devised to address needs areas of both the students and the businesses they aspire to enter. For example, Java is a system for which applications are quickly evolving. We create a quick-response course to address a specific application, and in the process of teaching it to both students and professional technical people, we find out how to refine it to the point where it gets added to the broad curriculum. Hence we accept the responsibility to play a monitoring role as well as an innovation role.

How do you feel Asian SMEs will respond to technological change?

For more than ten years now we have been looking at the problem of some SMEs' reluctance, largely for financial reasons, to introduce advanced technology in their businesses. The result is two methods we have found to work quite well—in fact, so well that today more than 90 percent of SMEs with more than ten employees are computerized.

The first method is direct incentives to adopt IT in their business. Over that decade we set into place funding mechanisms whereby SMEs can study and implement the IT that will improve their businesses. We did not simply offer block grants hoping for the best, but instead devised a context-specific system in which a consultant first assesses a company's condition in light of what is happening in its industry. We offset the study and implementation costs of any SME interested in this service. We then help arrange for loans to buy new IT equipment and train employees. The result is a responsibility-sharing arrangement in which the government (via the NCB) absorbs information-providing costs while the SME company provides its own capital-improvement costs.

The second method is to work with SMEs on a sectorial basis. For example, our ShopNet system ties together retail shops under a common IT system. BookNet ties together the retail book shops. The link-up between shops and wholesalers on an industry-wide basis made the retail supply chain more efficient and therefore cheaper. At the manufacturing level, we have done the same with furniture makers.

In effect this is a meta system that can be broadly applied to many and quite different sectors, then fine-tuned with each to the point where it establishes a kind of benchmark IT standard. The financial support for this comes from the NCB and various industry groups acting on behalf of their members.

One effect has been to maintain the firewall between government and business. Companies do their own IT and computerizing, while we work with them in the area of sectorial standards and refining applications.

What future exists for cross-border engineering and manufacturing?

That subject has been on our minds in Singapore ever since we realized that a value-adding manufacturing system supported by IT technology pays no attention to borders. We developed a system called EDIMAN in which an industrial sector can adopt a uniform system for supplies and the like. In effect it is an EDS (electronic data system) adapted to the needs of large-scale manufacturers working with many suppliers and many projects.

What stored-value technology applications do you feel will end up the most socially productive?

We are working on two applications in this area. The first is the traditional smart card. However, beyond the card itself, we plan to provide every SingONE user with a smart-card reader which can be used to make electronic payments based on value stored in the card. This can be placed anywhere in the network to (a) top up the card from one's own bank account, and (b) pay for products or services electronically. The point of sale can be a retail shop, the office of a professional service, or in the case of on-line purchases, one's own home or office. The transaction's actual money transfer takes place through a banking organization called NET, which also issues the cards.

Another is an electronic Giro-like system called FEDI (Financial EDI). This system does not store money. You have a relationship with a vendor in which what you purchase is deducted from your FEDI account to pay the vendor. The smart card in this case might be more accurately described as a transactional card enabling you to do business, but without stored value within the card itself. Settlement is done by NET.

How will electronic commerce impact daily life?

We are studying what people want out of e-commerce and how they want it. The results are not in yet, but it is safe to say e-commerce is still in its infancy. The early adopters are likely to be those already exposed to the Internet. Cybercafes and computer stores are excellent points for introducing e-commerce to people, so we have approached those (as well as public areas like malls and public fairs) with the idea of placing a computer there so people with an Internet account can be exposed to e-commerce in public. We feel this will attract curious bystanders as much as the computer cognoscenti.

At the NCB we have a working group called "IT Culture" whose purpose is to bring all this exposure to the populace. It is a road show that sets up at community centers, malls, schools, libraries, and so on. We even have a little mascot to make the rather abstract nature of content more soft and warm for the noncomputer person.

Is Singapore the IT test bed for the rest of Asia?

We have long known that the size of our populace and island is too small to sustain certain kinds of business development. The intention of IT2000 was to position us well in the area of multimedia. How can we advance Singapore's future economic growth through better physical infrastructure, applications, and workforce talent? We look at SingaporeONE as a test bed. If it works in Singapore, it can be exported elsewhere. We are achieving some success at this already. The company that created the Magic School Bus series built their software here in Singapore and tested the system in Singaporean homes. It is now being marketed internationally. Microsoft is thinking of an Asian version of Sidewalk to be sited in Singapore.

It is in our long-term interest to attract higher and higher levels of creative, value-adding enterprises to Singapore. One of our great advantages is that we are a jumping-off point for customizing for the Asia market services and ideas which originate elsewhere.

16

Singapore Anxiety, Singapore Ferocity

Singapore's demographic history has little of the drama of Malaysia's. The endless statistics of a meritocracy making a case for itself are frightfully dull reading, yet yield a dynamic city. As with the tedium that accompanied the history of the rise of modern Paris over the last century, Singapore, too, is a recitation of boulevard making (and strolling), the drains being put in early and properly, efficient transport, and exhortations to public cleanliness and order. Why do Westerners so gibe at Singapore's laws against littering while finding so charming Paris's legion of *Defense d'Affichier* ("Forbidden to Poster") signs?

In 1997 Singapore was ranked the world's most competitive economy for the second year in a row in the *Global Competitiveness Report* of the World Economic Forum in Geneva. Transparency International ranked Singapore and Hong Kong as Asia's least corrupt countries. Singapore will soon, at $30,000 per head, surpass the United States in terms of individual wealth.

Yet a surprising sense of anxiety wafts through Singapore. It impels the island's populace to strive constantly to improve. Themselves, their island, their economy. And above all their children, who are confronted soon after toddlerhood with an educational meritocracy unlike any in Asia save Japan. Yet unlike Japan's, Singapore's education doesn't suddenly dematerialize after a crushing secondary school but rather gets more stringent through university years.

It is hard to imagine a populace more honed by hard work. Yet astonishingly, for all its competitive prowess and economic transparency, Singapore is surprisingly anxiety-prone. It is aware—perhaps too well aware—of a small island's considerable geographic and economic vulnerabilities. An enclave of modernity and internationalism in a multitudinous region beset with the politicization of tradition, an immense history of denial, and periodic wafts of economic jealousy fanning the flames of racial exceptionalism, Singapore fears it is simply too smart, works too hard, and is moving too quickly for its neighbors. Malaysia's political scoundrels wave the kris of cutting off Singapore's water supply whenever they dislike something the island does. Yet Singapore's response, curiously, is not to invest heavily in labor-intensive industries in the region where the water is produced or form interlocking corporate directors with the political authorities and Sultan of Johore.

Indonesia often resembles a great *wayang kulit* (a dramatic form) tragedy in which denial of one's flaws inevitably results in their victory. Malaysia peoples the news pages with Lears of impotent rage and Iagos whispering jealousies and a cabal of Brutuses manipulating the market for an Antony named Renong. Singapore resembles a great voyage epic of the Odyssean type. It plugs its ears when it recognizes the sirens of the semiconductors for what they are, plunges an IT stake into the one-eyed giant of corruption, touches this shore of management theory and that shore of capacity expansion, then hurries on before any one idea becomes a trap too tempting.

The demographic psychology driving Singapore is a sociological magnet at once attracting and repelling: size anxiety. Singapore is demographically small and can never grow large. This anxiety is all but an obsession, never fully sublimated by success, and magnified all out of proportion by every wheeze from the lungs of progress. Historians point out that many capacity-restrained states have a similar record of trembling unduly from their fear of smallness, and overcompensating accordingly. Just look at Athens, Sicily in the time of Roger II, Japan just after the Meiji Restoration, and Britain just about any time. Being small kept them on the ball.

Rather than erect grand monuments exalting its self-image, Singapore appointed a panel of government officials and local and international business executives to devise ways to shift people away from the idea that only figureheads at the top may do the deciding while everyone else's job is to do as they're told. Just after Singapore's secondary students scored among the highest in the world in science and math, the government was already fretting how to get them to think more creatively.

Some of Singapore's anxieties are well founded. When its economy slowed in 1997 to a minuscule (by prior standards anyway) 7 percent growth, the sector hardest hit was electronics, from which half its manufacturing output came. In fact electronics did turn around a year later, par for the course. But it is still a boom-and-bust sector in an Asia in which China's manufacturing might and emphasis on science in education are likely to turn many a boom-minded Asian wannabe into an anemic once-was.

Lee Kuan Yew personifies the endless striving—and insecurity—of the island. Although he long ago turned over the reins of acting power to Singapore President Goh Tok Chong and his technocrats, Lee retains a charismatic presence of the sort once wielded by the late Deng Xiaoping. In 1997 he made some trenchant observations about managing Singapore's economy as it copes with Southeast Asia's political liabilities:

Leaders in China and Hong Kong say they want to emulate
Singapore. What is the essence of the Singapore model?

What Chinese leaders found attractive was cleanliness, both physically and in administrative terms. As an administration we run a clean ship. Our workers have a stake in home ownership. We have a free market and are able to grow. We have trade unions that play a part in productivity with management and the government. C. H. Tung knows Singapore. He's been back and forth over the years. My guess is he also disapproves of laxness in society and would like a certain propriety of behavior in public.

Is firm political control part of the Singapore model?

Firm government is part of it. You've got to take tough decisions. We had to change people's habits. When we were turned out of Malaysia in 1965, we knew a way of life had come to an end. We were the entrepôt center for Malaysia and for Indonesia. The Confrontation [a 1965 political squabble between Indonesia and Malaysia] was on. Malaysia had established its own direct trade, and so we were really on our own. From being the hub of the British Empire in Southeast Asia, we were now a head without a body. We either perished or found some new way to pump in blood to keep our circulation going.

By 1968 we settled on two strategies: First, leapfrog the region and link up to the developed world—America, Japan, and Europe. Get their multinationals to come here, set up shop, and export back to the industrial countries.

That strategy meant we needed a better-educated, more cooperative workforce. So we had to change attitudes from communist, noncooperative unions to cooperative unions.

The other strategy was to make Singapore a First World base in a Third World region, with standards of administration, health, education, security, and communications that would approximate what they were in Europe, America, and Japan.

The infrastructure was put in, but the people's behavior had to change because we were a rough-and-ready society. That required not an overpowering government but a government that was able to make hard decisions and get its people to support it. They responded well because they knew that if we didn't change, if we could not make a living on our own, we would perish.

We had four official languages: Malay, Chinese, Tamil, English. Now everybody learns English as the main language of instruction, and their mother tongue as their second language. We geared the work force to the international community. That is the reason we got here.

Is what the World Bank terms the "East Asian miracle" fading or
slowing?

We are all dependent on external demand. We are not an economically self-generating region yet. Without the American market, our miracle can't complete its course. In another fifteen to twenty years—after the Japanese have deregulated and opened up, after ASEAN has become a free trade area, after the WTO has progressed further with China—then it may be a different matter. We will not be so vulnerable to things like a slowdown in electronics in the United States. That was the reason for all of us doing poorly in 1996–1997.

SINGONE AND EAST–WEST ISSUES

Singapore has more in common with the business practices of the West than those of Asia. Singapore is trying to externalize its economy by encouraging local businesses to spread their wings across the region. To fuel future growth, it has invested billions of dollars in Asia. Singapore is well known for its efficiency and its intolerance for corruption. But this could hinder its efforts to expand economic links with the region. Singapore's transparent business environment had attracted foreign companies and contributed to its economic success. This very strength could increasingly become a source of weakness as Singapore attempts to expand its economy by interfacing more closely with the rest of Asia.

Nurtured in a transparent business environment, Singaporean businessmen find it hard to adjust to the ways of their colleagues in other countries in the region. Although Singapore may disagree with the West in the debate over Asian values, in business it has more in common with Western ways of doing things than with Asian ways. In most parts of Asia, administration is rarely efficient, corruption a way of life, commercial laws are vague, contradictory, or inconsistently enforced.

Singapore's advantages are its huge foreign currency reserves and cash-rich companies eager to seek out overseas investments. But their experience suggests that these advantages may not be enough. For example, Singapore launched its investment in the Suzhou industrial park project near Shanghai in 1994 with great enthusiasm, believing Singapore's can-do reputation in the West would attract multinational clients. But warm enthusiasm became a cold shower after differences arose over the way China perceived problems and made decisions. New foreign investment in the park dropped after April 1996 when foreign companies were abruptly required to pay tax on imported capital equipment.

Looking toward the other side of Asia, Singaporean businesses that invested in India have ended up with headaches. Not all local governments in India share the enthusiasm for economic reform and foreign investment that the Centre in New Delhi does.

Singapore Airlines' proposal to start a domestic airline in India and a plan to build a new airport in Bangalore both suffered setbacks; the SIA deal was dropped altogether after India's refusal to allow international competition to Air India. A technology park in Bangalore opened in 1997 to tepid response.

Singapore's mixed success in traditional business ventures may well erode the enthusiasm of Singapore IT companies for being agents of economic development beyond the island's borders. Many Asian countries are approaching a level of development where Singapore's "Asian" expertise may not seem as attractive as dealing directly with IT companies.

Singapore could find itself in the position of having built a state-of-the-art multimedia delivery system for its citizens only to find it doesn't translate well to the rest of Asia. The rest of Asia might well prove less interested in importing a system devised in Singapore than building from scratch a system of their own. The Suns and Microsofts and IBMs and Oracles have already established bridgeheads in the major Asian markets and can handily replicate Singapore's architecture and hardware just about anywhere, free of Singapore's beta-stage glitches, and help create locality-specific software that even Singapore, for all its Asia-prowess, can't code as quickly. Borrowing or buying someone else's success is the kind of behavior that Microsoft excels at, and even Singapore can't do much about it.

The most serious problem Singapore faces is not internal. It is the bad odor being given to all of Southeast Asia by Malaysia's Prime Minister Mahathir's sour pronouncements about George Soros, the international rules of investment, and anything Western. These have had two effects:

- Mahathir gives verbal validation on the international stage to those Asian businesses and governments who do not want to reform their business methods, thus enabling them to dig their heels in further.

- Mahathir gives non-Asians a very poor and unfair image of Southeast Asia as a region of backwards autocrats who want easy investment money and international market access while ignoring the rules of international commerce whenever it suits their interests. The advanced state of information usage in Singapore has all but been forgotten by the world press as it seizes on Mahathir as the symbol of regressionism in Asia.

No one who considers Southeast Asia as a future investment site should overlook the fact that SingaporeONE's business, government, and entertainment databases comprise Asia's first, finest, and most sophisticated working multimedia network. It is all the more remarkable because it was invented by a government to stimulate the intelligence of its own populace.

PART III

Delivery Systems: Malaysia's Multimedia Super Corridor

17

Malaysia's Multimedia Super Corridor

No Asian IT project has provoked more debate than Malaysia's Multimedia Super Corridor (MSC).

Listen to Malaysian government officials and the MSC is the steppingstone to a Southeast Asian economic future freed from export dependency and the corrosive values of Western business methods and cultural ideas.

To international consultancies based in Malaysia, the MSC has been considerably overpromoted in relation to Malaysia's technical competencies and has no definitive strategic information-enterprise plan beyond a handful of projects whose cumulative effect is to increase the government's control over its citizens.

To international stock market investors, the MSC is a good idea in the wrong hands, namely Malaysia's old guard of politically favored business cronies who have little taste for the transparency and competency required by international business.

To proponents of regionally-based economic growth, the Malaysian government has ignored the MSC's greatest asset as a culturally sensitive information flow-through site from sources throughout the region to the myriad niche languages and cultures of the Asian marketplace.

To companies that would like to set up in the corridor, the MSC is a virgin market for technologies like smart cards and telemedicine whose technical problems were solved long ago. Yet the Malaysian government appears willing to pay dearly for them without demanding too much in the way of technology transfer in return.

To economists, the MSC is an expensive infrastructure investment that makes no effort to solve problems like low worker productivity rates, misallocation of wealth to unproductive sectors, government-dictated banking practices, opacity, denial, and market issues such as how to satisfy the consumer demands of a rapidly rising middle class.

Technology assessment experts deem the MSC a creature of 1995–1996 technological thinking which, by the time the MSC is fully installed, will be slow and inefficient. They have misgivings that MSC has been turned over to sole-service providers like Telekom Malaysia, whose record and vision are only marginally competitive in today's IT world.

Urbanologists consider the MSC's all-of-a-piece, take-it-or-leave-it government/technology park a new Brasilia with a high risk for turning into a horrendous mistake with heavy social implications. Urban planners feel that so-called cyber-states like the MSC are state-imposed solutions that will not work in today's free-market global economy. They observe that the Cyberjaya IT enclave is not being designed as a future information technology delivery platform but as a cheap-land government-sponsored industrial park not markedly different from, but several years behind, Malaysia's Penang electronics assembly enclave.

To Malaysia's Chinese business community, the MSC was conceived as a way of removing the country's IT future from its promising start-up phase in Chinese-dominated Penang, thus ensuring that Malaysia's system of racially motivated economic preferences would be extended into the IT sector.

Southeast Asian business people see the MSC as the brainchild of a prime minister who has never worked in the business world and who takes nearly all his advice from a close circle of friends whose wealth has been accumulated by political manipulation, not free enterprise.

Legalists are dubious about Malaysia's intellectual property guarantees given the way the country's private-enterprise schools require their students to buy pirated software and photocopied texts. They also feel that Malaysia's court system is arbitrary and unpredictable on freedom-of-information issues, and that claims about the MSC being a haven for freedom of information are an outright deception in light of what can happen when information escapes the shielded enclave of the MSC into the country at large.

The world's news media are concerned about the reliability of a country's media when it claims that its political leadership created the MSC, though it is commonly known in the IT community that the MSC idea originated from McKinsey & Company and Kenichi Ohmae.

Venture capitalists say that in light of IT developments in the rest of Asia, the MSC's star has cooled before it could ignite. The cause was not that the MSC was swept down the drain along with the other expensive boondoggles that contributed to Southeast Asia's economic woes, but that it was poorly structured and deceptively promoted from the outset.

These are the things outside observers are saying. What does the Malaysian government say? The following section describes the MSC as represented by statements from the MSC's website and government FAQs.

THE MALAYSIAN GOVERNMENT'S OFFICIAL PORTRAIT OF THE MSC

The MSC evolved both conceptually and physically at a fairly rapid pace through 1996 and 1997. This made it difficult at times to follow exactly what the project entailed. The following information was provided by the Multimedia Development Corporation (MDC) as a state-of-the-art synopsis of the MSC as of August 1997.

(Updates to the official government information in this section can be found on the Multimedia Development Corporation's website, http://www.mdc.com.my, and via e-mail at info@mdc.com.my.)

The MSC is to be a regional launch site for companies developing or using leading multimedia technologies. As of 30 November 1997, the Malaysian government had awarded seventy-nine Malaysian and foreign technology companies Multimedia Super Corridor, or MSC, status, which gives them, among other benefits, a tax holiday of up to ten years. Those companies were chosen from 167 applicants.

The MSC is intended to unlock multimedia's full potential by integrating groundbreaking cyberlaws and outstanding information infrastructure in an attractive physical environment. Driving this initiative is the Multimedia Development Corporation, a one-stop shop focused on ensuring the unconditional success of the MSC and its companies.

MDC will shape the MSC into Asia's technology hub. It will be a place where innovative multimedia developers and users can harness Malaysia's unique competitive advantages that arise from its multicultural links, committed leadership, and proven track record in developing products and services for regional and global markets.

The MSC Site

The MSC will be sited in a fifteen-by-fifty kilometer (nine-by-thirty mile) zone extending south from Malaysia's present national capital and business hub, Kuala Lumpur. The nation has devoted this massive corridor—larger than Singapore—to creating a perfect environment for companies wanting to create, distribute, and employ multimedia products and services. The MSC brings together three key elements:

1. A high-capacity global telecommunications and logistics infrastructure built upon the MSC's 2.5–10 gigabit digital optical fiber backbone and a massive, new international airport.

2. New policies and cyberlaws designed to enable and encourage electronic commerce, facilitate the development of multimedia applications, and position Malaysia as the regional leader in intellectual property protection.

3. An attractive living environment in which careful zoning plans integrate infrastructure "mega-projects" with green reserves to create environmentally friendly, "intelligent" urban developments.

To speed the MSC's evolution, the Malaysian government has targeted seven multimedia applications for development by the year 2000. These "Flagship Applications" are:

- Electronic government
- Telemedicine
- Smart schools

- A national multipurpose card
- R&D clusters
- Worldwide manufacturing webs
- Borderless marketing centers

The government is seeking assistance from leading local companies to develop and implement these applications. Companies wanting to join the MSC can apply to the MDC for "MSC Status." Companies with MSC Status are entitled to operate tax free for up to ten years or receive a 100 percent investment tax allowance, and enjoy other incentives and benefits backed by the Malaysian government's Bill of Guarantees.

The MSC is the ideal platform for multimedia developers and users to launch their export operations by leveraging Malaysia's competitive strengths of multiculturalism, political stability, and reliable support services.

As a cornerstone of its move into the Information Age, Malaysia is transforming its legal and regulatory environment to support companies undertaking multimedia commerce. The first steps include drafting the Multimedia Convergence Act, which creates an up-to-date communications framework.

Supporting the MSC is a high-capacity, digital telecommunications infrastructure designed to the highest international standards in capacity, reliability, and pricing. This information network is part of an integrated logistics hub enabling rapid distribution of products along modern land, air, and sea links.

Key telecommunications network features that will link the MSC to regional and global centers include:

- A fiber-optic backbone with a 2.5–10 gigabit capacity, which is more than enough network power to support virtual boardrooms, remote CAD/CAM operations, and live multimedia Internet broadcasting
- High-capacity links to international centers to ensure that information, products, and services flow freely and quickly between MSC companies, their overseas partners, and export markets
- Open standards, high-speed switching, and multiple protocols including ATM that bring power and flexibility to the development and implementation of multimedia applications
- Best-in-class performance guarantees including installation of telephone services within twenty-four hours, ATM circuits within five days, and a 99.9 percent service availability
- Competitive telecommunications pricing including flat-rate, low pricing for basic network services compared with other regional centers, and an open-entry policy for value-added network services to ensure the MSC maintains its competitive edge
- Integration into the new transportation projects such as a dual "smart" highway and rapid transit rail system, linking the new MSC cities of Putrajaya and Cyberjaya with Kuala Lumpur and the Kuala Lumpur International Airport (KLIA)

The act will be implemented by 1997 along with the following five high-impact cyberlaws:

1. The digital signatures cyberlaw enables businesses and the community to use electronic signatures instead of their hand-written counterparts in legal and business transactions.

2. The multimedia intellectual property cyberlaw gives multimedia developers full intellectual property protection through the on-line registration of works, licensing, and royalty collection.

3. The computer crime cyberlaw provides law enforcers with a framework that defines illegal access, interception, and use of computers and information; defines standards for service providers; and outlines potential penalties for infractions.

4. The telemedicine development cyberlaw empowers medical practitioners to provide medical services from remote locations using electronic medical data and prescription standards, in the knowledge that their treatment will be covered under insurance schemes.

5. The electronic government cyberlaw allows politicians, public servants, and the public to communicate electronically with each other using established and secure formats and standards.

The Physical Plant Site

The MSC extends from Kuala Lumpur in the north to Malaysia's new national airport in the south. The MSC's "green" development plan will ensure that present and future urban developments blend with the natural environment to create a beautiful and functional region that breeds innovation and excitement.

At the MSC's northern border stands Kuala Lumpur Tower, which houses the region's tallest telecommunications facility, and the Kuala Lumpur City Centre complex, which includes the world's highest twin towers and a self-contained "intelligent" city-within-a-city. Both developments use dedicated fiber-optic cables to plug into the MSC's broadband multimedia network.

Malaysia's new national capital, Putrajaya, is currently being built at the MSC's center, next to the new road and rail links between KLIA and Kuala Lumpur. Putrajaya will showcase multimedia technologies to create a "paperless administration" for interaction between government departments and with the public. The national government, led by the Prime Minister's Office, will move into the new capital next year. The city's population is estimated to exceed seventy-five thousand by the year 2000.

Occupying a full one hundred square kilometers (thirty-six square miles), KLIA will be Asia's largest airport. Upon opening in 1998, the airport will handle more than seventy-two flights per hour on a two-runway, mixed-operations system, and have the capacity to receive and dispatch more than a million metric tons of cargo. This capacity is, in part, due to a sophisticated electronic information network that will be integrated with other MSC projects. In addition to serving as a regional logistics hub, KLIA will form the center of Malaysia's emerging aerospace industry.

Due to be opened next to Putrajaya, Cyberjaya is the MSC's dedicated "intelligent" city for multimedia companies. In addition to excellent office facilities and business-friendly enterprise zones, Cyberjaya will have first-class resort hotels, serviced apartments, hillside houses and condominiums as well as excellent shopping and recreational facilities.

Located at Cyberjaya's heart is Multimedia University, established to undertake high-level teaching and next-generation research in multimedia and information technology.

The Flagship Applications

Putrajaya, the new seat of national government under construction in the MSC, will use multimedia technologies to become a paperless administration. Leading the initiative is the Prime Minister's Office, which plans to become paperless by the year 2000. Eventually, most interdepartmental communications and interactions with the public will be conducted via electronic and multimedia channels, including card-based birth and marriage registration, and driver's licenses.

Selected ministries and departments will also be equipped with multimedia mobile offices, video conferencing, digital archiving, shared databases, and digital signature facilities. The project will involve linking up to one hundred thousand government employees to a variety of multimedia applications and training them to use the technology effectively, as well as providing links for businesses and general citizens.

Through the Telemedicine Flagship Application, multimedia technologies will be incorporated into Malaysia's health care system. Applying the latest communication technology will improve the quality of Malaysian healthcare and create an opportunity to build a regional telemedicine center of excellence. The key elements of the Telemedicine Flagship Application include: distance learning; remote consultation, diagnosis, and treatment; virtual patient records; and a national, electronic medical network. An R&D cluster of universities and companies focused on developing new applications will position Malaysia as a center of excellence in telemedicine. Scheduled for completion in 1998, the first flagship hospital will be in the city of Selayang. This pilot hospital will lead the move toward using multimedia systems in other Malaysian hospitals.

MSC laws, policies, and infrastructure, coupled with the Malaysian population's multilingual capabilities and multicultural links, will help MSC companies serve their customers in the fast-growing Asia Pacific market. The MSC will serve as an excellent platform for companies' customer service operations, such as telemarketing, technical support, backroom data processing, and local customization of marketing materials.

Companies can use the MSC to establish regional hubs to control, monitor, and deliver operational support to their regional networks of design, manufacturing, and distribution centers. Using the MSC's low-cost, high-performance information and logistics networks, regional operations can be linked with operations across the globe twenty-four hours a day, 365 days a year. In the future, these telecommunication links will enable companies to have real-time operational control of product development and customization, manufacturing, marketing, and distribution operations around the world from a central MSC location.

Malaysia plans to be at the forefront of research and development of next-generation multimedia technologies by developing collaborative R&D centers between corporations and universities. Multimedia University, located at the MSC's heart, will catalyze a dynamic research community able to use the MSC's unique environment to test new multimedia and IT applications.

Investment Incentives

The Multimedia Development Corporation was created to make the MSC a success. It is a unique, performance-oriented, client-focused corporation possessing all the necessary implementation powers to ensure that the necessary conditions are in place to meet the needs of each company interested in joining the MSC. It will also drive the rapid development of the MSC and the flagship applications.

The MDC is to be a facilitator and partner of companies choosing to operate in the MSC. It will cut through red tape to expedite permit and license approvals, provide information and advice on the MSC, and introduce companies to potential local partners and financiers. The MDC will also market the MSC globally, shape MSC-specific laws and policies by advising the Malaysian government, and set standards for the MSC's information infrastructure and urban developments.

All companies that create, distribute, integrate, or use multimedia products and services can apply for MSC status. The MDC guarantees a thirty-day turnaround for applications, and will coach companies through the selection process. Companies awarded MSC status will enjoy the government's Bill of Guarantees and other compelling incentives, including:

- Substantial financial incentives, including zero percent income tax for up to ten years or a 100 percent investment tax allowance, and no duties on multimedia equipment.
- The right to tender for key implementation contracts for flagship applications. Only companies with MSC status will be able to apply for these contracts.
- Support from the MDC's one-stop client center that will expedite visas and other licenses and permits.
- Direct access to Malaysia's top leadership through membership of the MSC's International Advisory Panel, chaired by the Prime Minister, and the Founders' Council, chaired by the Deputy Prime Minister. (First movers to the MSC will be invited to sit on these high-level councils.)

The Malaysian Government commits the following to companies with MSC status. It will:

1. Provide a world-class physical and information infrastructure,
2. Allow unrestricted employment of local and foreign knowledge workers,

3. Ensure freedom of ownership by exempting companies with MSC status from local ownership requirements,

4. Give the freedom to source capital globally for MSC infrastructure, and the right to borrow funds globally,

5. Provide competitive financial incentives,

6. Become a regional leader in intellectual property protection and cyberlaws,

7. Ensure no Internet censorship,

8. Provide globally competitive telecoms tariffs,

9. Tender key MSC infrastructure contracts to leading companies willing to use the MSC as their regional hub,

10. Provide a high-powered implementation agency to act as an effective one-stop super shop.

18

The Malaysian Government's Answer to Competency Questions

The Malaysian government's official statements have not gone unquestioned. Many of the viewpoints that appeared in the beginning of this part have appeared in the international press and on the Internet, with little or no response from the Malaysian government.

Below are some questions and responses put to Tan Sri Dato' Dr. Othman Yeop Abdullah, Executive Chairman of the Multimedia Development Corporation, implementation body of the Multimedia Super Corridor, in August 1997.

Is there a parallel between Malaysia's cultural development during the time of the sultanates and the MSC today?

Not from the cultural perspective, no. People look at the MSC from its social transformation level rather than culture. When we talk of social transformation, it covers all the dimensions—education, health, economic, as well as pure business relationships across borders. The MSC cannot be viewed from purely an ethnic perspective. We do not see the MSC from Malay cultural adaptations. It cannot be viewed that way, because the nation and society have reached that level of sophistication that things are not viewed from ethnic viewpoints any more, at least from the Malaysian perspective. It is a measure of the maturity of the society now. For one, it is not purely an ethnic perspective. Second, it covers a very large dimension, not purely cultural. It is a social transformation covering all the areas. Malacca became what was considered to be a trade emporium. The idea of the MSC as a hub with networks with various other hubs is a different concept—a cyber emporium rather than actual physical interactions.

Will cyberlaws change the way the Malaysian legal system works?

The cyberlaws were created to support multimedia. They are related to data network security as well as clearer definitions of the various activities that cover the electronic media. Again these are social dimensions that cut across business to the way we live, the way we relate to each other. This reinforces my earlier point about the social transformation of Malaysian society and how the MSC facilitates that transformation.

Does Prime Minister Datuk Seri Dr. Mahathir's statement, "Those who don't come on board now may find it tough going later" imply that the government's role will dominate the MSC's development?

This statement is taken out of context. It refers to the speed with which the whole project is being undertaken. He was referring to those who are slow in taking advantage of the possibilities the MSC is offering. We can't afford to wait. The nature of the IT industry is that there is tremendous speed by which products are changing, that if you are not on board and the train speeds to its next destination you will not arrive at it. The Prime Minister's statement was directed to local companies more than the foreign ones—in fact, specifically to the local companies here. He's not actually trying to put a cap that you must come in or otherwise we will not be giving you any contracts whatsoever. He was essentially referring to the speed by which we are embarking on the development of the Multimedia Super Corridor.

Are the flagship applications too weighted towards government services, at the expense of business services?

There are two aspects to the development of the Multimedia Super Corridor. One aspect is the flagship applications. These provide the focus, as well as the opportunities for businesses to come in and bid for government contracts.

The other aspect would be the business sector, which is huge—the service sector, banking, insurance, transport, private hospitals, private schools, and actual systems development in order to increase the productivity level of manufacturing and the other industries. These are ongoing. By creating the Multimedia Super Corridor and coming up with the infrastructure, both soft as well as hard, the business sector can develop the applications for both. I believe the government sector is small relative to the private sector. So there are two aspects here you cannot miss.

What business-support databases are presently available?

The databases such as the small- and medium-scale enterprises in this country, yes, we have. And the database for companies which have applied for MSC status, we also have. Databases for the investments for the first to fifth year, databases relating to the revenue we project for the next five years, the requirements for various categories of knowledge workers, applications that we are interested in, whether they are investing in R&D or not—we have these as well.

The Malaysian news media convey the clear impression that the MSC was solely Prime Minister Mahathir's idea, that he was the creator and founder of the MSC. What is the chronology of the MSC's early conceptual history?

The Multimedia Super Corridor is not proprietary to anyone. When you ask whether it was invented by somebody, that somehow somebody came up and discovered something, this is not so. This is an evolving thing. When Prime Minister

Datuk Seri Dr. Mahathir came up with Vision 2020, you will observe that Vision 2020 is on a different level, fairly abstract, and we needed something very focused to follow through the objectives of Vision 2020. That search was on right from the start when Vision 2020 was launched by the Prime Minister. He had discussions with various people, including Kenichi Ohmae, and as a result of those discussions the McKinsey group was enlisted in order to do an analysis of how Malaysia can sustain its economic growth and move from one strategy to the next, looking at the global changes. So McKinsey came up with a concept paper, how to prevent Malaysia from being hollowed out by emerging countries that have a comparative advantage with Malaysia. Following from that, a number of consulting firms like McKinsey, Booz Allen, A. D. Little, Nippon Telephone and Telegraph, Mimos, Telekom Malaysia, and the Economic Planning Unit participated with studies. They did the analysis and our concept paper came out from that. It was fairly cohesive, drawing various timelines, and how we proceed from one level to the next, what should be the operational plan.

What came out from there at that time was not in context. A great deal of detail work and elaboration needed to be done. We then came up with a business plan for the Multimedia Development Corporation, and through continuous interaction with the Prime Minister the plan was further elaborated and we have come up to the present stage. It is a continual process. As it stands now the MSC at this moment is quite different from the MSC that was started. The next five years, too, the MSC will change.

The Malaysian government continues to review its economic plan. The economic plan covers various aspects. You look at infrastructure, you look at trade patterns, you look at the IMP (Industrial Master Plan), and then you look at education as well. So most crucial at that particular time was looking at the competitive position of the country. The competitive position of the country examines whether we should go purely on manufacturing, the position of commodities, plus all the other support required to move the country to a different level of economic sophistication. At one time the new industries identified that were given high priority even now remain constant—like biotechnology, aerospace, advanced materials, and microelectronics. They still maintain their priority. But overall we see the IT sector and the multimedia.

How quickly do you feel technological change will find its way into governmental thinking?

The NITC (National Information Technology Council) was set up around 1994. It came out with this national plan. Through this the MSC was taken on board. It all started in 1994 when NITC came into being. The NITC was the one pushing and fine-tuning and interacting with the consultants. If you ask me the landmark on the whole thing, it was the setting up of the NITC, and was chaired by the Prime Minister. He would push very hard for focus.

The flagship applications were devised in 1995. The MSC is a homegrown product not related at all to Singapore. Singapore is embarking on a different road compared to the MSC. It is not related at all.

*Is SingaporeONE moving ahead so quickly that it is outpacing the
MSC's progress?*

The MSC is a completely different concept from SingaporeONE, a different
concept entirely. We discussed earlier about social transformation, the setup of the
cyberlaws. There is no set of cyberlaws in Singapore. We talk about the soft and
hardware infrastructure, and we talk about the community of highly creative people
working together developing content. Those are not there in Singapore. We talk
about flagships like electronic government, single multipurpose cards, financial
services and financial applications, we talk about telemedicine and smart schools—
elements of all these are in Singapore but not in a comprehensive way. They cannot
be compared with what we are trying to do. It is very unique, you cannot find it
anywhere. This is recognized not by us, but by the captains of industry, MIT, as well
as the intellectual community. When we promoted up to this point, the MSC overseas, we promoted it at the University of California at Los Angeles. We also had a
special forum at Stanford University. In London we had it at the Imperial College.
Again, another university. The whole idea is to drum up the intellectual communities, and interact at the same time with the business people. Everyone came out in
full support. Everyone described how unique the MSC is with what's being done
right now in the media hubs of the world. So you cannot compare this with what
Singapore is doing. At the same time we are not competing with them. Companies
are coming, developing solutions, the flagships, see the advantage. The solutions
are nor proprietary to us. We can replicate this in markets outside.

*How do you evaluate the follow-on market for MSC services,
sometimes called the "rainbow" market?*

What is happening is that the companies coming in do not have the solutions to
all the applications. They come in and operate as consortiums. The flagships that
we have put in place for the companies to bid, the big companies are coming in together with the small ones. This is how the concept of Web Shapers has come into
being. This is how Silicon Valley developed over the years. You have the big companies and the small companies operating together. Sometimes they cooperate and
sometimes they compete. When they cooperate they narrow down, come up with
media solutions. When they compete they improve on the solutions. They make a
highly creative environment. That's how technology is propelled forward.

The first thing that is happening here, these companies coming in and applying
for MSC status, they are always asking if they can work together with the SMEs,
the smaller companies, whether locally or abroad. So they don't come in singly.

That's one area. The other is that, if you will notice, there are also a number of
telecommunications companies coming in. I wouldn't be surprised if the MSC developed into a major telecommunications hub. That would mean there would be a
tremendous inflow and outflow of content, whether it is education, entertainment,
health, applications for purpose of electronic procurement as well as electronic
commerce. Then you would see that this thing would be moving across borders. As
I see it—take as an example the multipurpose card, telemedicine, and electronic

commerce—I wouldn't be surprised to see the MSC and SingaporeONE taking the lead for ASEAN. The platform is there; we've been trading together a long time. It makes a great deal of sense for the two countries to elevate to a higher level of efficiency, to benefit the business community in the two countries. If we don't do that, we will be hollowed out by somebody else. The same thing applies with the other ASEAN member countries. Nothing to stop trading of commodities through electronic medium. That would be another application, to do away with the middleman and link up the transportation with the banking and insurance sectors. So there is a great deal of excitement in the sense that a number of people have identified vast opportunities to participate, to capitalize on the spin-offs from pure technological solutions.

In light of the problems with forged cellular phones, stolen credit cards, and software piracy, is putting an individual's entire relationship with the government onto a single (or pair of) cards a wise idea?

Multipurpose cards and some of the other applications would be meaningless without adequate securities put into place. We have to protect the transactions through the network, and at the same time protect the databases containing private information on individuals. They must be in place. This is very important. Otherwise the whole thing will fall flat. The security system will have to be enhanced. One part of the flagship application for the multipurpose card is the system for the encryption and security. The other is the digital signature legislation as well as the computer crime act. Quite a number of companies are actively involved with us. We have been discussing with them, looking at the security system. We have a newsletter that describes these developments, "msc.com," which is available to interested parties.

Can you comment on concerns in the international IT and investment community that the MSC has been oversold in relation to the actual services it is likely to deliver?

I am surprised that the question of whether a timeline has been achieved or not. You will recall from our literature that on the basis of the launching of the MSC the timeline was that the first phase of Cyberjaya would be completed by September 1999. We have since then changed the timeline. We have pushed it one year ahead. The first phase is to be completed September 1998. It is purely on our calculations that we just want to move faster. We could have very well stuck with 1999 and moved comfortably to make that timeline. I myself was directly involved. I feel the pressure. I also feel comfortable that we can deliver here.

Let's look at the indicators. We promised we would come up with the set of cyberlaws. Some countries have taken two or more years and have not yet come up with the legislation we did. We did it in a year. The second point is that we cannot ensure that we won't be able to get the CRFPs [Concept Request for Proposal] out in time. We met that deadline ahead of time. People still say, "No, it takes a year to do that." People never give us credit for these things. Third, we set the target that we would be able to attract by the year 2000 fifty leading-edge companies to invest in the MSC. Up to this point [August 1997] we have forty-one leading edge companies, plus 107 applications. Again we have gone beyond the targets that we have set out. People have never given us credit for all these things. They have got to be very precise with the indicators that we have set out.

With regard to the human resource component, we recognize this is one of the critical areas that we should advance. The Bill of Guarantees provides that in the short term, companies that have been given MSC status will be allowed to engage foreign knowledge workers according to their needs. That is short-term. With the Multimedia University, the first students will be coming out in three or four years down the line. The other universities have increased their intake. The Universiti Utara Malaysia will be producing about seven hundred IT graduates a year; they intend to increase this, I believe, to about one thousand. The same thing applies to the Universiti Malaya and Universiti Teknologi Malaysia. We will not be able to meet the entire demand of the multimedia enterprises in the MSC over the next four or five years, but we will be able to stabilize beyond the period from 2002–2003. The most important thing to keep in mind is that we can't wait. We have to work for all the elements to be put into place or we will never get started.

Are there concerns that technology will not be transferred as promised?

Not for the IT sector. You will observe that most of the multinational companies in this country employ local IT staff. Take Motorola, for example, most employees are Malaysians. With Hewlett-Packard, most employees are Malaysians. It's a question of supply. The more qualified Malaysians we have, it makes a great deal of sense for them to engage locals. It is less costly for them. Even in Silicon Valley there is a tremendous transfer of technology all around. It is a highly cosmopolitan society. That's how technology has been able to move so fast. Rather than being insular and confined to any single company. I don't see any problem with technology transfer for IT sector.

Is there information liability safety beyond the MSC firewall? What assurance does the MSC information provider have that situations like the Murray Hiebert case won't occur if information protected within the MSC intentionally or accidentally escapes it?

Some of these issues will be addressed by the Multimedia Convergence Act. There is a need to improve on the legislation, take care of some of the discrepancies. The difference between inside the MSC and outside the MSC will also be addressed. There are plans to address the firewall problem.

What are your personal feelings about the MSC and your role in it?

The MSC cannot succeed without the other major hubs being linked with it. This is a prerequisite. If the MSC is developed in isolation, it will not flourish as much as we expect it to. The MSC should be the shared vision of everyone in the country. There has to be tremendous effort on our part and all the other agencies and industries to spread the MSC and allow the groundswell to take place. Something that has cascaded down from the top can only be purified if the bottom swell comes up. It cannot be one-way here.

The third element for success would be the MDC, ourselves here in this room. We are a one-stop shop that is the driving force behind the thing, and is highly mandated. The success of the MSC depends on how the MDC manifests its commitment on the path to development, fulfills its professionalism. If we here at the MDC lag behind or falter, then the credibility of the MSC can be tarnished.

Finally, of course, there is the continuity and the drive of the top political leadership. This is the element that has been pushing the whole thing.

These are some of the things that we have identified that we should provide for, to capitalize on some of the strengths manifested by some of these successful hubs. In terms of organizational structure and the steps that should be taken to ensure success, there is no recipe, no established art. We have to play by ear, put our nose to the ground and smell, and try to get as much feedback as we can and respond accordingly. It is difficult to say this will be the success formula, the recipe that we should use. I don't have the answers. We proceed along together and discuss, and come up with the actions that we should try to avoid—that would be on the firefighting side.

On the proactive side, we just make projections and hope for the best, and try to position ourselves accordingly. As an example, the setting up of the Technology Centre that we proposed. That, to us, would be vital to push the country ahead, as well as to anchor the MSC in something which is indigenous as we move forward, rather than being dependent on the outside. So as we move along we try to learn from our experience, to draw cumulative wisdom from each other.

If you just depend entirely on consensus, that would be an abdication of leadership. Ultimately, I have to make that decision. Sometimes it is difficult to get consensus. You have different views, and the leader has got to come in and decide, to make a stand. Still, the desire is to try as much as possible to get consensus because that is what strengthens the implementation process. If everyone agrees on something, then implementation would be easier. Everyone is committed to the line of action to be taken.

19

The Thinking of
Malaysia's IT Players

Malaysia's businessmen—especially in the Small and Medium Enterprise sector—resist the personal and financial investment necessary to be competitively innovative and technologically oriented. The average SME businessman is slow to invest in research and development. Some 68 percent of the country's manufacturers have a low level of automation by industry standards. These companies assume that cheap (and often illegal) foreign labor enables them to compensate for low levels of technology with high levels of labor to justify their resistance to innovation.

The SMEs have traditionally operated without much in the way of government help. They are mostly Chinese-owned and managed and must be approached by people who can communicate effectively with them in the manner they are accustomed to. In general they are wary of government officials, whom they regard as tax collectors and environmental enforcers.

Still, SMEs are the mainstay of Malaysia's industrialization efforts and cannot be underestimated. It is difficult for the government to convince them to use more technology when the stock reply is that if the government wants it, the government can pay for it.

The nonexport sectors are even worse off, with reliance on cheap labor having evolved into what amounts to an addiction to cheap labor, with all the denial and withdrawal problems of addiction of any kind.

One obvious withdrawal problem is how the Malaysian government can persuade both investors and business owners to phase out its labor intensive industries and move into capital- and technology-based industries. Most analysts from the academic world suggest the usual array of fixes—improvements in quality, more investment in machinery, reallocating capital resources from low productivity to high productivity sectors, and workforce training—but are frustratingly silent on how this should be achieved.

Malaysia's MSC was intended in part to inspire investment by local SMEs in IT products and services. How is this encouragement being translated into reality? Here are four profiles of Malaysian players that are not particularly tied to the country's politically connected business elite.

HITECHNIAGA SDN BHD

Hitechniaga Sdn Bhd (http://www.hitech.com.my) describes itself as a "systems integrator for electronic commerce." (In Malay the word *niaga* means "trade.") The firm was established in August 1987 by George Gan and Zurina Datuk Zubir. Today the firm comprises 340 employees in twelve offices in Malaysia, one office in Hong Kong, three in China, and one in Vietnam. The corporate headquarters is at Enterprise 3, RU1A, Technology Park Malaysia, Bukit Jalil, 57000 Kuala Lumpur.

Hitechniaga's venture into electronic commerce began in 1995 when Mr. Gan sensed that the digital economy was emerging and that information technology could bring about a significant shift in the way businesses operate. Gan and his team felt Malaysia represented a sizable untapped market for e-commerce. Gan was (and still is) convinced that one problem with building an e-commerce business in Malaysia was that while many people know the right buzzwords, very few of them know how to translate those words into a workable business model. Accordingly, he focused Hitechniaga on building and implementing e-commerce models specific to the Asian business market's needs. The key market segments he chose were payment systems, security for data centers, and the integration of smart card technology into electronic commerce.

He entered into partnerships or business ventures with IBM, Verifone, Connect, Oracle, Andersen Consulting, Sun Microsystems, and Motorola. Today Hitechniaga is one of two companies in Asia (Fujibank of Japan being the other) sitting on the International Advisory Council of Mastercard's e-commerce venture, which sets the standards of e-commerce. Hitechniaga is also doing a pilot project on SET (Secure Electronic Transactions) conformity in Malaysia. SET is a standard established by Visa and Mastercard to ensure the creation of a standard form of payment, as well as a secure environment for payments, on the Internet. Hitechniaga is also working on projects in the United States with Connect. The two companies recently installed an adaptive website for *Reader's Digest* that differs from the conventional website in the way it adapts to the preferences of the user and enables the seller to push products to the user. A software cookie follows and records each user's browsing and buying habits. Based on that data, the site markets products and services through e-mail and on-line advertising. As of early 1998 Hitechniaga was well positioned in the retail and Internet electronic banking market. The company is setting up an Internet banking system with a local bank and is working with Mimos Bhd, Malaysia's umbrella organization for IT development in the country, to create a full-featured cybermall for Jaring, Malaysia's first ISP. The other is TM Net, a venture under the auspices of Malaysia Telekom. Both services are the source of considerable complaint by Netizens. As of February 1998 the Malaysian government had no immediate plans to increase the number of ISPs in the country. This policy is interpreted as a way of maintaining the government's control over the IT market. Hitechniaga is also working with overseas banks to develop electronic banking delivery products. The goal is electronic banking systems accessible for everyone through the Internet. The company foresees a future in which business people can apply for trade financing electronically, without the need to meet a loan officer—even without leaving their homes. The company has targeted Taiwan, the Philippines, and Indonesia as future markets, although no projects are expected to materialize until the 1997–1998 economic crisis has settled down.

Mr. Gan feels that although commerce via the Internet is generally seen in terms of the relationship between businesses and consumers, the major impact will be felt by businesses. "The whole process of traditional business is expensive. Worldwide surveys show that the average basic transaction cost is $250. So even if we buy something like a pen that costs $1, the overhead cost is still $250. But if I use e-commerce, all my product information is in my commerce-enabled web site. I also invoice my clients electronically. The overhead cost of doing the same transaction using electronic commerce is $16."

It may be cheaper, as Mr. Gan's hypothetical figures illustrate, but is it safe? "Security is an issue that inevitably crops up with regards to electronic commerce. I am confident that the payment security will be satisfactorily addressed by SET. It ensures that the buyer's credit card information does not reach the merchant. Under SET, both the consumer and the merchant hold an encrypted electronic key. This in turn is authenticated by the certification authority (the bank), which holds the master key, thus ensuring the credibility of both the consumer and the merchant."

Mr. Gan is more concerned about Internet fraud, where, for example, a RM1 million loss could be experienced through a million individuals each stealing RM1 from the organization. In many circumstances even a loss of this magnitude could be untraceable. The solution Mr. Gan advocates is to put in a gateway where information can be screened before it enters the server.

Although e-commerce is gaining ground in Malaysia, companies are not jumping onto the bandwagon. The government was disappointed even before July 1997, and SME interest in investing in anything has plummeted since then in spite of the government's R&D grant schemes designed specifically to boost SME performance. Some firms are leery of the Net because they have encountered (or more likely, have heard about others encountering) disappointing results from their Web pages. Mr. Gan attributes this mostly to companies that hype themselves into believing fantastic promises of millions in profit, which then do not materialize because the companies do not have an adequate marketing plan. "They do not have the right payment system, they do not give enough product information to attract sales. So while many people may visit their site, too few buy from it."

Mr. Gan feels that the future for Malaysia will be greatly affected by the MSC, but that the gain for Malaysian companies will not come from innovating in core technologies. "It is unlikely that we'll come up with a Windows 95 or with a Java.

Core technologies will come from the USA because that is where they get established." His view is that Malaysian companies should ride the wave of these core technologies. "The challenge is identifying the right core technologies for Malaysia and how to apply them in business applications. Understanding the technology means that you can either apply it or sell it to other companies. If you believe in electronic commerce, then you have to believe in the global marketplace, the idea that everybody, everywhere in the world, is your market."

CN CORPORATE NETWORK HOLDINGS SDN BHD

CN Corporate Network Holdings Sdn Bhd (http://www.corpnetwork.com.my) is a diversified corporation with a strong slant towards information technology and "total solutions for companies." The group consists of ten subsidiaries, each of which concentrates on a specific aspect of business. CN was established in mid-1996. Its headquarters is Penthouse T2 & T3, Centrepoint Bandar Utama, Lebuh Bandar Utama, Bandar Utama, 47800 Petaling Jaya, Selangor Darul Ehsan, Malaysia.

The CN Group's most visible entities are (a) Hot Java, a restaurant-cum-bar that screens the KLSE on-line during the day and music videos and advanced computer graphics by night, (b) CompAsia, a computer superstore; and (c) Walk, a one-stop mobile communications center.

A little more behind the scenes are Web Asia Inc., an advertising firm; CN Interactive, a multimedia solutions subsidiary; and CN Eminent Systems, a subsidiary that deals with corporate and high-end IT solutions.

CN's most important contribution to Malaysian IT future is Corporate Network Database, the country's first corporate information database available on the Net. As of late 1997 the project had been two years and some RM3 million in the making.

Mr. Raja Singham is chairman of CN Corporate Network Holdings Sdn Bhd. Aged thirty-one in 1997, he is a example of the very young IT entrepreneurs Malaysia is producing whose ideas and thinking are years ahead of the country's political-business establishment, and yet who are ignored—largely for racial reasons—by that establishment. "Our idea is not to be Malaysian-based only. Ultimately, what we are going to do is cover Malaysia, ASEAN, and selected countries like India and South Africa where Malaysians are going to be doing business. One problem we face is that there is so much information on the Internet that often there are problems with its accuracy. There are millions of pages on the Net, but many are unvalidated pages. How can someone extract information from such a database when we don't know whether it is accurate or not? Another problem is that each source of information is presented in a different format, so users waste time getting used to each system."

Corporate Network Database's solution to this problem is to create a Web-accessible database of information about the business environment in Malaysia from various sources such as the Malaysian Industrial Development Authority and the Malaysian media. To this Mr. Singham's database adds tax policies, investment incentives, and similar material that is available over the Malaysian government's databases but is assembled by CND into a systematic Java-accessible format. The database includes search features like thematically defined article contents in which users instruct the search agent to find and update all articles on a particular theme; the search engine alerts the searcher to its updates at every log-on.

CND is a subscriber-based product aimed at the corporate sector, notably banks, financial institutions, securities companies, private limited companies, business people, and insurance companies. "The database will enable companies to be better informed about their competitors as well as potential clients, and thus be better placed themselves," Mr. Singham points out.

The CN Group has just been awarded a contract to facilitate information exchange between Brunei, Indonesia, Malaysia, and the Philippines. It is also setting up borderless marketing centers within the MSC.

Mr. Singham sees a bright future for e-commerce in Malaysia. "We expect the market to really grow—the number of people interested in what we're doing is phenomenal. The key to technological advancement in e-commerce will be the spending power of consumers. Success in e-commerce will reward those who have the patience. Although a great deal of technology is presently available, right now consumers are not ready for it."

Mr. Singham believes the solution lies in changing people's mind-sets through training. "Already, we are seeing this happen as more and more parents encourage their children's participation in IT courses. CN Corp. seeks ways to incorporate education into our business plans. The information age is over. We are now entering Asia's communication age. Products are becoming less and less demanding to use. Once people are friendly with them, they'll be delighted."

THB ASIA CONNECT SDN BHD

THB Asia Connect Sdn Bhd (http://www.asiaconnect.com.my) began in 1995 as an Internet solutions provider. Today it has fifty-five employees and is located at Menara SMI, Level 6, 6 Lorong P. Ramlee, 50250 Kuala Lumpur.

Raymond Cheng is president and CEO. The company's range of products and services includes network consultancy, database development, website design, content development, multimedia production, and Internet marketing consultancy. "We're an infrastructure builder," Mr. Cheng states. "We build the servers and license core technologies."

The company became the only Microsoft Internet services provider in the Asia-Pacific region in 1996. By early 1998 it had produced over eighty large websites for both the local and overseas markets—clients such as Sukom '98 (the 1998 Commonwealth Games to be held in Malaysia), Malaysia Airlines System Bhd, Pitman Distance Learning of the U.K., and Aquascutum, a water purification/filtration firm. THB worked with ITT Sheraton to deliver Internet servers into the rooms of Sheraton's Asia-Pacific chain.

The company was set up in May 1995 as one of five subsidiaries of Tongkah Holdings Bhd, which is involved in IT services. Tongkah, led by Mokhzani Mahathir, the prime minister's son, owns 70 percent of Asia Connect.

Asia Connect's biggest project is PenangNET, a public/private sector initiative to bring the Malaysian state of Penang into the digital economy by interactively wiring Penang's government, business, and private citizens. THB Asia Connect has also joint ventured with Binariang Sdn Bhd, a private wireless telephone provider, and Telekom Malaysia Bhd, the government's provider, in PenangNET's deployment, design, and architecture. PenangNET Work Services, a subsidiary whose partners include Asia Connect, Binariang, and Penang Development Corporation, will manage the network. All this illustrates the hazy boundaries between government, business, and the necessary presence of political *nomenklatura* that typify Malaysian business style.

When PenangNET is fully operational it will enable Penangans to inquire about their taxes, withdraw money from ATM machines, and use their television sets to pay traffic fines and water bills and send e-mail. "Consumers will be able to access PenangNET from their TV at home; corporations will be able to exchange electronic documents," says Mr. Cheng. "Electronic commerce, facilitated by the MSC and regional networks like PenangNET, will have a great impact on the way business is done in Malaysia. It will change everything in the buyer-to-seller relationship and completely wipe out the middleman. Everything will be done at the speed of light." Not only will IT bring a bigger market for the seller and more choice for the buyer, it also promises greater efficiency through more competition. "Businesses will face a level playing field worldwide, and those which are less competitive will be forced out of business in a very short space of time. Quality and price are not competitive edges anymore. To stay competitive, businesses will have to invest in promoting and marketing their websites and generate sufficient content so that people will want to visit them."

But despite popular belief, e-commerce will not eliminate the need for face-to-face contact. "A lot of people think that with Internet commerce, all of us can just sit at home, or sit in the office and do everything. That's not what is happening now. People interact more, people talk more. I still need to shake your hand when I go out, I still need people interaction," says Mr. Cheng.

Although e-commerce is quickly becoming the fastest growing segment of the Internet, users are not ready to fully embrace this new technology. Cheng believes there are many reasons for this. "Users do not understand the benefits. A lot of them get caught up in the hype." He says vendors make this worse, spending too much of their time "pushing boxes and coming up with buzzwords, making revenue and riding on hype, rather than delivering realistic solutions."

For e-commerce to really take off, a few basic criteria need to be met, Mr. Cheng believes. "PCs must be much easier to use, and the web more user friendly. But the evolutionary process will be quick. It took the telephone seventy-five years to reach its current state. It's taken the web three years to get to where we are now. It's just a matter of time for these things to arrive, and once we take them for granted, true e-commerce will happen."

SILICON COMMUNICATIONS SDN BHD

Silicon Communications Sdn Bhd (http://www.silicon.net.my) was established 31 July 1996 and as of December 1997 had eighty employees. They describe themselves as "Business solutions provider and JASP (Jaring Access Service Provider)." Their office address is 15.01–15.04, 15th Floor, Central Plaza, Jalan Sultan Ismail, 50200 Kuala Lumpur.

Kho Han Mien, Silicon Communication's twenty-five-year-old (in 1997) CEO, believes, "The Internet poses endless possibilities for business. This is the one business I know that can let you grow your customer base from one person to one hundred thousand in one day. It is a medium to communicate and disseminate information, and we can open up to a wide range of markets."

Since its launch in August 1996, Silicon Communication (SC) has grown rapidly, ranging from an agreement with Mimos Bhd to be one of four JASPs, to a project with EasyCall Malaysia Sdn Bhd to provide an Internet Paging Service. SC also has a tie-up with KLSE (Kuala Lumpur Stock Exchange) Chilong Systems Sdn Bhd to provide real time share prices on the KLSE and direct real time trading via the Internet. SC's major bid for an e-commerce presence is its tie-up with KLSE Chilong System, which will provide the raw data that SC will put on the Net.

Kho's reasoning for these ventures is: "People are looking at some form of trading relationship across the Internet. What we aim to do is to give people from all over the world, through the Internet, a means to access real time information." He says, "What we are doing with KLSE Chilong is to come up with a solution that allows any person to trade. You can choose any broker you like, any brokerage company, and even choose a *remisier* [stockbroker] whom you want to trade with. With these two things in place on the Internet, you can look at the pricing, select a price, and place your order."

SC's services will ultimately cover the KLSE main board, second board, Mesdaq (a Nasdaq-like over-the-counter service), and the futures market and will enable the user to monitor his or her portfolio, sector performances, and composite indices. SC plans to eventually incorporate value-added services such as company annual reports, information, advice, brokers' opinions, predictions, charts, and technical graphs into their product.

Kho says that far from replacing brokers, the service will widen the scope of investment in the market by providing an opportunity for people around the world to invest in small volumes and enabling brokers to deal effectively with all callers, big and small. According to Kho, the service will be easily accessible. There will be several restrictions, such as a minimum age limit of eighteen and proof that the user is able to pay for his or her purchases, probably through the depositing of sufficient funds in special bank accounts.

Kho believes the scope for commerce is phenomenal: "Just like the Nasdaq in the United States, which through the Internet receives four million visitors every day. If just one percent of them decide to trade, and out of that one percent, everyone does half a lot of shares, and each share averages US$10, that figure is quite huge by any standard," he says.

For now, SC's concern is to develop a system that is resilient and secure enough to handle a high number of visitors, as well as many people buying and selling.

What kind of response does SC expect? "I'm not very ambitious but we hope that after one year of operation, we can have anything between 20,000 and 40,000 visitors a day."

SC aims to carve a niche for its product by offering services that present providers don't. The KLSE Chilong and Bernama (Malaysia's government-controlled national news service), which are licensed to provide the raw feed of information, do not allow the user to disseminate information and trade on the KLSE. Proprietary services such as Bloomberg, Reuters, and Knight Ridder tend to be too expensive for the average user. "They are more like financial information services companies. They provide you with a series of information. If you want to buy and sell, you have to call up your broker. You even have to buy special terminals to get their services. What we want to do is make the TV and the computer open. We want to make the cost so low that everyone can buy and sell."

As of late 1997 SC and its partners, TechnoChannel Sdn Bhd and Philips, were developing a service to deliver the Internet to Malaysians through their television sets. Called NetChannel, the service would "use an access device plugged into TV sets attached to a phone line linking the user with the Internet service provider (ISP). NetChannel users can surf the Net by using a remote control device or a wireless keyboard."

TechnoChannel is providing the server system software and client application software while Philips is designing and producing the hardware. SC is the local ISP. Kho says NetChannel's aim is "to let the people who cannot afford the computer have access to the Internet. We wanted to narrow the gap between the Internet haves and have-nots. A box is about 900 ringgit, while a PC and modem costs RM5,000 and up."

SUMMARY

The statements of the latter two firms in the above sound very much like someone so caught up with explaining ideas that he neglects to look at the market. For example, nowhere in Mr. Kho's enthusiasm for the technology of on-line trading is any mention of luring the middle-class market into shares trading with deep-discount services. This is odd in a market as price and value conscious as Malaysia's middle class. Indeed, there is a notable absence in Mr. Kho's statements of references to market research into the informational needs of shares buyers. One gets the very clear impression throughout much of Malaysia's IT community that people are far more comfortable with talking about what technology can do than they are with talking about what markets want it to do.

With the exception of Mr. Singham above, the foregoing conveys quite clearly the sense of romantic idealism and airy planning that characterizes so much of the Malaysian IT community's public utterances. Compared with the very rapid deployment of meaningful databases by SingaporeONE, the vague visions of Malaysian businesses—especially those that have involved themselves in close ties to political elites—give the impression of a community that feels a greater obligation to say it well than to do it well.

20

The MSC as Viewed by International Managers, Investors, and Consultancies

The following three compendiums of interviews were distilled from interviews conducted by the author in person in June and August 1997, with follow-ups by e-mail through February 1998. Of the people who contributed to the amalgamate responses below, the four managers were Japanese and Korean managing directors or production supervisors of manufactories whose parent companies were in their home countries. The investors represented three Western companies interested in high-technology ventures, and the chief executive of a European-based petroleum products company. The consultancies were Arthur Andersen, Coopers-Lybrand, Price-Waterhouse, and Frank Small Associates, plus two that did not wish to be identified. Ernst & Young in Kuala Lumpur declined to contribute in any way to this study, the only company of all those contacted to do so. The typescript of all interviews quoted in this book was returned to the principals for fact-checking and error correction before being condensed into the format below. Except for those named, most interviewees asked not to be identified by name or organization.

MARKETING CONSULTANCIES

What has been your experience with the MSC?

Our projects involved research on (a) which MSC services have the most appeal, and (b) the likely consumer uptake of the smart card. In addition we have also done research on the paperless government.

I'm not sure the general population understands what the MSC is about and the opportunities it presents. Our own uncommissioned research on pure awareness issues [done in mid-1997] reveals that the term "Multimedia Super Corridor" itself is still disappointingly low in the national awareness. The national average is 30 to 40 percent levels of awareness when giving an explanation of what the term and the project mean. This is disappointing given all the publicity about the MSC that has appeared in the press. We find that much work has to be done on the level of basic public awareness before we can talk of people adopting and using the MSC's services.

The indications are that once people understand what the MSC is about they will respond well to it. We spent some time with them explaining the MSC's proposed services. When they were given the basic facts about the MSC and we asked how it might affect them, their responses were very positive. There was a clear willingness to make the mental leap into using these services, even if they had no direct experience with similar ones. This was very positive. It also reinforces the familiarization issue and the need for a lengthy and consistent public awareness campaign. Once people become aware that the MSC is not a threatening technology, the "not-for-me" effect will dwindle. Once the fear-of-the-medium issue is resolved the services to be delivered by it will most certainly appeal; the services themselves really aren't all that new.

Is the MSC being oversold to international investors?

We are very concerned about what our clients are being told. We don't want them coming to Malaysia unprepared for the realities of what they're going to find. It is not a question of whether the infrastructure can be put in place, it is the time gap and the technical competency of Malaysia's workforce. When the government markets the MSC, my concern is that international small players will take government statements at face value and get on an airplane ready to sign deals with local companies with little experience in information technology. The MSC will take shape as promised—the government has a good track record in coming through on infrastructure—but in about four to eight years from now, not next year.

What stumbling blocks do you see?

Fear of technology is a major problem in Malaysia, and indeed, all over Southeast Asia. There is still a very low penetration of PCs into Malaysian homes—the latest figures [mid-1997] are 7 percent on the Peninsula. That is a staggeringly low level, especially considering the reach into the homes the MSC requires if some of its flagship applications are to be commercially viable. Some people counter by saying that PC growth has been exponential and likely to remain so. However, exponential growth doesn't mean all that much when it is starting from a very low baseline.

The Net PC also does not appear to offer much of an alternative to high PC costs at this time. Our work for computer companies on the feasibility of a Net PC priced in the low- to mid-hundreds of ringgit (roughly $100–$200) indicates that even that relatively low price plateau will still be a stumbling block.

Another consideration is that we are not yet sure whether those involved in the strategic planning and early promotion of the MSC are fully clear how its services are going to be offered and how well the system will actually function. Anyone who's undergone the frustrations of dealing with Malaysia's official Internet provider Jaring wonders how the MSC can be such an improvement, particularly when the same officials who oversee Jaring also are on the MSC board of directors. Significant problems with Jaring haven't been adequately addressed, much less resolved. Indeed no one seems to be sure how quickly they *can* be resolved. If Jaring is any example of how the MSC will operate, that isn't much of a confidence-builder.

Wouldn't it have been better to first perfect Jaring than to launch yet another new project an order of magnitude more complex and technically demanding?

Internationally the MSC has had a major impact. All the major IT companies have approached us for major market search data. They are very excited about the MSC as an idea, but considerably more dubious about Malaysia's technological acumen. The Singaporeans are disturbed and frightened by all this. There is a lot of argument both there and within Malaysia whether Malaysia should go it alone or work out a partnership with SingaporeONE. Foreign investors feel this would be a good approach, in large part because Singapore is seen as Southeast Asia's technology hub and Malaysia something of a backwater.

What about Malaysia Telekom's monopoly inside the MSC?

The MSC is supposed to develop into a world-class high-tech park. However, there are concerns about the abilities of the country's support mechanisms, particularly telecommunications. We believe that the way Malaysia plans to build what has been proposed may not in fact be workable given that Malaysia Telekom has been designated sole provider. Telecommunications is at the heart of everything the MSC promises. Multimedia applications depend on broad bandwidth. The companies within the corridor need to choose telecommunication services according to their particular needs. Instead they are getting a pure monopoly for Telekom Malaysia within the MSC for ten years. Equal access—which allows telephone users to choose among different companies' services by dialing special codes—will not be available within the MSC. The MSC is to be an "island to itself," as one Telekom official explains it. There is apparently no government interest in things being any other way. The country's telecoms regulator, Jabatan Telekom Malaysia, and the agency in charge of the MSC, the Multimedia Development Corporation, will approve all rate changes, and that's the end of that.

Outside the MSC, however, equal access conditions apply. We see this as giving a company whose competency is far from proved a monopoly over the most important telecoms-related project in the country's future while opening the rest of the market to competition. Why? A monopoly limited to one provider controlling one part of Malaysia is technically and legally difficult, and unfair for MSC residents demanding a choice.

What about the lines that Telekom's competitors have already installed through the MSC area?

We doubt Telekom will get to keep the ten-year monopoly. Even if MT was able to keep its monopoly, we doubt Telekom would earn huge profits from the MSC, if indeed the government is committed to rates that can, as the MSC website puts it, "compete with U.S. telecoms rates." Malaysia's leaders want to give the MSC a first-class, globally competitive telecommunications infrastructure to entice leading IT firms to invest and to elevate the skills and aspirations of all Malaysians. This is already an iffy proposition the way the government is meddling with the project. A telecommunications regulatory regime that gives Malaysia Telekom a monopoly within the MSC and equal access to the rest of the country represents a barrier to those goals.

What is your evaluation of the e-commerce market?

We are surprised with how few of our Malaysian clients have an e-mail address and how infrequently we are asked to use it. They still prefer to communicate by fax. It is difficult to determine whether this is a matter of old habits dying hard or unwillingness to shift to a new technology. There appears to be a belief that the paper bureaucracy is still very important and hard copy has what you might call a "validity standing" that electronic communication does not.

In any Malaysian governmental or financial institution, the paper bureaucracy is huge, signatures are still required for minute details, and work performance is often calibrated by how many pieces of paper one processes.

What e-commerce obstacles do you foresee?

The public attitude we see developing towards e-commerce area will resemble that which developed when ATMs were first introduced. Suspicion and fear of theft abounded when ATMs were first introduced. Today, several years after their introduction, ATMs are still not accepted as a part of everyday life. The phrase we use to describe this is "cybervoid."

MSC cybervoid problems are going to be even more formidable because of so many uncertainties about the nature and the quality of the services its developers are planning for it. If people are frightened of the ATM, what are they going to say about telemedicine?

How would you describe the Malaysian entrepreneurial mentality?

There is huge cultural dichotomy between Malays and the Chinese. The latter have a strong business ethic, a strong money identity. Malays don't display this to nearly the same degree. If you look at the locally based SMEs that have grown in the last twenty years, the entrepreneurial ones have mostly been Chinese. The *bumiputera* companies have grown largely because of their government contract work. This has resulted in the little appreciated but vital fact that the entrepreneurial spirit is vested in roughly 30 percent of the population while the biggest market growth opportunities are vested in 60 percent of the population. So far, no inward investor in the MSC has shown us signs they grasp the implications of this fact.

What cultural reactions do you foresee concerning the MSC?

There is much inference to support the fact that cultural reaction may be a problem. In the Malay business community there is a sensitive and emotional reaction to foreigners, particularly Western ones, coming to snap up business opportunities. This is especially true since the Chinese in Malaysia are responding a lot quicker to the MSC and its business opportunities than the Malays. Hence Malay-versus-Chinese feelings could be converted into anti-West expressions. If they are to succeed here, Western businesses need to do a lot of homework on respecting local values, particularly Malay sensitivities to being bypassed or ignored.

What are the relative strengths and weaknesses of Malaysia versus Singapore?

The two programs have fairly congruent technical goals—two T3 connections to the United States, one to Europe, one to Japan, and lower bandwidth connections throughout Asia. Malaysia has a somewhat similar social program they wish to see the MSC address as Singapore is addressing with SingaporeONE. Beyond that commercial considerations enter into the picture. Malaysia has an obvious advantage in labor cost, but it is unclear how this will affect the bottom lines of businesses obliged to import a lot of expatriate skills to make up for Malaysia's technical shortcomings.

Singapore, on the other hand, has technical skills costs somewhat lower but still roughly commensurate with those of the United States. Singapore has much higher land, buildings, and infrastructure costs compared with Malaysia. Hence the base costs of setting up an operation in Malaysia are certainly advantageous.

This said, Malaysia's downsides are formidable as well. There is still the lack of a skilled workforce. Despite the claims of the Ministry of Education about the schools gearing up to teach a bright young crop of graduates, that crop won't actually have diplomas in their hands until 2001. They won't have any genuinely useful real-world experience until after 2005. Overseas companies will have to rely on costly imported technical talent for five-plus years. This may well price Malaysia very highly compared with Singapore.

This places a considerable burden on Malaysia to provide a truly efficient and problem-free IT infrastructure if Malaysia is to compete head-to-head in investment efficiency terms with Singapore. There are doubts even in the Malaysian government that this efficiency will occur.

What about the gilt-edged cast of MSC investors—Microsoft, NTT, Sun, and the like?

Many Malaysians believe the MSC can be refined with enough financial investment and technical assistance from the MSC's pioneer investors like Microsoft, Sun, Oracle, and so on.

The problem there is that Malaysia is unlikely to get cutting-edge technology from these sources, leading Malaysia into the same transfer-of-technology trap that has bedeviled the country since the days of the rubber barons, which was replicated when Mitsubishi kept stringing Proton along with secondhand auto technology in the late 1980s and early 1990s.

Geographical issues are somewhat brighter. When Kuala Lumpur becomes more accessible internationally with the new KLIA airport and Port Klang seaport, many of the barriers that made Malaysia a geographical backwater will disappear.

In terms of internal markets, Singapore is a wealthier market and one whose aggregate middle class purchasing power is roughly commensurate with Malaysia's.

This equation is beginning to change as Malaysia's middle class grows—and it is growing more quickly than any other in Southeast Asia. The physical size of Malaysia's twenty-million-person domestic market is larger than Singapore's 3.5 million, but there is considerable concern about the ongoing levels of credit-card debt in Singapore.

What kinds of problems do you find in Malaysia's Small and Medium Enterprise community?

One of the strategic mistakes of Southeast Asian governments in general has been to neglect the importance of small and medium enterprises. In Malaysia, SMEs comprise 92.6 percent of the total manufacturing establishments in the informal sector. These are mostly family-owned SMEs that rely on anchor contractors, use labor-intensive production processes, operate in less regulated environment, and function in highly competitive markets where there is little ease of entry.

Their restricted capital, limited technological capacity and capability hinder their growth. The SMEs are not efficient producers due to inadequate production management skills, low labor productivity, low labor skills, and low marketing skills.

Malaysian SMEs dislike globalization. They see it as changing the fundamental way they operate while simultaneously reducing the policy options that the government has to promote SME interests. The two major challenges they face are (a) how to deal with rising market demands that are beyond their experience level, and (b) how to prosper in the post-1997 intensively competitive environment. Though competition is not unknown to Malaysia's SMEs, they are used to "old boy's club" competition, not the inflow of sharply more efficient foreign companies.

SMEs have to change their production structure and acquire the necessary expertise such as high skill levels, mastery of new technology, and flexibility that will make them more competitive. There are significant hindrances to this, mostly arising from the SMEs' treatment at the hands of their anchors (see the responses to the next question). The government recognizes this and has devised a number of programs to support the SMEs. The most urgent is to increase their access to finance, since they are often under-capitalized and cannot raise funds for investment due to inadequate collateral.

A second priority is to help SMEs adapt to standardization and ISO 9001 types of quality assurance procedures. A third is to open up public procurement markets to SMEs. The SMEs find it difficult to compete effectively for contracts because of the onerous administrative requirements of Malaysia's tender bid system.

Many fear that globalization will kill off a large number of Malaysia's SMEs. They point to the influx of large international supermarket chains with their efficient management practices and low costs (through economies of scale) that have forced out many small retailers.

However, the future of SMEs is not totally bleak. As the markets increase, there will be greater need for specialization. SMEs are in a good position to provide subcontracting services to large-scale manufacturers. However, the practices of large manufacturers have to change considerably (see next question).

New technology, which is an integral part of globalization, can assist in the development of SMEs that are particularly suitable for small scale production. Industry sources say that SMEs have to specialize in specific areas to survive the intense global competition. R&D should form an integral part of SMEs' business strategy, but SMEs are hamstrung by their inability to invest huge sums in R&D.

The Malaysian government should introduce policies to assist SMEs to integrate and compete in the globalized economy. We have long suggested that:

- When introducing deregulation measures, particularly in the financial sector, governments should ensure that the SMEs are not marginalized. They must have access to capital at reasonable costs.
- The development of high technology SMEs must be encouraged through the availability of venture capital. Small-sized high technology companies have a good chance to succeed but often have an insufficient long-term performance record to help them raise debt capital. This is the ideal territory of venture equity capital, and it needs to become a much greater part of the Asian system of business finance.
- Adequate IT facilities and support should be made available to the SMEs.
- Skills training facilities need to be increased.
- In future trade liberalization negotiations, governments should give serious consideration to the effects of their measures on SMEs.

The biggest problem SMEs face beyond enough money is that there is often little or incomplete attention paid to the basics of computer and IT thinking. Things are consistently done on the cheap—buying cheap-quality hardware or software such as underpowered processors; cheap keyboards, receipt printers, and scanners; insufficient memory; and computers with no repair contracts. There are often unprotected systems; old or worn-out diskettes; disks exposed to magnetic fields; no virus scanning, passwords, or locks on floppy drives; and no backup of data. Another problem is absence of an uninterruptable power supply (UPS), which results in lost data, incomplete backups, and incomplete polling.

The persistent practice of pirating software results in wrong or modified software, features that are missing, software that has been modified in such a way that it makes an upgrade impossible; and software that does not talk to other software. Software is customized without regard to consequences. There is an unwillingness to read hardware and software documentation and commercially published self-help manuals like the Sybex and even "Dummies" type. The results are underutilized software, wasted time, and no understanding of how to fix errors. Too often the response to a simple problem is, "Call technical support!"

How would you describe the behavior patterns of Malaysia's SME anchors?

Detestable. Most SME companies produce industrial components and parts to be supplied to anchor companies concentrated in the automotive, electrical/electronics, plastic, rubber, machinery/engineering, wood-based, and shipping industries. The principal defect of the relationship is that anchor companies usually provide financial backing for the projects undertaken by their vendors. The reason is that Malaysia's capital markets are notoriously insensitive to the needs of small independent businesses while overly considerate of the needs of politically connected conglomerates. In practice this gives anchor companies a degree of control over their vendors that can be accurately described as a stranglehold.

On the plus side this arrangement means that vendors' products are assured of their market. Yet the Franchise and Vendor Division of the Entrepreneur Development Ministry indicates that the production capacity of Malaysia's SMEs is markedly inefficient compared with that of the major industries and SMEs in Singapore and Taiwan.

The principal reason is not enough money to invest in new and more efficient equipment because the source of that money is a tight-fisted anchor company. Vendors are shabbily treated by their anchor companies in many ways. Anchors give them the lowest-profit contracts or contracts with narrow margins (independent small entrepreneurs could obtain much higher profits for similar products in the open market). The result is vendors being squeezed between high production costs and poor returns.

Anchor companies are also reluctant to transfer their technologies. Those who do usually impose extra charges or high fees. Some anchor companies refuse to fulfill their obligation to their vendors, despite having signed agreements with them, knowing the vendors can do nothing about it. The glitzy retail shopping sector is so badly regulated that retailers take up to a *year* to pay their local vendors.

Even Entrepreneur Development Minister Datuk Mustapa Mohamad has raised doubts as to whether the vendor development program launched by the government several years ago will achieve its objective of developing the small and medium-scale industries. He questions whether giant companies are interested in the fate of their vendors or transferring the latest technologies to ensure the survival of the SMEs.

Generally, the vendors feel that these weaknesses could be rectified if the government was serious about helping them. This does not appear to be the case. The principal reason is seen as the Malaysian government's legacy of politically connected financial preference and the government's selection of political loyalists as business leaders.

What about the state of Malaysia's R&D community?

Despite Malaysia's success in many areas of economic achievement, the state of science in the country is all but poverty stricken.

In a study covering a fourteen-year period from 1981 to 1994 based on the Science Citation Index published by the Institute for Scientific Information, the world's seven largest economies (the G7 nations) spent 1.2 percent–2.5 percent of their GDP on R&D. In terms of the total output of scientific papers between 1981 and 1994, the greatest growth rates (more than 10 percent per year) were achieved by Hong Kong, China, Singapore, South Korea, and Taiwan.

Based on an index called the Relative Citation Impact (RCI), the United States achieved a ratio of 1.42, the United Kingdom 1.14, Japan 0.78, and Malaysia 0.38. Malaysia contributed 0.064 percent of the total world output of scientific articles. Although Singapore, the Philippines, Thailand, and Malaysia had RCIs averaging about 0.4 for the period 1981–1985, the first three countries showed a consistent increase in RCI and improvement in scientific quality, while Malaysia's RCI declined. This suggests that Malaysia lags its regional neighbors.

Malaysia is in the middle of an ongoing decline in student interest in scientific professions. Too much R&D funding is devoted to dedicated projects and too little is devoted to research.

What kind of market response do you foresee for the MSC's services?

Slower than what MSC vendors would like. Market response comes back to the question of public awareness and understanding, which clearly aren't there. There is still a lot of suspicion and uninterest.

The fact that other countries have gone through the same public mistrust scenario and evolved strategies to overcome it does not seem to have registered with the Malaysian authorities. For example, there has been no indication the MSC officials have consulted the Spanish and Catalan authorities about how their populaces responded to the high-tech innovations associated with the world sports games in Seville and Barcelona. Both these involved a massive effort to build a sports and a high-tech infrastructure simultaneously, just as Malaysia is proposing to do.

Although transplanting lessons from one context to another may not be entirely appropriate for cultural reasons, it is surprising that the Malaysian authorities are going it alone to the extent that they are. This may be *Malaysia Boleh* ("Malaysia Can") at work, and if so, let's hope it works. There is a defensive mental attitude that any Malaysian product is better because it is Malaysian. There is a waving of the flag that you don't need to buy overseas because we make it here. Malaysia's Chinese are less ardent. They do not depend on the flag like the Malays do.

To what extent can Malaysian market response to the MSC be quantified?

It is too early to speculate on that issue. We have done a fair amount of work of projecting Internet market growth in Asia and the response to our studies shows that Asian growth rates are well behind the growth rates in the United States and Europe. The revenue projections in the United States are in the billions of dollars. Despite Asia's much greater population size the figures we show are minuscule compared with that.

Are Malaysia's restrictions on entry to the MSC a form of censorship?

The Malaysian government and the Jaring Internet service providers don't seem to be aware that international commerce on the Net is very much correlated to freedom of information. If access continues to be filtered, screened, or censored the way it is now, Malaysia's—and indeed all of Asia's—Internet commercial potential will never reach its true level. There are doubts that Malaysia's commercial potential will even achieve critical mass. If this happens the reason will be lack of freedom of information, not any inadequacy of infrastructure.

Moreover, in early 1997 the director of the Ministry of Telecommunications and Energy stated in print that it would "probably be necessary to register Internet users in Malaysia." He eventually backed down, but the point was clear: The Internet is highly mistrusted by the Malaysian government. They want the MSC to attract overseas investment in programs to be distributed by the Net, but also want the Net to distribute only information that the government approves. The Net isn't about having your cake and eating it, too, it is about information creation and delivery. To whomever, whyever. Malaysia's government sees information technology is an economic stimulus, when in fact it is a social stimulus. Social stimulation is something the government doesn't want.

What about market stratification?

We see a very interesting development in the under-twenties as a market, and the scions of the wealthy families especially. There is a tremendous mental struggle going on in the minds of the teenagers and young singles. Their own culture is dominated by Western icons—food, fashion, music—and they are hugely excited by it. KFC (the new name for Kentucky Fried Chicken) is as much a meeting place as a restaurant.

The downside is that mentally they haven't come to terms with family pressures that want them to remain Asian, especially in the Chinese community where the bond of family is very strong. We see this generation being pulled in different directions and they haven't resolved it. They buy Western products, but domestically they are pulled back to their predominant family culture and its values. All our work tells us this identity problem is far from being resolved.

The Malay youth seem to have a dadah (heroin) problem much higher than other ethnic groups. Why?

An estimated 90 percent of Malaysia's addicts are young Malays. This number is increasing at roughly fourteen thousand new recorded addicts a year; no one can guess how many go unrecorded.

This appears to be associated with a lack of internal strength, social direction, and life purpose among Malay youth. The Chinese have a very strong focus on achieving in business, on accumulating wealth, and on displaying the obvious signs they are progressing materially and educationally. Malay culture doesn't offer that gratification stimulus for its youth. Indeed, it is difficult to tell from the media exactly what Malay culture *is* offering its youth. With no focus to their lives they succumb to boredom and mental lethargy. This manifests itself in high levels of dadah (heroin) abuse and Saturday-night motorcycle terrorism.

How should MSC investors market their IT ventures?

One of the biggest stumbling blocks is that Asia doesn't exist except as a term. There is no one set of values. Except in the minds of politicians, there really isn't a universal set of beliefs or practices called "Asian values." Asia's cultural and be-havioral diversity is quite dramatic—much more so than in America and the Euro-pean countries. Even internally there is much diversity. A lot of American companies don't really understand that. They believe that what they do in the States and how they do it will simply translate into Asian terms. Too many articles in the American business press are written from the point of view that America is just wowing the pants off these Asian folks—the "McDonalds-is-taking-over-China" syndrome. This cultural self-centeredness has contributed to big mistakes in the past and has lost American business interests a lot of friends.

The major players that have made this mistake are fast food franchisers, fol-lowed by more general food and domestic consumables marketers. I don't want to point fingers, but some companies have displayed a total lack of concern over coming to terms with individual tastes within Asian countries, especially disre-gard for religious sensitivities. The secular educations of American business peo-ple give them no clue whatsoever to the tremendous power religion exercises in Asia.

In the areas of banking, finance, and communications, Westerners harbor the delusion that what appeals to the Western consumer will translate straight into Asia. For example, the concept of customer service is a holy grail in the West. But you can't just lift the customer service strategies of the United States and implant them in Asia. The we're-all-equals candor of America runs up against the psychology of face, caste, and hierarchy in Asia. Surprisingly, the Asian psy-chology of face or hierarchy has not been studied or written about very much even in Asia.

On the other hand, a lot of Western psychological terms and the suppositions and ideas behind them—terms like sublimation, inferiority complex, passive ag-gression, and relational displacement—are hard even to translate linguistically, much less culturally. Westerners are unaware, for example, that the Chinese judge as much by a person's facial expression during the act of greeting as by more ex-tended interactions such as one's conduct throughout a meeting.

To cite another example, *feng shui*, the Chinese geomancy of space and design, is an important part of Chinese relational thinking. People won't move into an of-fice if it doesn't have the right *feng shui*. The idea of hiring a geomancer to lay out a business office seems preposterous to Americans—rather like hiring an as-trologer to pick one's stocks. But to the Chinese, *feng shui* is vitally important. It governs the harmoniousness of space. They say that Peregrine Investments in Hong Kong fell because of its offices' bad *feng shui*, which affected personal de-meanor, which affected attitudes, which affected decisions. Who's to say? The point is, add *feng shui* to face, and life in an Asian office becomes very compli-cated to the uninitiated.

In the household area—things like the household cleansers—Westerners haven't come to terms with the fact that the market is structured very differently. European marketers for firms like Unilever are far more astute about marketing research in India than Americans are about the more "Western" Southeast Asia.

For example, the upwardly mobile middle class—supposedly an obvious market for home-care products—backs away from being associated with "the maid's" products. A lot of money can be wasted simply by communicating a good product to the wrong people. One study, for a domestic consumables manufacturer, assessed a household's jobs—surface cleaning, sinks, toilets, and so on. The researchers were stunned at how radically different everyday practices were. For example, most Asian washing machines and dishwashers don't have a hot water connection. Running hot water is available in only about 10 percent of kitchens. So a lot of the company's claims about product formulations that made sense in Western markets had to go out the window.

What about the quality of Malaysia's business press?

Vapid in content and quality. One section in the *Star* on Saturday is pretty good, but that's about it. There is a dismally repetitive emphasis on local success stories and next to nothing on market research, trend analysis, product development, or innovative problem-solving. There is absolutely no criticism, even of the positive kind. Readers are led to believe Malaysian business people are founts of wisdom who never make mistakes. There is a combination of denial and dream-world fantasizing that makes for some of the most uninformative business reading in Asia. In contrast with India's business press, which is the best in Asia, Southeast Asia's comes across as bootlicking. Mauritius's business press is more informative than Malaysia's.

On the other hand, the business press does make possible a lot of opportunities for marketers and advertisers to take high ground in consumer marketing. The editors are actively looking for more articles on marketing in the daily press but don't have authoritative writers who can provide it. CNBC's half-hour program on advertising is the sort of focused information that is needed to raise the profile of the region.

What broad consumer trends do you see?

We are seeing changes in where and how consumers buy. There is a quickly developing trend away from buying from street stalls and wet markets and toward supermarkets. Part of this has to do with the succession of bad press hawker stalls have been getting on health and environmental issues. The government is so concerned about the health issues it plans to move all hawker stalls off the streets and into sanitary centers with water and cleaning facilities by the year 2000. There are predictions, sometimes accompanied by nostalgic hand-wringing, that the traditional wet markets will disappear. Others say that, given how filthy they are, they *should* disappear. The upshot is that advertisers need to look at other venues in which to market their products.

There are also rapid shifts in spending patterns. One is the shift away from "Eastern" product categories to "Western." This is especially notable in the arena of electronic products. Five years ago people went to Imbi Plaza in Kuala Lumpur, a building in which most computer and computer ancillaries like CD-ROMs and software retailers are gathered together. One result was that Imbi Plaza became

Malaysia's largest informal price-fixing cartel. It was also the place to buy cheap do-it-yourself computers you could bolt together yourself. (The joke was that their running time in hours equaled the purchase price in ringgits.) Now the rise of megastores in the suburbs—CompAsia being a case in point—is taking away Imbi's business, even though its branded products are twice the price of Imbi's. Branded products have introduced the belief that warranty support is a good idea after all.

What about Malaysia's record of rentier practices in which politically favored individuals are allowed to monopolize a market?

Let's look at how it affects daily life. Every office has experienced the major drama that occurs when a copier breaks down. Trying to get spare parts and service is maddening. When the service does come, the personnel are not as competent as in other countries, notably Singapore.

This expands to a broader range of office equipment as well. Office equipment and computer franchises are one of the most evident rentier-driven industries the foreign business person encounters in Malaysia.

On the more macro scale, in the automotive sector, Proton is obliged to relinquish its government patronage by the year 2000 and compete openly with other brands. Proton has dominated the market for so long that it has created a mystique among Malaysians about what automotive realities are like around the world. We are inundated with research projects for Japanese and European car manufacturers. Their focus is largely on improved customer service, not improved product (product speaks for itself compared with Proton). They are inquiring about the feasibility of twenty-four-hour services, on-the-road services, spare parts inventories, customer support hotlines, and similar customer-service issues, rather than color, engine size, and so on. Proton has no idea, or even apparent concern, about what this will do to their market share.

Is Malaysia overpromising and underperforming with the MSC?

To the extent that in 1997 the Prime Minister went around the world promising far more capability than his country was capable of providing by the year 2000, yes. But to the extent that Malaysia has had a good record pulling rabbits out of the infrastructure development hat before, no.

This said, it is also true that Malaysia's formidable infrastructure development was largely low-tech and built by politically connected contractors using hordes of cheap immigrant labor and paying for it all with borrowed money or oil pumped out of the ground. There are limits on how much one can extrapolate from having built the North-South Highway under budget and before deadline, to building an enormously complex and sophisticated technological IT infrastructure like the MSC. The performance record of Jaring and Malaysia Telekom is not encouraging.

There are substantial warning flags in the very high number of usages of the words "will do this" instead of "does this" in the government's press releases and official speeches. The glowing reports about a skilled workforce being trained look a lot different when you visit the campus and find it is mainly bare earth and that the first-year students are studying at a temporary facility in Malacca, many of them using textbooks photocopied from already superseded originals.

There are clear concerns over the fact that the same group of companies that built Malaysia's highways and high-rises are now building the MSC, and they don't seem to have done much consulting with the builders of smart buildings in other parts of the world.

Malaysia's chilly relations with Singapore, Southeast Asia's most advanced technology culture, also are not comforting.

What can MSC investors realistically expect here?

Longer time frames and higher costs, especially costs associated with acquiring a competent workforce and penetrating local markets.

The government has become giddy with the vision of where the MSC will lead Malaysia. They have neglected their homework on how this vision is to be achieved in nuts and bolts reality. Consultancies are concerned that the MSC may all fall flat and powerful people will have egg on their face. If that happens it will be because the end vision clouded daily diligence. But instead of admitting to that and going on, what will likely happen is that scapegoats will be sought, and Western investors in the MSC—especially Americans—are likely to be it.

It is hard to imagine more self-destructive behavior than Prime Minister Mahathir's response to the 1997 currency crisis. Everything that could have been done wrong was done wrong. Everything that could have been done right, by the simple fact of admitting a mistake, was ignored. Prime Minister Mahathir and his advisors have been shielded by two decades of perks, easy money, and a fawning press. The chances that they will start to get real now are remote. Malaysia's upper echelon of government officials, by and large, don't know what the real world is, and the advice they are giving Mahathir shows it. These are the people who decided who was going to take over the Proton automobile company while enjoying a business jet flight over Burma.

FINANCE AND ACCOUNTANCY CONSULTING FIRMS

What are the prospects for the flagship applications such as
telemedicine and smart schools?

Within Malaysia, everyone realizes that there are considerable implementation problems with the telemedicine and smart schools applications. The problem is not at the information delivery side but the costs of installing an end-user infrastructure. Telemedicine capability in every clinic is a massive investment, and no one has really quantified it yet. Smart schools will be even more costly. The government is talking about every school being on the Net. Presently there is one computer for every three thousand students. The country does not have the financial resources to put a computer in every classroom—not to mention training the teacher how to use it. We don't see telemedicine and smart schools taking off for a long time. Perhaps telemedicine can be fully implemented in Kuala Lumpur in ten to fifteen years, but not the whole of Malaysia.

From the overseas investor's point of view, the applications Malaysia is in love with are relatively unimportant. Telemedicine isn't international and certainly isn't cutting-edge IT. Malaysia's flagship applications have a highly specific local character. They are irrelevant in the international marketplace. The Malaysian market is too small for most foreigners to work with, and Malaysian telemedicine won't travel beyond its borders.

A third reason is the government's refusal to relax its censorship mentality. Malaysia's response to satellite TV is a case in point—India has more free access to TV than Malaysia. If you make access to the Internet via any medium cheap and available, you will also make most everything on the Internet available. The government's main concern isn't pornography getting into kids via TV—although there are certainly plenty of misgivings about that. The kids are already getting all the porn they want via X-rated clips buried within the "Movie Player" applications of CD-ROM games sold at the local video stores.

What the government really doesn't want is news that reflects badly on politicians and bureaucrats. Pornography is just an excuse to censor political content. The country's heroin problem is far more grave in terms of real damage to the community, but it is not viewed by the government as anywhere near the problem pornography is.

Will Net TV work in Malaysia?

There are doubts how widely and in what form the government wants the information on the MSC to filter into society at large. Today the people with access information are primarily English-speaking and urban. This is a middle class that is in theory anti-government but isn't at all about to jeopardize their comfortable lifestyles. They can digest adverse information about their government and yet be counted on to rock no boats.

What the government worries about is the man in the *kampung* [village] learning from his TV that the government is more responsible for the country's economic and social problems than George Soros ever was. Combined with the erosion of *bumiputera* privileges and a vanishing youth on job flight to the cities, the last thing the government will permit is dissent among the *bumiputeras* in the *kampungs*. The government's safety net in the *kampung* is language—Malay, and often colloquial Malay at that. The government feels that as long as the MSC's information dissemination is kept to English except in noncontroversial matters like telemedicine, it won't much penetrate the kampungs where the government's most solid support base lies.

Will there be MSC technology transfer benefits beyond the IT sector?

Right now so much is undefined that no one is really certain where the expertise trade-offs will occur, even though we know they will. Some people think the

MSC initiative will end up costing more than the tangible benefits Malaysia will eventually derive from it. However, in our discussions with academics at the universities, we have been surprised by how much they want to see the MSC take off. They want to see tie-ups that can use and enhance their current research facilities. They want to tap into the software, joint R&D, and technical collaboration that the MSC should make possible. The academic community believes this will eventually come about once investing foreign companies see that they have a natural stake in encouraging local expertise.

Reading between the lines on this, what the academics really see the MSC doing is providing them future jobs. They don't necessarily see these jobs as integral to the economy. Few of them have any interest in the world of business. They do not necessarily link research with production. Investing companies are going to need local technological and marketing expertise. There are, for example, several thousand local postgraduates who are a significant basis for manpower. This is where academics see their cut of the IT/e-commerce pie.

What are the prospects for the MSC as a flow-through technology
funneling IT resources to Asia's myriad special markets?

The government has not said much about the flow-through potential of the MSC. Nor is it being discussed much at the university level. The feeling is that Malaysia must first address more fundamental questions associated with putting the MSC in place—real estate, mortar and bricks, infrastructure. Much of the government's thinking is presently shorter term and fairly precisely focused—educating the future workforce, the benefits that will accrue to local universities, building an adequately prepared SME vendor base, and so on. While everyone realizes flow-through is where the ultimate market is, the potential looks as if it won't start happening before five or more years down the road.

What are the principal obstacles within Malaysia?

Malaysian bureaucrats live in great fear of making a public mistake. Investors have to understand that. We let clients know that they may not get the bandwidth that's being promised as fast as they're being told they will. We are not sure investors will get the manpower they're being told is available, or whether they will ever see the Immigration Department granting them visas for expat employees in the three days they are being promised. Investors must be prepared to bear with the start-up blues for four or more years. Though the government says Cyberjaya will be in place by mid-1999, it is not realistic to expect to tap into fully equipped, smoothly functioning IT infrastructure there until, say, 2001.

Is Malaysia Telekom up to the technical and managerial task they've
undertaken?

MT has to get the MSC into place and running because the Prime Minister is breathing down its neck. There are significant concerns over the quality of MT's work. As with so many entrenched organizations suddenly confronted with the demand to rapidly change, the elite at the top can talk up change very readily, but that facility doesn't extend very far down into the hierarchy. It is at the third to fifth levels of bureaucratic decision making and public contact where the obstacles lie. It is very difficult to pin down where responsibility lies at this level when things get held up.

There are also technological obstacles. Until quite recently MT had a fixed-line monopoly. They are used to having a dominant market position. Now the wireless operator Binariang is putting in fiber-optic cables. Like all communications service providers—hard-wire, wireless, satellite—Binariang has a rate-of-return mentality that MT does not. MT is not responding to competitive pressures in anything like the attentiveness they do when the Prime Minister barks and they talk. Given that the new international airport and government headquarters at Putrajaya are being built in a hurry whether or not Malaysia Telekom approves, MT has no choice but to comply. The problem is, what kind of quality is being installed? The MSC's equipment is supposed to last to 2020 before needing replacement. We are not sure whether MT has the competence to make such a guarantee.

What about the quality of local infrastructure outside the MSC?

Malaysia's performance has been very good with mega-infrastructure projects—highways, dams, ports, and the like. But those are mortar-and-brick technology that can largely be bought out and brought in. These also financially benefit in fairly easy ways—land acquisition, construction licenses, cheap immigrant labor. The MSC's kind of infrastructure can be done quickly and well if there is a political will at the level of the middle bureaucracy. There was such a will with previous infrastructure because so much money benefited so many along the food chain.

But the MSC stands to benefit relatively few old-line firms and very few bureaucrats. Information—especially information over which they have no control—is something that frightens most Malaysian bureaucrats. They are used to the sultanate mentality in which it is treachery, or *derhaka*, to disagree with authority. While the state leaders make aggressive pro-MSC statements, I see mid-level political interference on issues of *bumiputera* policies and the authority of entrenched bureaucracies. Mid-level state bureaucrats, for example, have considerable powers to obstruct when issuing local licenses.

Where will the most difficult bureaucracy problems likely arise?

The great bulk of the MSC will be built in the state of Selangor. We are not sure how aggressive and keyed in these two state bureaucracies are, especially toward foreign investors who have been given to believe their investment plans can be implemented with few hassles. Bureaucrats dig in their heels when they feel they are being pressured by anybody, much less foreigners who act as though their projects as being accorded special government privilege—which is exactly what the government is promising overseas investors. Putting something into place quickly is simply not going to happen.

Why shouldn't investors turn to the SingaporeONE site, which is technically more sophisticated than the MSC, and what's more, up and running?

Singaporean government administrators have the perception that Prime Minister Mahathir is too far ahead of his functionaries, that his people—and Malaysia in general—will not be able to deliver what Mahathir is promising. There's some truth to that. Singapore simply cannot be competed with.

But there is also reason to believe Malaysia will surprise the Singaporeans. People at the universities want us to deliver. We have faced and overcome these issues in the past. A particularly Malaysian attitude is understanding your strengths sufficiently so you don't give into your weaknesses. Foreign investors indicate that Malaysia is favorable but consistently loses out to Singapore because of Malaysia's bureaucratic inefficiencies and the government's hostility to the Western financial community. The question is whether our local administration can become sufficiently organized in the next three to six years to give Singapore a run for its money. Malaysia's biggest enemy is its sociology, not Singapore.

What are Malaysia's strengths for foreign investors?

Many would prefer to locate here. Singapore is easier for the developed-world business to do business in, especially in the matter of Singapore's better services. But Singapore has its downsides. In spite of Malaysia's being not in complete agreement with unrestrained free speech, in comparison with Singapore, Malaysia offers somewhat more freedom for political expression and dissent. An investor in Singapore does not dare publicly state a contrarian point of view. Singapore is also very high-priced for what you get, though that may change after the cold bath of the 1997 crisis.

Just how ironclad are the cyberlaws on freedom of expression?

Not as much as the government implies. There is no clear governmental guideline or legal ruling on the matter of what happens when you disseminate matter protected in the MSC by the cyberlaws out into the Malaysian community at large. Malaysia has a record of arbitrariness on the dissemination question. The word "dissemination" here means any public utterance, whether printed or verbally stated to an assembly of people. A formidable array of slander, libel, and religious laws come into play when anything is "disseminated" in Malaysia. The question for investors is whether anyone in Malaysia outside the protected arena of the MSC Malaysia who takes a dislike to something said on-line (electronic "print") can bring a libel or slander suit and make it stick. If they can, this will have a very chilling effect on investment.

The whole point of the Internet is that it eliminates economic borders the same way as it does geographical ones. The government's response to that thus far is hoping that the free information flow within the MSC will remain there. The implication is that the MSC is where economic benefits will remain as well.

Hence the dissemination issue is a question of lower-level leaders coming to terms with the responsibilities set forth higher up. The degree of arbitrariness among state political leaders on freedom of expression issues is very counterproductive for Malaysia's investment future. The case in which the Chief Minister of Selangor was banning Michael Jackson one week and the next week getting caught with nearly a million dollars in cash on his way to New Zealand says a great deal about how Malaysia construes the relationship between power, money, and information. The spring 1997 corruption housecleaning was supposed to be a clear signal that the government wanted an evolution towards more personal freedom, including freedom of dissemination. That housecleaning lasted about two months. Two months after that Mahathir was telling everyone that foreigners were to blame for all Malaysia's troubles.

What about the response of Malaysia's Small and Medium Enterprise community?

To the SME community the MSC is a sales opportunity more than an IT technology opportunity. The Chinese and Indian communities are eager for the MSC; they see enormous opportunities for their naturally entrepreneurial work-hard proclivities. I have heard of students who want to know how they can make a million by the time they graduate. Brash attitude, yes, but absolutely necessary.

The big question is whether the government will mandate that SME vendors must be sourced by racial preference—whether the *bumiputera* SMEs will be granted mandatory participation quotas as has been the case in the past. If the government accepts it can no longer interfere with the market the way it has in the past via the *bumiputera* [Malay exceptionalist] laws, then the MSC will benefit commensurately. The government is trying to put into place *bumiputera* incubation projects, but these will take time to reach fruition. If they don't fruit fast enough, there will be political pressure to return to the days of *bumiputera* preferentialism. The inefficiencies of the *bumiputera* system will drive investors out even if their projects are otherwise promising.

What kinds of things should overseas investors plan for when dealing with the bumiputera community?

Dealing with the *bumiputera* environment can be a very different experience for those who have not done their homework on Malaysian history and the exceptionalist model Malays have created for themselves.

Many *bumiputera* businesses enthusiastically court export orders from overseas but fail to organize themselves financially to fulfill them on time. A large proportion of temporarily unused capital goes into property or shares speculation rather than interest-bearing accounts. Middle-tier companies approaching the equity market often seek to list only a small portion of their equity, intending to keep as much as 80 percent under their own control. Borrowers often pay less attention to the business intricacies surrounding their loan proposal than the size of the cash pool it makes available. Lenders often pay less attention to the business plan than the political connections of the people presenting it. Business plans (when they exist) often predict first-year equity growth several times greater than GDP growth.

These imply a pattern of shortsightedness that carries over into operational management. Most vendor businesses will habitually focus on short-term goals and give low priority to strategic planning. Investors should not look for depth among the *bumiputera* community in terms of technical resources—software engineers, computer personnel, graphics designers, and the like. They should instead look for infrastructure providers—construction, furniture, office equipment, and office services such as bookkeeping and administrative management.

The easiest way for investors to best utilize the *bumiputera* community is to tie up with the universities and the Ministry of Entrepreneurial Development, all of whom have a charter to develop *bumiputera* human resources. The educational establishment at Universiti Putra in Bangi is in the lead in this regard. Universiti Putra has started a program to get into the MSC. Also, one or two of the twinning universities are interested in somehow using the MSC as a training ground for their students. Sunway College comes to mind. These institutions see great benefit for everyone training the teenager of today for R&D capability.

What about the quality of Malaysia's educational system?

The Malaysian government is trying very hard to raise educational standards. It has to focus on tertiary education facilities that are perceived as competitive in a global sense. Presently they lose much of their talent overseas to students who never return. Retaining the best and the brightest has to be a long-term focus.

Our study on literacy rates showed that there is a problem with self-defense—some say pride—in showing the world Malaysia is not "behind." This came from the United Nations report showing Malaysian literacy to be below its neighbors. In fairness to Malaysia, our own study showed higher literacy rates than the United Nation's study.

There is an understanding that Malaysia must address these issues. The *Malaysia Boleh* attitude hints at the underlying ambivalence about ability to perform. If they can do it, why don't they just do it instead of talking about it?

What management models and experience can investors introduce
that will most help Malaysia?

Malaysia has little experience with channeling the culture of free thought in a socially productive direction. They need to learn how to unleash creativity. Our educational establishment has been structured with a top-down, hierarchical mentality since the 1970s. This has evolved into a "big brother" mentality that still exists in too many educational institutions. Today there is a growing perception that top-down thinking is counterproductive. Why, for example, should an educational institution forbid a lecturer from developing software as a private venture on the side? Yet they do.

The more astute educational institutions realize that they should encourage people to do what they want to do, be what they want to be. If this attitude can generalize, it will be the single most important factor contributing to the development of a support base for the MSC. Silicon Valley grew out of tinkering at the universities. This is now generally accepted as a good thing by Malaysia's better universities. Our financial institutions should also support this kind of thinking, but they need to work on this a little harder. The best thing anyone can do for Malaysia is to encourage the culture of thinking.

What about the bumiputera *attitude that it is OK to rewrite the rules of an agreement to suit themselves after the project is underway?*

Unfortunately, a lot of *bumiputeras* educated in the mid 1970s and 1980s are convinced that the rules must be adapted to them rather than that they adapt to the rules. When the New Economic Policy that was inaugurated in the 1970s to encourage *bumiputera* self-development was replaced by the New Development Policy in 1990, it was the beginning of accomplishing in fact what Dr. Mahathir has long encouraged: Malays need to face competition on the world's terms, not terms they set up for themselves.

The MSC will vastly accelerate the need to move out of self-protective *bumiputera* thinking into global thinking. This will involve some pain and some time. In particular the *bumiputera* youth of today will have a rough time relinquishing preferential rules that give them privileged access and an easy life. A foreign investor is going to be unimpressed by an employee who believes just by being *bumiputera* he should get preferential access to technology. The investor will be impressed by someone who knows what to do with the technology before demanding that it be handed over.

Unfortunately, all this was thrown into jeopardy by the government's response to the currency and shares market crashes. So much anti-West hostility erupted that many believe it was never being properly addressed, that despite the lip service to internationalization there was a hidden undercurrent of resentful statusquoism. Only time will tell for certain, but at present [late 1997] it appears that Malaysia is going backward, not forward.

What about Transfer-of-Technology (TOT) problems?

In the software arena, TOT benefits are very real. The government has promised it would allow unfettered access to IT professionals. What I fear is Malaysians ending up performing only the second- and third-tier jobs and being shut out of the really creative areas. That will create a massive and permanent technology backlash to match 1997's investor backlash.

What about the possibility of certain foreign multinationals, Microsoft being the chief case in point, bedding down with politicians to create monopolies for themselves in Asia's absence of antitrust laws?

Microsoft is getting a lot more out of Asia in market presence than it is putting in in technology transfer. If they're not careful they can become as unpopular as the Japanese. Many inward investing companies think a lot more about their importance to the region than the region's importance to them.

The possibility of a powerful company buying up every local software developer and in effect shutting out every product but their own definitely exists. If Microsoft goes on an acquisition program the way it has in the United States, local

software competitors will certainly complain. It is uncertain how much the
Malaysian government would interfere, since local software innovators would be
making a lot of praiseworthy Malaysian success stories in the press. Matters are
not being helped by the fact that Microsoft is being allowed to get away with aggressive acquisition in the United States, so what can Malaysia possibly say?

The Malaysian government wants investment with social responsibility. The
whole idea of investing in the MSC is investing in Malaysia. The investors get substantial Asian market presence in return. We have had our experiences with the rubber barons in the past and don't want to see it repeated by electronics barons today.

INVESTMENT CONSULTING FIRMS

*Have you compared the markets of the MSC and SingaporeONE and
the time frames these markets will materialize?*

The Malaysian government is trying to pretend SingaporeONE does not exist.
It is trying to pretend *Singapore* does not exist. We have not seen any comparisons
of the markets for the two systems. It is natural for people promoting their own
product to avoid comparisons. The MDC avoids answers by promoting their own
product, the MSC. In Malaysia there is a tendency to drive from the top end, so the
market tends to get ignored. No one in the decision-making echelons of the
Malaysian government has much experience in business of any kind, and certainly
not marketing.

From our view, the biggest difference between the MSC and SingaporeONE is
who is attracting the creative professionals. The living environment in Cyberjaya
will be quite secluded and supportive, a sort of long-term retreat site.

This type of environment has already existed for some time in Penang. We are
not sure what motivated the Malaysian government to ignore its existing IT support base in Penang and try to build one from nothing at Cyberjaya. Some believe that locating Cyberjaya next door to Putrajaya was an important concern.
At first sight this would mean lower infrastructure-building costs by not stringing fiber optic all the way to Penang. However, that is not really a large investment item.

Hence the consensus is that the government is trying to keep the capital that will
go into Cyberjaya out of Penang hands, since Penang has always been the power
base of the opposition DAP party, and Penang business has always been very independent and international. Penang has never had problems with cluster-type venture-
capital vehicles, and the electronic industry in Penang has always seen itself as a
flow-through site for electronics manufacture to locales like Kuantan and Kuching.

*How would you describe the level and quality of demand forecasting
that has been done vis-à-vis the MSC and SingaporeONE, either by
the Malaysian government or potential investors?*

We have requests from clients in other countries, studies on foretelling medicine, insurance software, web products. Our clients are attracted by the growing IT

markets in this region and want to know the economic reasons why they should invest. Our studies show that the IT market will go to $3 billion from $1.6 billion between now [August 1997] and 2000, driven by software at 34 percent annum and hardware at 32 percent. The real market is for software for industries—financial, distribution, transportation, and retail.

There is no doubt of the R&D potential of the MSC. However, the government tends to be more visionary, less interested in hard numbers. When you talk about selling something as different as the MSC, you have to be visionary, true enough, but the MSC is being tied to the flagship applications, not what Malaysian businesses need.

With only 150,000 of its populace ever having been on the Internet, is Malaysia being unrealistic by investing so heavily in Net-based enterprises without determining what they will do for the country and the economy?

Basing an information enterprise on the Internet user market is very short-sighted. The MSC's potential is much larger. Malaysian companies that want to make money have to think in more expansionary terms. Though *CompuTimes* and *The Edge* [Malaysian newspapers that deal with IT issues] talk about the web as a potential avenue of communication, it is only one of many. Direct selling is a far larger market. Our market studies show that retail stores comprise 60 percent of the software and hardware market in Malaysia.

What kind of profit margins do your clients anticipate and what time frames are they looking at to make any money from their MSC investment?

It depends on the type of business, but most are predicting ranges between 15 to 35–40 percent. It will take one to two years for these to materialize.

What kinds of retention incentives should investors offer Malaysian employees?

Two simple words: Stock Options. On an annual basis, and in volumes that keep on increasing with seniority. There is no better way to dilute the urge to job-hop. Letting them hop was fine when Malaysia was a low-cost manufacturing site; one assembly line worker was not much different than another. But intellectual labor is of a very different caliber. Companies must be prepared to part with equity to keep talented people.

Companies can also be very astute by internationally posting employees who stay a given period of time in overseas areas that excite them. MSC companies—across the board—should adopt a policy of sending promising employees to Silicon Valley and other profession-enhancing overseas locales as appropriate. Taiwan is already the leader in this, but there is no better way to train better technologists and management than by sending them to the parts of the world that are still dream places to them. Companies should also accept Asians who want to transfer to subsidiary companies worldwide. Motorola and Intel already do this, and find it to be very cost effective.

What non-Cyberjaya organizations are most likely to be positively affected by the MSC? Have you estimated the size of the ripple market for MSC-related investments in Malaysia?

We don't know and we haven't seen any government figures.

Do you see the introduction of new business processes at the MSC level filtering down into Malaysia's other businesses? What might some of them be?

We have heard people talking but no plans.

Do you feel court-sensitive intellectual-freedom issues like the Murray Hiebert case pose a stumbling block to information providers?

Better talk to the Attorney-General about that.

21

The MSC as KFC

An important issue that Malaysia has not addressed is who will define and carve out arenas of market share in what everyone agrees will be a sizable Asian IT and e-commerce market developing between 2000 and 2020.

Too much ink is flowing over the technological feats the MSC plans to accomplish, and too little is flowing over who will buy the information the MSC provides.

The market Malaysia has ignored is the myriad niche markets of Asia. Malaysian information companies are far less aware of this potential than the information content providers of the United States and Europe. This is why U.S. companies are willing to put up with the uncertainties that the MSC will perform as billed and with the bombast of Prime Minister Mahathir. They know Mahathir will soon be gone and wiser heads will take over. But what then?

BUT THE BANDWIDTH DOESN'T YET PLAY

Of Malaysia's 23 million people, fewer than an estimated 150,000 have ever been on the Internet. How does Malaysia plan to match Singapore's booming fifteen-year-old IT industry and its experienced workforce?

Malaysia hasn't specified where exactly the MSC's workforce is to come from and what skills it will arrive with, although offshore investors are invited to bring in all the employees they want. The government's FAQ reply on the Internet reads, "The skilled workforce needs of companies in the MSC will be met by a combination of (1) unrestricted and user-friendly work permit policies for foreign knowledge workers; (2) a dramatic increase in the number of technical and business professionals graduating from Malaysian universities; (3) a growing number of technical graduates from the MSC's new Multimedia University and the MSC campuses of top IT universities; and (4) the creation of university-company partnerships to educate and train potential employees in specific skills."

Only the first of these is anything like a proven resource. The latter three don't even exist yet in the form of first-year students declaring science majors, much less the "MSC campuses," which as of mid-1997 were still hectares of trees.

There is also the matter of cheapskate investment policies in the country's many private schools that purport to train computer, IT, and design professionals. For instance, as recently as mid-1996 the computer lab manager of the Limkokwing Institute of Communications Technology in Kuala Lumpur required his students to buy photocopied PageMaker 5.0 manuals provided by himself at RM 30 ($12) each. Students joked that it was hard to tell which is the worst offense, conveying the message that piracy is OK because the lab manager says so, or teaching them such an antiquated version of PageMaker. LICT is one among the many Malaysian private schools that have purchased their curriculum modules from overseas institutions. While curriculum sellers like the Royal Melbourne Institute of Technology are happy to see their name associated with a Malaysian "educational" institution, they exercise only modest control over the way their curricula are implemented and turn a blind eye to Malaysia's endemic private school problems like underpaid teachers, mediocre libraries, and horrendous intellectual piracy attitudes.

DYSYNERGY WITH SINGAPORE

Synergy with Singapore has never been easy to come by on the Malayan Peninsula. The 1997 Malaysian mishandling of Lee Kuan Yew's rash statement about Johore's crime rates is a case in point. Lee apologized unreservedly for statements that everyone agreed were taken out of context and then blown out of proportion. However, that wasn't enough for the Malaysians, who went on and on about it for months afterward. Analysts outside the region say they wonder about working in a country that insists on rubbing its neighbor's nose in it even after the neighbor has been contrite. What's going to happen to the Western investor who makes a mistake given Malaysia's prickly anti-Western pronouncements over the years?

WHERE'S THE MONEY?

Malaysia's Multimedia Super Corridor started off as a formidable idea. The core technology was to be a 2.5–10 gigabyte optical fiber connecting Kuala Lumpur's Petronas Towers/Kuala Lumpur's City Centre complex with the new Kuala Lumpur International Airport (KLIA) to the south. Linking into its middle was to be a massive governmental headquarters called Putrajaya plus a technological R&D and manufacturing complex called Cyberjaya. Cyberjaya was to be an intelligent city that would house two hundred fifty thousand inhabitants working on the MSC's various information technology projects. A multimedia university was also planned for Cyberjaya. All this will cost RM 50 billion ringgit ($20 billion in 1996 dollars), including the fiber optical system and an integrated transportation system. Companies like Oracle, IBM, and Microsoft would be attracted by a ten-year tax holiday, not to mention the favorable press in the local papers. All this would come to be within three years and work flawlessly.

The air of unreality aside, there was only one problem with this vision. A business person would spot it right away: Where is the money? How is this thing going to pay for itself? Did Malaysia really think they could recoup a $20 billion investment from the profits of R&D devised by overseas companies who have already been informed they have no obligation for things like taxes or technology transfer?

To sum up the Multimedia Super Corridor as seen in the minds of international business people, here is a quote from one of these investors: "Malaysia wants to invest $20 billion in a high-tech infopark, grant business people one-hundred per cent tax exemptions for ten years, sees no substantial exports potential from the type of services these companies will build, asks them to serve an insignificant home market of 80,000 Internet users and fewer than one phone for every seven people, introduce informational services of use almost entirely to the government—and calls this the IT business opportunity of the century? Who do they think they're kidding?"

The fact is that Malaysia's leaders have been kidding each other (and their people) for a decade. The country's business success is largely "KFC Success." KFC is Malaysia's most successful fast food franchise. Its product is tasty, cheap, and appeals to everybody. A KFC franchise owner counts the enormous amounts of cash his business brings in, and the apparent ease with which it is coming to him, and pats himself on the back for being such an accomplished business person. The profits are proof, aren't they?

The reality is that the KFC idea, the business plan, the franchise idea, the recipes, the image, the equipment, the training, the management system, the operating procedures, and the architecture and color scheme—all were developed somewhere else and imported for a fee. What the local businessman did was provide the location and the money.

The biggest monument of Malaysia's idea of success is the Petronas Twin Towers. They are indeed the tallest occupied buildings in the world. Yet the architect was Italian. One tower was constructed by a Japanese consortium, the other by Koreans. Most of the construction equipment and finishing products such as the stainless steel cladding and the elevators was imported, as was a hefty portion of the concrete. The construction labor was mostly immigrants from Indonesia and Bangladesh. The truck drivers were mostly Thai and Indian. The money to build it was pumped from the ground (Petronas or "Petroleum Nasional" is Malaysia's national oil company). The mystical exterior lighting scheme was designed by Howard Branston and Partners in the United States. The Petronas Towers are not a testimony to a great industrializing nation thrusting into the skies a monument to its prowess, they are image packaging on a grand scale. They are testimony to contriving an international identity by importing it.

Malaysia could get away with its KFC mentality when infrastructure projects required cheap immigrant labor and cheap capital from Japan. However, an IT infrastructure is an order of magnitude greater. Yet the sole candidate for building the MSC's fiber-optics link is Malaysia Telekom, whose performance in the consumer telecoms sector hardly inspires confidence. Virtually all the infrastructure work was parceled out to politically favored construction companies and old-time cronies who headed key supplier companies. Every significant participating company was decided at the outset, without apparent tendering process, down to the lowliest air-con vendor, as much as three years before their services would be required. The words "sole provider" after so many vendor names is a warning flag to people who know the performance histories of Malaysian rentier and monopoly companies.

The MSC's vendor selection process suggests a governmental assumption that directives and a politically favored elite are what make an economy, not competitive bidding and performance benchmarks. In most countries this approach to a complex investment with significant national-image value in the international arena would have brought considerable press scrutiny. But Malaysia's business press is a mix of thinly disguised public relations masquerading as profile pieces, glowing reports of company and economy performance, lots of nice pie charts and graphics, and almost no trend and opportunity analysis. There is next to no criticism of the way business is conducted in Malaysia, although features on corporate jets and the lifestyles of their owners are prominent. Articles are so blandly written to avoid political repercussions that they are all but unreadable, especially to anyone bred on a diet of the *Economist* and *Fortune.*

Newcomers are surprised at how provincial the Malaysian business press is when it comes to Southeast Asian markets and business developments. There are few articles about business developments beyond Malaysia's borders, and those that do get printed all too often fall into the category of the "Excellent Opportunities in Cambodia" category, illustrated with a factory picture and a smiling VIP. The effect is like reading the U.S. press if you're interested in Canada or the German press if you're interested in Belgium. Many business pieces published in Malaysia originate in the public relations departments of organizations that benefit from the favorable publicity. During the publicity run-up to the MSC's opening in 1997, the following subjects did not get press attention in the Malaysian business press:

- Why does the Malaysian government insist on an infrastructure project when the market needs a service delivery project?

- Isn't there a problem in the fact that high-tech stocks account for only around 0.5 percent of stockmarket capitalization in Southeast Asia compared with 5 percent of Japan's?

- Where is the advantage to Malaysia's economy when the government courts exports investments from companies without requiring them to value-add anything?

- The Malaysian government apparently assumes that R&D brings in business and business brings in income; where are the studies that demonstrate tangible sector-by-sector benefits to the Malaysian economy?

- Why does the term 'e-business' never appear in the MSC prospectus, and why is the term 'e-commerce' treated as on-line shopping?

- Has the government or anyone else ever done a demographic study of the Malaysian IT market to find out what it wants?

- What are the consequences of selling the Malaysian people on the idea that the MSC would transform the country into an IT giant with little effort from themselves?

- Won't the enclave character of the new administrative capital Putrajaya end up making the country's bureaucracy even more remote and elitist than it already is?
- How can the complacency embedded in Malay exceptionalist *bumiputera* laws suddenly blossom into a dynamically competitive economy?
- Why are the most important support services of a techno-economy so conspicuously neglected in the MSC's plans—services like how to expand production to improve economies of scale, launch new products regularly, create effective and eye-catching product design, build stronger service marketing, devise better delivery systems?
- How does the Malaysian government plan to turn a country whose populace is so unaccustomed to consuming technology into a world informational technology center?
- How, given the fact that Malaysia's government is so inefficient, can it prepare for the demands information technology will bring?

The above are fairly tangible issues. The intangible ones are even more important, yet equally unaddressed. The purported goal of the MSC is importing higher levels of technology and inducing the kinds of wealth-building that the term "Silicon Valley" represents. Most government officials do not want to deal with what happens when people learn the things their governments don't want them to know. It was easy to hide the defects in the country's social and political fabric when the main engine of the economy was the overseas investor and the ignorant and frightened immigrant. But the MSC will bring a massive influx of sophisticated thinking in the form of the expat employees and financiers. These will be Malaysia's new wealth engine, and they will be far more observant, analytic, and blunt than any wealth-builder the country has ever experienced.

In the A. D. Little Company's 1997 survey of Asia's fifty most competitive companies, the highest (and only) Malaysian company on the list, at twenty-sixth, was Genting Bhd.—Malaysia's only casino company. No other Malaysian company made the list, which included such luminaries as Sony and Acer at the top and Korea's Pohang Iron and Steel at the bottom. In *Business Week*'s 7 July 1997 "Global 1000" list of blue-chip firms, Singapore listed eleven and Malaysia none. Singapore's telephones-per-person ratio is 1:2; Malaysia's 1:7. Singapore is first on the list of world competitiveness; Malaysia is ninth.

Why does Malaysia, for all its economic-hero self-image, have such a mediocre performance record in reality?

One reason is the relative thinness of the layer of top performers. The Malaysia, Inc., system works well for a handful of companies and cronies, but the 95 percent of Malaysian businesses that fall into the SME or family-owned and operated category invest little, manage poorly, monopolize whenever possible, and regard consumers as hostages. Malaysia's business problem is not the cream of its bureaucratic and corporate crop, but the vast layers of mediocre to nonperformers who really don't see why they need do business any other way.

While the country's public relations performance during the 1997 crisis was not particularly noble, neither was it particularly dangerous. Behind the scenes, however, it reinforced the strong authoritarian imperative arising from the country's determination to preserve at all costs its two-decade record of Malay exceptionalist and crony-driven economic development. These have given rise to a high concentration of wealth and authority in very few hands at the top. The result is poor world awareness at all levels below the top layer. One does not see the phenomenon of middle managers jetting around on company business that you see in Japan and the West. You get middle managers who have spent most of their life in their own offices reading reports about business developments elsewhere. Malaysia's vision problem is not at the top, but in the vast ranks of middle and upper middle management. Malaysia doesn't need more top decision makers in five-star hotels, it needs more middle managers in three-star ones. Yet there is no mention of a systematic program of upgrading management skills in the MSC flagship applications.

Many Malaysians are romantics. They long for the could be, should be, might be, will be. This is painfully evident in the vaporous, airy quality of the MSC's brochures and the *New Straits Times* and *CompuTimes* articles describing progress on the project. But romantics are not much interested in what is, they are interested in what might be. The Malaysian government is simply not ready for the degree of truth its MSC will import along with the digital switches and R&D labs. An anti-Western backlash is almost certain to occur. There is already a deep pool of anti-West resentment, fed for years by the Prime Minister and the press seeking to deflect attention from the political establishment's shortcomings. Anti-Western attitudes can flood in just about any direction when the inevitable storms begin to rage over the country's inadequate social infrastructure and its excess of narrowly distributed wealth. The Malaysian people have received very little ROI for their sweat equity in comparison with countries like Taiwan and Singapore, and one of these days they are going to learn that fact. At whom will their disillusion be directed?

Information technology is about end users, about consumers. The decisions being made about the MSC are preoccupied with what amounts to components. At some point one has to package components as a product. The MSC's organizers are not thinking about what that product should be. A country's greatest asset is not its ability to amass information, but its ability to turn information into material well-being. It is hard to see how a society as overregulated as Malaysia's can excel at something that demands the organizational inventiveness of information technology and e-commerce. Unless there is a serious relook at the purpose and direction of the MSC, Malaysia may do well with the technology but is setting itself up to fall flat with the content.

PART IV

E-Commerce's Sociological Complexities

22

Meet Your New Market—III

Bangsar Baru and the Taj Mahal

On-line technology changes the way people interact. But does it change the way they are?

Will the people who write the software that controls the way people communicate today introduce a view of the world that will supersede the view held by people in the past? As software code more and more determines the way information is organized and transmitted, will it become a regulatory mechanism more powerful than the law? In an information age, is progress the arbiter of order?

In the suburban townhouse developments and condos popping up in clusters around Asia's infrastructural cores, Mat and E.J. and Cik and Pammy are creating colonies of people absorbed in similar interests. Call them Bangsar Barus ("New Bangsars"). The term is a generic name derived from a trendy, over-dressy, and tedious suburb south of Kuala Lumpur where Asia's cyber*varna* first came to be noticed for what it is. The term "Bangsar Baru" is generic the same way McDonalds is generic: wherever you are, it looks and smells and tastes much the same.

Bangsar Baru, by Mat and E.J.'s understanding, is Asia's future. The old core cities that the tourists adore are slipping into the stuffy pretense of political old boys and their business-boy cronies who do deals at the Shangri-La yet neglect to notice how filthy the streets have become. Asia's Bangsar Barus, not the redolent museums or the old downtowns, are the magnets for today's new attitudes and subcultures. Bangsar Barus draw people from all over the world to work in industrial research, communications, databases, image enhancement, and anything to do with marketing. They have the trendy shops, thriving cafes, pub culture, fake French boulangeries, Tex-Mex eateries, skimpy young things in beige, real-estate imbeciles in BMWs—and the satellite dishes, cybercafes, newsletters, and financial opportunities. Kebayoran Baru in Jakarta has so many rooftop sat-dishes you think the place is some kind of enormous national R&D project.

It is. The government just doesn't know that yet. It is a testbed in how to be modern without showing it.

Sat-dishes are culture R&D. Marketing is where the money is, but culture is where the market is.

Mat and E.J. are real people. They are also about to become, under different names, market identities—those demographic profiles that market research firms use to designate the upbeat, future-forward, twenty/thirty-something middle class with a penchant for pioneer purchasing. "Mat" is Malay for "Guy" or what Spanish cyber*varna* members call "Hombre." Cik and Pammy will soon become transmuted into whatever ad agencies decide is a good, wholesome generic name for a career woman destined to end up a housewife with very clear ideas on where the kids are going to be educated. (India's marketers are already ahead of Southeast Asia's: her name is "Mati," short for "Srimati India," the Indian housewife.)

These about-to-be market identities may be a cyber*varna*, and their Bangsar Barus may be the looming generica of Asia the way Mountain View and Cambridge are the generica of California and England, but make no mistake: Mat and E.J. and Cik and Pammy are middle class to the core. The only difference is that, given the credit, tax, and consumer constraints placed by their societies, they choose to live without the car in order to have the computer, not the other way around.

Middle class too, but in a vastly different way, is the Karnataka or Orissa or Nam Dinh or Kedah or Guizhou or Jiangsu or Bandar Acheh villager who sleeps on his bed of woven twine but has a new tractor parked under the tin roof that used to house his goats. The goats, accommodatingly enough, find that sleeping under the tractor is no worse than sleeping under the tin roof.

This is the unseen, unknown, unheeded, unstudied, and unquantified rural middle class slowly growing in affluence all over Asia like fire-tree blossoms in Spring. They know that, behind the veil of dust and sun and distance that shimmers over the vastness of Asia's rural plains, they are missing out on something. They see it on TV.

The Toyota or Proton or Maruti is only a dream. But the wife has a "mixie"—an electric blender—and here, "right here in this ad, my Husband, do see it right *here*, it says that Kelvinator and Electrolux have brought their fridgie prices down to almost the same prices as washers and what's more, offer interest-free credit payments. Do you *see* that, my Husband! *You* got the tractor. When is it *my* turn?"

Interest-free, the husband would like to say, until you add up the total number of payments you have to make. But what's a husband to do when he is reminded that the tractor was on time payments too—40 percent every three months from the moneylender.

Rural middle-class Asians are cut from very different cloth than the urban bourgeoisie. They are its almost totally ignored market, and the one with the greatest long-term potential for the kinds of middle-price, middle-class, middle-longevity products that an economy thrives on over the longest spans of time. The rural bourgeoisie is rice (and rice products) to Asia the way it is bread (and bread products) to Europe.

Many Asian rurals have enjoyed a steady income rise courtesy of the Green Revolution in agriculture. They love their houses brimming with ultra-budget consumer goods—soaps, cleansers, cookies and snacks, the contenting niceties that make for good looks and full tummies. They are cheerfully materialist in their public appearances, but not in their private outlooks. They dislike strong statements. They hate change. In lieu of drama they love domesticities—hair dryers, pressure cookers, microwaves. They give their treasured possessions cutesy nicknames like the ones dowagers give pampered pets: the "mixies" and "fridgies" we already know about, but one of these days you'll be hearing the term "nettie," meaning the little box on top of the TV from which they find out how to buy and pay for those things they see on the TV.

These are the "Mixies," not really a class and certainly not a *varna*, but a part of the Asian inevitability of a gigantic populace turning inexorably toward gigantic change upon the wheels of marketing. Asia's middle classes are not really aware of it, but they are the only social buffer that exists between Asia's abusive power addicts and the dozing mammoth of ignorance still sowing rice. In India there are said to be half a million Bangsar Baruans, another 50 million people who qualify as middle class, and still another 200 million in the Mixie category who would qualify as budget yuppies if the definition of "middle class" were expanded to include the ability to buy a set-top cable-cum-Internet box to go on top of their existing TV.

Beyond these are 750 million who haven't a clue.

That is the case for India, the country enjoying the sharpest-researching business reporters in Asia. No one knows what the numbers are elsewhere (the numbers advanced by the international consulting and market research firms are at wild variance with each other), but it is probably not far off the mark to say that three-quarters of Asia have seen something on TV they wish they could have, but can't.

Marketers amend that to: can't have *yet*.

All this is dazzling. It also is delusory. Marketers are dazzled by Asia's Bangsar Baru and Mixie classes. Politicians and religious leaders deplore them. Old-time Asian nationalists are scared to death of them. Demographers are scratching their heads trying to figure out how to turn them into predictions. Foreign companies and investors want to tap the market they are.

It is delusory because resentment against the urban middle class runs high in many rural communities. Locals say that city dwellers consume too large a share of government revenue, natural resources, and energy, while they, the country's food producers, are neglected. Rural electricity is often available for only a few hours each night, but air conditioners hum round the clock in the cities. The farmers also see the markups in the prices of their produce in city markets and wonder why those big profit margins should go to someone else. (Yet they unwittingly make their own contribution to those profits by demanding subsidies in both buying supplies and selling goods, and withholding supplies from government procurement centers and the bazaars until the price is high.)

It is also delusory because so many would-be marketers haven't lived in their market. Some, for example, are of the opinion that the main barrier between their products and Asia's consumers is not poverty but politics. They cite India as an example of their view that governments don't want informed people because information shifts the power balance from politics to business.

Hogwash. The problem with the Asian market is the Asian marketplace. For the record, this is the problem:

The average Asian shop is one of a dozen to a hundred practically identical stalls on both sides of a street through which autos careen past oxcarts, sending dogs whining and chickens skrawking out of the way. There are no curbs or sidewalks, and in the rainy season all this is a rutway of mire.

The neighboring shops will be the likes of haircutters (one mirror, one razor, one comb), vendors of agricultural implements (many forged from sheet iron in the back) and purveyors of poisons, one stall selling tea but no soft drinks and the next stall selling soft drinks but no tea (product stratification being ever present in the business world), and chemists who sell just about anything without need of approval from some physician.

Most customers buy for the moment, whether it be an analgesic for a headache, a disposable razor, a cigarette, or the vegetables required for the next meal. Fronting the stall will be an array of banana bunches dangling on strings from metal hooks. There may be as many as twenty varieties of bananas ranging from a few varieties of dull-green, hard-fleshed ones used only for cooking to a fairly exotic species with a skin the thickness of paper and that tastes like perfumed honey.

Aside from the bananas (mostly well past their prime) there will be an array of oranges, mangos, mangosteens, papayas, etc. (likewise mostly well past their prime) in slivery wooden bins, a metal wire bread display with six shelves that hold dozens of jars of marmalades, and polyethylene sacks of cookies.

Inside it looks like retailer's convention reduced to the dimensions of a stall roughly the size of a living room but twice as high. Nowhere is there a square foot of empty anything, except perhaps for the floor, where spare foot room often as not is partly taken up by two kittens or a pup lunching on Mom. Shelf space amounts to cardboard boxes with their tops cut off and stacked on top of each other, gaping cavernously for attention. Bags of Pampers and boxes of tampons hang from the ceiling on strings, onions vie for attention with half a dozen brands of hand soap heaped on a plank nailed to another plank nailed to a wall. You can hardly find the counter (there being no cash register) behind the facade of coffee packets and bags of dried mango slivers and onion flakes. One wall will be a garishly colored escutcheon promoting milk powders or insta-noodle soups. In between are tins of peas, sacks of lentils and garbanzos and red beans, and things labeled in local script that might be either pig's knuckles or sheep testicles, it's hard to tell from the pictures.

Around the periphery, brooms hang from hooks, fire extinguishers lie next to boxes of matches, tea, toothpicks, dried chilis in frilly bunches that any good photographer could turn into art objects, two-liter bottles of cooking oil, hopsack bags of sugar and semolina spilling their cargoes all over on floor. Don't step in the spill of brown sugar. The proprietor intends to sweep it back into the sack momentarily.

The entire affair is coated with dust, the grime of the roaring river of diesels just outside the door, and gecko (lizard) poop decorating everything like icing on a birthday cake.

The locals wouldn't dream of shopping anywhere else.

Veteran marketers see this as unparalleled opportunity. They have seen new consumer markets create themselves out of stallholder verisimilitude before—Spain after Franco, Russia on the coattails of Yeltsin; Taiwan, Hong Kong, and Singapore since the 1985 Plaza Accords. They are very well aware that Asia's urban and rural middle classes are culturally conservative at heart, no matter what they might put on in a moment of mania inspired by *Cosmopolitan*. E.J. and Pammy might be computerized to their teeth, but they live in Tampines and see the shops with their perpetual sign wars over prices but no signs proclaiming new products. E.J. and Pammy aren't particularly fooled by either of these worlds. Instead, they see them as opportunity.

In India the members of the so-called "Maruti Class" are the largest purchasers of ethnic art and artifacts. In Malaysia the "Proton proletariat" almost single-handedly keeps alive the historical craftsmanship of the country's traditional weavers, potters, jewelry makers, and folk artists. Just ask Cik. She regularly goes out into the *kampungs* of Trengganu and the riverine villages of Sarawak to find motifs for her pewter designs. Just ask an architect like Hijjas Kasturi of Kuala Lumpur, who has transmuted the ancient visual motifs of Malay crafts into buildings of history-making visual power and grace. Thais and Filipinos, as much as they adore the playthings of Western culture (not to mention the salaries), realize that their culture is a unique, ancient, and very valuable one. They are not about to see it thrown to the marketing wolves of Coca Cola and KFC. It didn't take Manila's Jollibee long to figure out the easiest way to a better-selling burger was not what went inside it but the wrapper that went outside it.

In short, Mat and E.J. are Western in words but Asian in deeds. To visitors reading the icon publications of their culture—*ID* and *Her World, Metro*, and *Jakarta Express*—it is easy to mistake Asia's cyber middle class for the investment and managerial middle class.

Yet these are words, not ideas. They represent things in life, not change in life. A digital decade is not an information era. No one knows when or how—and, for that matter, if—Asia's e-commerce era will come. Investment strategists and marketers are certain that Singapore's IT 2000 and Malaysia's Multimedia Super Corridor will be among the locuses of where it comes. But when, how, and to what effect are as enigmatic as the mandala and the arabesque.

What is known is known quite certainly: Mat and E.J. will opt for modest innovation—that curious blend again of the conservative and the liberal.

Modern Asia is changing. It isn't just a country of the Taj Mahal and Bali and Borobudur and the beggars and the cows and the shrines and the paddies any more. Specialists in research organizations chart social development in Asia by looking at what and how much people are purchasing, not the monuments politicians erect. Selling by brand name on television, billboards, or in glossy magazines began with soaps and toiletries, proceeded to basic foods, branched into motorbikes and household appliances and decorator bathroom fixtures and fashionable clothes; and now is well into soft drinks, snack foods, fashion, irons, and TVs.

Whatever Asia's economic future, the new way its urban middle classes perceive and use economy and the media is altering politics invisibly but with finality. The 1997 economic humiliation was caused by all those local pols building palaces for themselves in Australia with the money that was supposed to be used for computers in schools. Multiply these by a thousand similar stories—which is what TV does—and you have a sea of change. In percentage terms, middle-class Asia is not large—perhaps a tenth to a third of its populaces. Mat and E.J. are nearing critical mass with their very different sets of values. They rely on images, mediagenicity, substance, new ideas, realism, unsentimental truth mixed with reverence for the meaningful. Asia's political elders are seen as feudal monarchists who have neither sense of proportion nor true belief in the old cultures. Mat and E.J. sum up Asia's politicians in a quip: "Yesterday today." The same can be said of the Petronas Towers in Kuala Lumpur, and for the same reasons: too much show is the mask over the face of too much greed.

Mat and E.J. have—and know they have—the ability to alter the older political linkages based on caste, region, and religion.

All this has momentous implications. Earlier generations—intellectuals for the most part—saw all problems in East-West or North-South terms. They failed to notice that the most powerful and effective force for change—an informed populace—was growing in the professions and that professionals were networking themselves into colonies of Bangsar Barus with an entirely different way of communicating with one another.

Today the Asian power elite is dumbfounded by the notion that culture can proceed from things other than polity and authority. They don't know how to restrain the value-added ladder economy, which they can control, from becoming an information economy, which they cannot. Information turns timeless times into modern times. It is never easy.

23

Asia's Dissemination Structures

There are four basic dissemination structures in Asian social communication:

- *Corporate information* is hierarchical in character and transmitted up and down a functionary silo. One's worth is defined as the worth he or she has in the eyes of a decision maker. The worth of information is often that it has been validated by a boss.
- *Bureaucratic information* is disseminated in triangular patterns bridging two out of the many levels of the institution's hierarchy. One person in the higher layer communicates to a small group of subordinates (usually two) beneath, who communicate it across their layer to their colleagues. Information has to be validated within the triangle before it goes anywhere else. Hence the validity of information comes from the collective assent of many small niches. This is one reason why it can be truthfully said of bureaucracies that nobody decides anything because everybody does and everybody knows this because nobody does.
- *Urban information* is generated at one level of identity—say a social group such as neighbors or a club—and disseminated to others on the same level in the socioeconomic ladder, that is, between members of the same class, but not so often upward or downward into other levels of the social hierarchy. Hence the authority of information can easily equate to class approval.
- *Village information* is distributed evenly in every direction—up and down and across—though rarely beyond communal boundaries. Validation is largely communal. Knowledge from outside the system may be ignored or considered suspect because it has no local authority. The one external validation source is often the government's political representative, who doles out perks and, during elections, cash.

Asia isn't a marketplace. It is a cultureplace in which many markets exist. To think of the market without first thinking in terms of the cultures is fraught with dangers, of which the least troublesome is mediocre competitiveness. Although Asia's three basic cultures—Chinese, Malay, and Indian—are convenient reference points, they are simply three branches on a plant with great diversity.

Asia's complex mix of ancestral values, cultural niches, religions, folk practices, systems of family ties, superstitions, child-raising practices, attitudes about property, money-mindedness, and ceremonial rituals is a godsend for travel agents— and godawful for marketers. For example, in the middle of Asia's two bastions of Islam, Malaysia and Indonesia, there is a matriarchal culture, *minangkebau*. In the southern provinces of Mahayana Buddhist Thailand there is a strong Muslim culture, while in Theravada Buddhist Sri Lanka there exists such a rich potpourri of Hindu beliefs that there is even a class of temple, the *devale*, which graciously makes room for solemnly meditative Buddha statues under one tree and cheery elephant-headed Ganeshas under the next. Chinese Christianity mixes in a taste of ancient Taoism; ancient Taoism in turn has a hint of Buddhism. Even Western Christianity borrowed a whiff of the East. The Biblical figure of Jehosaphat is a distant derivation from Buddhism's Bodhisattva. Parts of the ritual of the Catholic mass were borrowed from ancient Mithraism, whose compassionate (though bull-slaying) deity Mithra was borrowed from Maitreya. Maitreya is title of the Buddha-to-be, the next Enlightened One in the series of twenty-five whose last reincarnation was that nice fellow Gotama from northern India.

Can you imagine what the cultures that produced this engaging mix of myth and humanity can do with the myths and humanity of the advertising world? Jollibee hamburgers outsell Big Macs in Manila, though there's not all that much difference once you get inside the wrapper.

Asia has so many niche cultures that the job of the e-commerce marketer is more how to respond to each on its own terms than impose a massive informational McDonalds on them all. For example, there is a marketing info-delivery challenge called the "village-server" model (see below). The job of the village server is find ways to address those billions of villagers from India to China whose only link to the IT and e-commerce world is one electrical line and one communal TV, around which the entire village gathers in the absence of anything more pressing to do. The TV-under-a-tree is a modern votive shrine taking up residence alongside the other tree-shrines of Shiva or Kuan Yin, benevolently guarding the village familiarities of the babies and young romantics and cooking smells and dogs racing through the dust. This is the *real* market of Asia.

Singapore might be getting it right in terms of installing an IT and e-commerce system that is effective, efficient, and informative. But no one, not even the Singaporeans, has any idea how to address the massive diversity of the Asian e-commerce market. Assuredly it will begin in the megalopolises and soon wend into the metros, but these are lucrative, easy markets tantamount to skimming the cream. The vast milk bottle of Asia is information delivery to the rural market.

The governments and big businesses of Asia have a different assumption than the one common to Western marketing gurus. Asians tend to place state and family leadership over economic markets and private enterprise. Hence the belief that government creates wealth and solves problems. The Chinese "Mandate of Heaven" idea presumes that one knows the government is good if local life is good. The Malay *devaraja* (god-king) ideal as embodied in today's sultans is that the ruler never betrays the people and in turn the people never betray the ruler. This explains the Malaysian adoration of Prime Minister Mahathir as an economic genius and why Indonesians find it easier to take out their frustrations on the Chinese than on the Suharto family. The enormous panoply of Hindu gods, which spill generously over into other religious doctrines by way of folk beliefs, is the idealized family, right down to the idealized wild-oats boyhood (Krishna and the *gopis* or maidens) and the idealized angry mother (Kali and her 108 swords).

All these are systems in which power and authority are exercised through hierarchy. Yet there is a congruent belief that a fundamental unity pervades all human beings (and in Jainism, all living beings). In Islam it has the name *ummah*, and in that belief system signifies the equality in brotherhood of all believers. The Hindu religion has given this belief a name: Indra's Net. The existence of all living things is a vast net of spiritual life force. At each crossing of the lines of the net a splendid multifaceted jewel exists in the form of a life. Each facet of each jewel reflects all the facets of all the other jewels, so that while we are unique individuals, we are also one immense web of commonalities. If we are to be whole, we must be both one and multitude.

NEEDED: THE RIGHT VILLAGE-SERVER MODEL

The pattern of information provision in most of Asia is centered on the fact that the village is usually served by only one electricity line and (sometimes) one telephone line. Everyone clusters around a communal TV in front of someone's home watching whatever fare it has to offer.

Serving this population with set-top servers or "Net TV" is sometimes called the "village-server" model. The idea of a "Net TV" (meaning the concept, not a specific commercial product) attached to the sole, or one of the few, television sets that dominate media life in many rural villages is obviously an attractive one. What are some of the cultural considerations marketers might have?

Presently rural television fare is news, sports, and popular entertainment, all of which is heavily predigested by governing authorities. Broadcast television largely ignores the village's formidable need for quick, on-call, noncommercial information of the medical, agricultural, prenatal, or emergency type. Yet village TV is perhaps the best vehicle for the kind of information in English and Chinese that can be most easily disseminated by Net TV.

There are three obstacles, however. The first is that the kind of information the villages most need is practical and noncommercial. Even with a willing government, a breathtaking budget would be required to equip villages with Net TVs and assemble the databases to be made available on them. The Web TV so popular among the urban digiterati is prohibitively expensive by Asian rural standards.

The second is the plethora of languages riven with regional and often highly local dialects. There is no technology that can easily translate the English-language body of international technical information into so many niche tongues.

The third and most serious is that, as we observed above, the communication dynamics of village life differ significantly from those of urban life. Information assembled and disseminated from governments, NGOs, or corporations can very well fall on what amounts to cultural deaf ears in the villages simply because it is not presented in the way villagers relate to.

These are potent obstacles to the idea of marketing social service information into Asia's villages by the typical urban vehicle of TV as authority surrogate. The solution lies in giving global knowledge the character of village validity. Unfortunately, the costs of turning English-language databases into village *patois*, socially as well as linguistically, are so high and bereft of profit potential it appears governments are the only probable venue. Unfortunately, the interests of too many Asian governments are in keeping the villagers ignorant, not informed.

IDEAS ABOUT AUTHORITY

Throughout much of the region's history, Asia's leaders have exercised power in two ways. In cultures that originated in Hinduism—meaning much of Southeast Asia despite today's overlayer of Islam—power was a relationship with a cosmic order (*rita*) ordained by other-worldly forces. The Chinese approach, on the other hand, asserted a this-worldly, human-centered, ethical-moral order.

Both emphasized the dominance of external, unseen, and often malevolent forces that could be harnessed only by a refined priestcraft or intelligentsia adept in the performance of the proper rituals. Unlike many early religions, which relied on appeasing the frightful forces in the world through sacrifice, the Indians and Chinese arrived at the solution of allying with these forces to draw into themselves their invisible power. Their appeal to these unseen forces was through ritual performance rather than striking bargains with them—like following codes of conduct such as the Ten Commandments.

This may seem abstract until you realize that in modern Asia the ideal power figure is seen to be aloof, remote, abstract, seldom seen or heard, and, who, when he does speak, does so in a low voice. The press reverently describes corporate leaders with adjectives like "secretive," "behind-the-scenes player," or "low-key." The contrast with the memo-spewing, terse, loud, domineering Western middle manager couldn't be more vivid.

In the history of Asian governmental practice, nearly all the Asian cultures exercised power through some form of ritual. Very early on they developed the idea that the most nearly perfect performance of ritual produced the most nearly perfect form of result. Those good at the prescribed rituals became the most powerful people of the community. In Hindu culture, people felt those in power deserved it because they had cleansed their karma of bad acts in previous lives by many good acts in the lives between. In Chinese culture, people believe those in power achieve it by hard work, earning their merit through learning and probity. This belief system is so ancient that unmistakable symbolic connections between acts of ritual and ruling can be found in archeological artifacts from the Indus River to Japan.

Modern life hasn't really changed things all that much. It is amazing how much authority a wizened elder in a Malaysian *kampung* wields by quietly doing things the way they are supposed to be done. The doing by itself is not important. In much of Asia, the ritual of doing things the right way is more important than what it is that is being done.

To take the example a little deeper into social expectation patterns, the sultanates era of Muslim Southeast Asia was (and in the case of Malaysia, still is) one of the most elegant and stylized eras in Asian history. Some formalisms were so magnificent that their residue motivates behavioral responses to this day. One of the most eloquent was associated with sending and receiving letters between the sultans. Because it was impossible for a sultan to make a long, arduous journey, letters were ceremonially delivered in their stead. This ceremony was a transference of the physical sultan in letter form, and had to be attended to with equal ceremony. The letters themselves were composed with great care and after extensive *muafakat* (concord among those participating). When completed, the letter would be sent by elephant to the accompaniment of music. The recipient would carefully listen to how the letter was worded, inquire extensively as to the manner in which it was sent, then pen his reply. When the envoys returned, the original sender would in turn ask all the details of how the letter had been received and re-sent.

Sultans put considerable effort into sending their letters so that the addressee, learning the details, would be properly flattered. The slightest hint of peremptoriness in phrasing or carelessness in the ritual of transmission could—and did—result in war.

The elaboration of these rituals paralleled court ceremony in many other parts of Asia, notably China. These images are not as archaic as one might think. Many of today's official functions are carried on with the same sensitivity to the tiniest ritual detail. Imagine how much preparation ahead of time goes into the tailoring of a host government's national shirt or garment which ASEAN members wear at their conclaves so that in the final group photo-op all of them hang to exactly the same level line across the image? And that's just the shirts—establishing who tees off with whom could be renamed "The Ballet of the Muftis."

These are extraordinarily old and powerful sensitivities. The combination of ritual and authority in Southeast Asia's states originates from pre-Muslim times when the region was ruled by a succession of Indian trader-potentates who asserted their authority via the trappings of *devarajas*. Their elaborate rituals were carried out with similar elaborate sacred paraphernalia. So were the rituals of the Emperor's court in China and Japan. The underlying purpose was to ensure that the structure of interpersonal relationships was in conformity with the forces that ruled the cosmos. If you want to see how alive this ideal of human concourse is today, get invited to a Hindu or Malay wedding.

Hindu-originated god-kings, through their rituals, were part of *rita*, the cosmic order. Everyone in society was expected to respect the forces of the supernatural by following the rules of their caste—their *dharma*—to improve the level of their caste in the next incarnation. The power of Indian rulers resided in the ceremonial rituals they performed.

This thinking was imported virtually intact into Southeast Asia during the great wave of merchant immigration during the ninth through the thirteenth centuries, a mercantile hegemonization that culminated in the region's first true political empire, Srivijaya. The name "Srivijaya" roughly translates to "honored victory" and this aptly named empire dominated the Southeast Asian maritime region from its home base in Palembang, Java, for several centuries. Bali and Borobudur are two of its legacies.

The complexity and precision of ancient Indian Brahminic costume and ritual were transferred almost intact to the Indonesian and Malayan potentates who arose during the great fourteenth- and fifteenth-century era of Malay self-definition after Islam's introduction in 1405. The elaborate position-defining array of titles, honorifics, clothing, and rituals of today's Southeast Asian political and business leadership goes back in a direct line to the *devaraja* concept, and with it the idea that the ultimate spiritual power guiding human behavior is articulated in a form everyday people can readily understand: rituals.

This idea that the will of the gods (or fate) and the exercise of human power reinforced each other was not unique to India. Chinese culture originated the same idea, but in China's uniquely appropriate way. From early times Chinese culture was centered on worldly matters. The emperor's power to rule stemmed from his duty to perform the rituals, which, when properly observed, made him the "Son of Heaven." The daily doings of humans were thought to be governed not by other humans but by external forces—Heaven, the Tao, the Way, or in the minds of the simpler folk, by fortune, luck, or chance. If all this seems exotically irrelevant, go to a Chinese astrologer anywhere in Asia and tell him your birth date is all the same number—say, 6/6/66.

In each system the basic principle was the same: finite human power became infinite by allying with a power greater than oneself—the heavens in those times, the government in these times. The Son of Heaven became a Prime Minister. Name change notwithstanding, he still is obliged to conduct himself in such a way that society will be protected from the consequences of fate's wrath. Indonesia's Suharto broke the rules by favoring his family over his people. Malaysia's Prime Minister Mahathir denied those rules, and in six months turned the image of Malaysia from one of a modern place to do business into one of an untrustworthy bastion of antiquated privilege.

Because the Chinese believe that the controlling forces of life and history exceed the power of any one person, the essence of Chinese political strategy was to design ways to ensure that one was on the side of the controlling forces, and that one's opponents would be defeated by the forces of fate. The key idea is "on the side of" those forces, not "in charge of" those forces. The collective identity is important; the individual's is not.

This is a major theme in Sun Tzu's *The Art of War* and the enduring handful of other Chinese, Korean, and Japanese leadership treatises penned over a thousand years ago. Their unifying idea was that meaningful power was linked to timing, to selecting the propitious moment, to understanding when to act. Secrecy in motive and intent is the key to awaiting the right moment. Today few foreigners dealing with Asia's Chinese business communities comprehend how primal their instinct for secrecy is, and why it is as such a striking part of daily dealings. To the Chinese, secrecy isn't about deviousness. It is about room for maneuver and timing. They are acutely aware their competitors are thinking the same way.

Few of these considerations appear in the theories of success through brute power penned by Western theorists. Those are devoted largely to considerations of force, dominance, and control. The idea of "guerrilla marketing" dumbfounds Asian marketers, who are far more concerned with timing a decision than imposing one.

This is a fundamental difference in the *aesthetics* of power. The fact of application is not the issue, the elegance of application is. The idea that business has a vitally necessary aesthetic component is one reason why Westerners find it difficult to grasp the Asian way of doing it. Five thousand years of elaborations on simple human themes of fealty and security are not going to go away just because some MBA comes along waving a diskette, any more than rice and fruit sales have been changed by the arrival of burgers and fries. The reality is that Asians are happily eating both.

THE ILLOGICAL MANAGER

All three of Asia's business cultures—Malay, Chinese, and Indian—dissociate two concepts that in the West are usually linked: power and responsibility.

Power is transferred from the fate realm to the human realm (from theory to practice) by the correctness of the rituals that exercise it (the letter of the law). Power without the proper ritual lacks precision. Lacking precision, it lacks meaning. The principle *behind* the rules is not important; the precision *of* the rules is important. It is useful to remember this when gritting your teeth at some bureaucrat who is correct on some insignificant point of fact but is wasting a lot of your time demonstrating it.

There is an anthropological term for this kind of behavior: *talismanic*. Talismans are the objects associated with the rituals—the game plans—that protect an organization or venture from mischance. Few Chinese or Hindu building contractors lay a foundation stone without consulting an astrologer to determine the propitious time. Many Chinese and Indians (but few Malays, due to Islam's proscription of icons) believe that the talismans *themselves*—the symbol of the game rather than the rules of the game—are what bring good fortune. People respond to the sight of flags, too.

If the notion that good rules and good luck are interrelated seems illogical, it is. The Asian response is, "So what?" The most difficult idea to grasp about Asian business style is that decisions don't have to be logical to be good. Asian academics point out that Western logic is no prize in the mental orderliness department, either. Logic begins with necessary assumptions. Assumptions are intuitive by nature. Sometimes they are insights that dawn in a networking session. Sometimes they are a bolt out of the blue. They often lead to great ideas or products when applied to logic. But they are totally illogical by themselves.

Most Westerners consider logical reasoning to be the only valid way to draw conclusions. Many Asians view rational thinking as merely one of many kinds of conclusionary methods, all of which are equally valid:

- *Reason* is deduction or induction applied to information supplied by the senses.
- *Intuition* arrives at conclusions by nondeductive emotional feelings and does not use sense information; typical intuition begins where logic leaves off—"My head said to do A, but my heart told me to do B."
- *Insight* reaches out beyond both mind and senses to the direct illumination of a natural law. Networking and focus grouping often result in insights that "come from nowhere."
- *Mystic*, which is the direct experience of God, the gods, or the One (the unity of all existence), cannot be explained by human experience. The Buddha's Enlightenment is one example.

Unfortunately for the newcomer to Asia, so many different and seemingly valid methods for arriving at a decision can result in decisions that seem—and are—illogical. It is important to realize that whether a decision is logical is not the point. The point is whether the decision is valid for the circumstances. While Asia's institutional memory can be extremely long (as seen in the durability of Confucianism and India's caste system, for example), many Asians have exceptionally short conclusionary memories; they often cannot recall—or don't care—which thought process they used to arrive at a belief.

Many associations that people today take as perfectly modern originated in folk mysticism. The earth deities of cyclical regeneration became associated with the cyclical change of the moon and the cycles of a woman's menses. From that mystical link they moved into the West via the Virgin Mary to the demanding but forgiving figure of Oprah Winfrey today. In India the earth goddess became protective mother figure via the milk of the sacred cow, thence to Mother India, to Indira Gandhi, and via her to today's Srimati India, the demographic name for the Indian middle-class housewife. In China the spirit of compassion and forgiveness came up through Buddhism's *bodhisattva* ideal of the compassionate helpmate into today's Kuan Yin. Intel knew what to do with Kuan Yin when it started sponsoring "PC Fairs" in different cities in 1995. School bands played (sometimes even in tune), and "PC Doctors" dressed in academic gowns (Confucian scholars) explained what microprocessors are and what they can do while "PC Nurses" cajoled children intimidated by the equipment by pulling up favorite puppets on screen and explaining that computers love them like their mothers love them.

High officials assume their duty is to act out their ritual roles for the good of all. Ritualized power—often reflected in specific garments worn on specific occasions—is a social symbol expressing the attitude that if a ruler behaves correctly, everyone benefits. When then U.S. Secretary of State James Baker once saw Dr. Mahathir wearing the distinctive Malay *songkok* hat at a ministerial meeting in Tokyo and commented, "Hey, who's the guy in the native costume?" Baker was ignorant of the fact that Mahathir was symbolizing to the Malaysian people watching him on TV that he was being precise in the ritual duty he performed when serving their interests. In performing the ritual thus, he was signaling that their interests were uppermost in his mind. To Asians Mahathir came off as admirable in the most exemplary way, while James Baker—and the United States—came off as uninformed.

Unfortunately, overdoing the rules of ritual has downsides. One is overaffection for the favored few, who often are better connected than they are qualified. In the past, Asian rulers were expected to be responsive to the concerns of the people. Hence they rewarded those they felt were best suited for the job of managing the people. Today the most visible vestige of this ancient behavior pattern is cronyism.

24

Chinese Psychology and Business Style

Chinese families embody more fealty bonds of the silo-hierarchy corporate type than other Asian family systems. More than anywhere else on Earth, "We" is "I." So much emphasis is placed on control by pragmatic adaptivity and so little on control by ideology that one can almost say that the Chinese talent for management is born, not made.

The nuclear family (*chia*) is generally the smallest silo within a much larger corporate kin group. Three basic types of Chinese families exist: (1) the small-size conjugal family, (2) the medium-size "stem" family, and (3) the large-sized "joint" family.

To elaborate on these definitions a bit, a conjugal family consists of a husband, his wife, their unmarried children, and sometimes the husband's unmarried brothers and sisters. A stem family consists of two conjugal units—the head of the family and with the son (usually the eldest) designated to be the stem of the family tree; the other sons move away upon marriage. A joint family is found mainly among the wealthy Chinese; it comprises the conjugal unit of the head of the family, his brothers, his sons, and his grandsons; all these conjugal units live in the same house and share the common property and food.

Beyond the family, there is also a clan system in which the numerous component families share patrilineal descent from a common ancestor.

The Chinese family of any size is patrilineal, patrilocal (the wife lives with the husband's family), and patriarchal. The family head is usually the father, but sometimes it can be the eldest brother or in rare cases the eldest son by delegation. The patriarch has absolute authority in control of common property, income of individual members, consumption, and conduct of the members. In poorer families the eldest son must bear the responsibilities of supporting and providing education for his younger siblings by entering the labor force early.

The property of a Chinese household is equally divided among paternal descendants upon the death of the head of the household or a family dispute. The inheriting members, together with their conjugal units, will then set up their own separate household.

Great emphasis is placed on the continuity of the family along the patrilineal line, as expressed in the Confucian philosophy that a living individual is the personification of all his forebears and of his descendants yet unborn. A Chinese family wants to have more than one son so the strength and prosperity of the family will be better ensured.

The Chinese kinship system stresses the importance of the male and of relationship traced through the male. With the unilineal descent and clan organization, the nuclear family (though common in the Chinese community) is subordinate to the larger family group. Hence a degree of group corporateness is maintained. Beyond the family circle, there are strong ties with kinship groups sharing a common surname and nearly as strong ties with members of the same dialect group. The principle is mutual help and obligation for common social and economic interest. The practical result is that one can find a place within many clan and dialect group associations.

Society's most fundamental needs are considered to be stability, continuity, and perpetuation. Strong family bonds contribute five value elements that reinforce these needs:

- the father-son relationship
- family pride
- the large family
- ancestor cult
- common ownership of family property

Today's social and economic development has introduced a number of changes to the above model of the traditional Chinese community:

- The patrilineal system has been largely replaced by a bilateral system in which the wife's relatives are as important as the husband's.
- Mutual obligations and social relations among kin are much less important than they used to be.
- Filial piety is widely accepted but has not been as strong as before.
- The conjugal type of family is preferred by an increasingly large majority of Chinese over the stem or joint types.
- Women have been emancipated from seclusion and complete submission to their traditional role, but they still usually center their interest and activities within the household.
- Marriage is now a matter of consultation between parents and young people, usually on the initiative of the latter.

- Divorce is still rare, but is not as strongly disapproved as formerly.
- Skepticism about spirits, demons, and gods has increased with the advance of education.

CONFUCIAN MANAGEMENT

Confucianism pervades the lives and thoughts of Chinese people. From about the mid-thirteenth century millions of Chinese have migrated from the mainland itself to Southeast Asia in search of a better living. Although the overseas Chinese (*hua chiao*) were assimilated into the other races and cultures, Confucianism remains a major influence in their thinking to this day.

The teachings of Confucius are broad. They range from humanity, filial piety (*haiao*), conduct (*li*), and character, to education, rites, and music—even how to govern a country, and today's modern equivalent of the small countries of long ago, the corporate empire.

Confucian teachings emphasize moral cultivation through human activity. Truth is distilled from much experience over long periods of time. The most important belief is that actions are more important than words. Confucian culture also embraces that other great world ethos based on practicality, capitalism. Hence Confucianism is an important guide to understanding the social and economic expectations of the majority of modern Asia's Chinese.

Chinese values with regard to managerial practices have evolved into a management system quite distinct from that of the West. An effective leader manifests competence in seven ways: character, conduct, enduring relationships (*ch'in*), caring, filial piety (*chung*), cleverness, and the Golden Mean (*Chung Yung*).

Character

Confucius's teachings focused on the fulfillment of life that comes with the full development of a person. He believed that family background or social order is what sets people apart. Humans must define their character early in life, then refine it through practice. Only through the "earnest practice of humanity" can a person merit the term *chun-tzu*, which roughly corresponds (gender being irrelevant) to the ideal of "gentleman."

An effective Confucian manager builds quality into an organization by transferring to it the high quality of his own character. He or she is flexible in behavior but firm in thinking. The phrase "practice what you preach" means little because the manager simply practices and lets the results do the preaching. The manager demonstrates commitment through self-discipline and self-restraint. The goal is to set a living example more than a spoken one.

A notable quality of the Confucian ideal of leadership is the manager's relinquishment of vainglory. The success of the organization as a whole is best assured if the manager does not care who ultimately gets the credit for his or her effort; results are their own reward. Thinking of others, forgetting self, and keeping a quiet profile are the primary characteristics of the enlightened manager. The power of a truly great leader is invisible yet powerful, like water.

Conduct

Confucius lived in a time of great *Li* or proper order in the world. In a world of *Li*, good conduct is the fundamental principle of all relationships, be they among family, society, or polity. *Li* is a complex term, rather like the French term *comme il faut* or "how things should be." It embodies the essence of personal propriety, orderliness, and good life. A *Li* society should be highly stratified. Different standards of propriety are obliged at different social levels, with the greatest propriety at the top.

Confucius taught his disciples that there were around three thousand rules governing each and every aspect of behavior. This is an interesting number, since in India the number of castes that have evolved over time to encompass the Hindu culture's range of personality types interpenetrating with lifestyle niches also numbers about three thousand.

According to Confucian management theory, politeness is the fundamental basis for all concourse. In conversation, the choice of words and the tone of speech are strictly controlled. Subtle language is a distinguishing character of many Asian conversational locutions, especially when expressing negative comments.

Good conduct is the fundamental principle for all harmonious relationships. An effective manager is well behaved. He or she encourages right conduct among subordinates (and superiors, should they go awry). Each individual in an organization must understand the need for the rules and regulations. Rules exist to promote uniform behavior, but they are supposed to be exemplified by action, not blindly or rigidly enforced.

Enduring Relationships (*Ch'in*)

A word difficult to translate well, *ch'in* is the foundation for enduring, meaningful, fruitful relationships, whether the relationship is between individuals, families, or business associates. An effective manager uses *ch'in* to arrive at proper decisions in daily interactions and business dealings.

A proper relationship begins with self-cultivation and proceeds through cultivating one's family to governing the country, thence to establishing peace throughout the world at large. An ancient poem sums up *ch'in* very well:

> *Where there is peace in the soul*
> *There is harmony in the person.*
> *Where there harmony in the person*
> *There is happiness in the home.*
> *When there is happiness in the home*
> *There is order in the nation.*
> *When there is order in the nation*
> *There is peace in the soul.*

The self is not an "I" standing alone in the world but rather the center of relationships that branch into an ever expanding network. Sincere consideration for others is the key to strong relationships and good networks. A manager does not discharge an employee as a form of disciplinary action because he believes that in taking such actions one should place *ch'in* before punishment. The wise manager uses *ch'in* to expand a business network and to gain the confidence and support of customers and others within the business circle (which Westerners often term "stakeholders") as well as other businessmen outside it. In difficult times, the manager relies on his or her *ch'in* to request assistance from others.

Caring

In Confucius's teaching, caring or *jen* is a key term that embraces a variety of meanings—humanism, benevolence, love, affection, and kindness. This rather diverse range of meanings hints that *jen* has different uses in different contexts.

Broadly speaking, *jen* is about the same as Christian *agape* and Buddhist *metta*—love without distinction. Love should permeate all human behavior: "A manager may be called a manager only if he or she treats all as equally as himself or herself." A wise leader does not take advantage over the weak or the less intelligent. Again, to use the image of the qualities of water, the manager pays full attention to all people around him without discrimination and distinction, the way water surrounds all parts of something within it. The manager sits in a chair at everyone's own level yet serves them with the highest sense of equality.

Filial Piety (*Chung*)

Another term that is difficult to translate, *chung* is roughly equivalent to "filial piety." *Chung* permeates and embraces all virtues and becomes the driving force behind our moral character.

The concepts of familism and filial piety have a very long history in Chinese culture. The family undergirds the whole structure of society. Respecting one's parents becomes an ever larger network of human relations involving siblings, relatives, kinfolk, society, and country. If a man serves his parents filially, he will serve his country loyally and thus be a good citizen.

Commitment to these moral values defines the employer's role as guardian and provider of the employee's welfare. An organization may have intelligent and knowledgeable people, but if they are motivated by a low sense of morality, the organization is poorer than one led by mediocrities. Hence installing a comprehensive system of controls—physical or moral—will not inspire ethical values or make people behave better. In fact, overt control tends to bring out the worst in people. It is vital to create and cultivate moral values that will inspire rather than govern human behavior. A truly great leader possesses the highest moral sense. He or she does not compromise on ethical matters. If an organizational leader does not act with morality in mind, the organization as a whole will not gain the confidence and trust of its people or its business partners.

Cleverness

As far back as two thousand years ago, education was strongly encouraged in China. China was the first country to set up a national examination system. The *Four Books* and *Five Classics*, which conveyed Confucius's teachings, were primary textbooks in school education and the basis of these national examinations.

Confucius believed the common denominator that distinguishes performance among individuals, companies, industries, and even economies is the quality of education. This explains why so many Chinese businesses and government organizations allocate such huge amounts in their budgets each year to systematically improving the training of employees. It also explains why Singapore, the Asian state run the most closely to Confucian lines, is the most advanced economy in the region. The Chinese believe that more than any other factor, education enhances overall organizational and economic effectiveness. It improves the quality of people, the technological and managerial competence, productivity, and the global competitiveness of an economy. Effective managers always view themselves as lifelong learners. They are strongly committed to learning from others and are not selfish in sharing their own knowledge and experience with them.

The Golden Mean (*Chung Yung*)

Underlying all Confucius's teachings is the principle of *Chung Yung* or the Doctrine of the Mean. It has worldwide correlatives in the Golden Rule and the Buddhist Middle Way.

Chung Yung focuses one's efforts on the middle way of human thought and action. It is important for a manager to balance words and actions. In action, the good manager adheres to the middle course between liberality and conservatism, spending and investing, production and training, adaptability and perfection.

In the West, qualities like courage, charisma, and discipline are considered good leadership qualities. In Confucian thinking, leaders should emphasize wisdom, patience, and tolerance. A wise manager maintains the balance between the good and the bad rather than striving to eliminate the bad or focus only on the good. Moderation is what keeps one immune from extremes.

CONFUCIAN MANAGEMENT IN MODERN EYES

The Confucian principles were ideals when they were first formulated.[1] Freshly MBA'd young Chinese management consultants will tell you even today that Confucius is the last word on Chinese management theory. Others see it differently. Today's young Chinese who study abroad draw on informational bases that embrace psychology, sociology, cultural history, even notions like Stephen Jay Gould's punctuated equilibrium theory and the anthropic theory arising out of cosmology in which the evolution of the cosmos and evolution of humanity are inextricably linked. With a long tradition of belief in the unity of nature behind them, young Chinese today are more likely to take seriously the Gaia theory (which views the earth as a single living organism) than their business-school counter-parts from the West.

Today there is something of a convergence phenomenon beginning to occur in which some of the young Chinese management theorists are relooking at Confucian ideas in light of the notions they are picking up from their Western educations. They are coming up with what they see as meaningful role models for the modern Asian business. Here are a few of them as understood by this writer. It is very interesting how the concepts of "leader" and "manager" tend to blend in these formulations.

The Futurist

This type of leader is a farsighted charismatic business manager who keeps one eye on the distant future and the other on the recent past. He or she sees the difficulties in trying to turn an imperfect present into a perfect future. The futurist sees that when Southeast Asian countries tried to graft traditional societies onto modern capitalism they encountered a goal clash between family and cultural duty and capitalism's duty to the market. The result was cronyism—governments dictating the allocation of capital to the markets instead of the markets allocating it to them. The Futurist sees that an ability to manage with a basic view toward distant future events is critical to Asia because when long-term goals are the basis for strategic organizational ties, successful response to opportunity is based on having the liquidity to move quickly. A clear strategic vision and direction for the organization is the guiding inspiration for all employees throughout the organization. In this type of leader's mind the business empire will eventually be inherited in the traditional manner by one's children (in particular, the eldest; less often a chosen son), but that inheritor will be more subservient to the strategic vision than in the past.

When planning, this type of manager focuses on long-term events; in implementation, he or she focuses on timing. The ability to visualize the future places great importance on acquiring a sensitivity for timing. The Futurist thinks of time in cyclical rather than linear terms. A cyclical view of business events leads him or her to regard lineage as more important than diversity. Based on that rationale, the Futurist works toward maximizing earnings with an eye to amassing a sizable liquidity pool rather than expanding quickly through debt.

The Intellectual

The intellectual manager possesses intelligence, a nearly photographic memory, rapid evaluation, astute prediction, and the ability to see useful ideas in batches of raw information. The Intellectual as a business leader is focused, sharp, and reacts very quickly to informational evidence. In the Confucian system, these abilities were thought to indicate a strong charismatic leader possessing supernatural powers. In modern eyes, these qualities can relate diverse and often remote organizational events to current situations. This makes the Intellectual highly sensitive to the opportunity messages concealed in accounting data or patterns of sales figures; hence they are often very good at mergers and acquisitions types of activity.

The methods and rigor of the modern Chinese system of extracurricular education should focus on memory, analysis, and prediction. In the traditional Chinese education, the student is required to memorize from textbooks from a young age. Some critics say that placing so much emphasis on memory turns schools into memory mills.

Perhaps so, but the Intellectual observes that criticisms of this type tend to focus on what's missing rather than what's there. The Intellectual's view is that building personal memory today results in institutional memory tomorrow. The opposite of a world based on rote memory is no better than one in which memory is sacrosanct. Can you imagine what would happen to a business run by the people who design logos? People tend to forget that an ideal of any kind needs a guidance system based on self-assessment and betterment. Where ideals go wrong is in listening to the people who have a vested interest in claiming them as the solution to everyone's problems.

Societies with ancient traditions behind them—be they cultures or governments or businesses—see themselves as perfected in some golden era of the past and come to believe they no longer have to evolve in the present. In the eyes of the Intellectual, what distinguishes a true civilization from a culture is the former's ability to remain vigorous in the face of great change and great variety. What distinguishes a culture from a government is the former's ability to survive its own worst ideas. What distinguishes a business from a government is the former's ability to change its direction without direction from its head.

Modern Southeast Asian business is barely a generation old in places like Hong Kong and Singapore, and much younger in the Tigers of Malaysia, Thailand, and so on. The value of institutional memory in strategic decision making is only now being understood. One reason the 1997 debacle was so swift was that so many decision makers and institutions from so many different countries made parallel mistakes. A number of those mistakes can be attributed to not having experienced this set of circumstances before—allocating assets based on privilege rather than responsibility, for example. It is one thing to read about the perils of real estate bubbles in *The Economist*, but another one altogether to discern the significance of debt-to-equity ratios rising more rapidly than loan refusal rates in one's own banking system. Nor did Asian business planners notice the implications of shifting debt more and more frequently between cross-owned stock holdings or trying to shuffle away the problems of debt by borrowing more money to serve the debt.

All these seem obvious because we see them in hindsight. So who can see problems in Stan Shih's archipelago model? Assuredly they exist. The Intellectual sees that the most important quality to business is pattern exploitation, the ability to discern and act on patterns in behavior—for example, that income growth occurs in predictable patterns in the marketplace but not the boardroom.

The Motivator

This is a charismatic type of business leader who does not manage by extrinsic factors like monetary or market growth. Instead, this manager uses psychological processes and emotional insights. He or she leads by action and behavior, symbol and image. Success comes with arousing followers to tackle challenging and difficult organizational goals. Describing a Motivator as a cheerleader is too glib. His or her real role is to provide role modeling and good example. In the Chinese business community, leaders tend to neglect hands-on management in favor of directorial management. The Motivator asserts a leadership style that is based on situational adaptability—for example, when you manage a wide variety of people you do it with images, not directives. This is a style that combines the hard skills of decisiveness with the soft skills of motivating by psychological insight.

To the Motivator, the distinguishing characteristic of the different approaches to the IT future embodied in Malaysia's Multimedia Super Corridor and Singapore-ONE is Malaysia's preoccupation with the value of the past and Singapore's preoccupation with the value of the future. Change is inherently unsettling—even revolutionary in the sense of the inexorable turn of the wheel. The Motivator, attuned to the longevity of symbol over words in most people's minds, sees that the primal symbols that define the cultures of Asia are the wheel for India, the dragon for China, and the mask for Southeast Asia. All three symbols are psychological shields against fear—the fear of loss, the fear of change, the fear of face.

The ancient Egyptians identified change with turmoil. Their principle of *ma'at* held that social order is worth more than its price in unhappiness. In ancient India change was managed by assigning specific functions to specific people in order to maintain *rita*, the Cosmic Order via the caste system. In ancient China, Confucius replaced social order based on one's birth to order based on one's earned merit. In ancient Malaya, leaders built *muafakat*, *mesyuarat*, and *gotong royong* (respectively "consultation," "consensus," and "mutual assistance") into the image shield of *hilm*, the combination of firmness, magnanimity, and conciliatoriness. To the Motivator, these defenses are unnecessary. What we know now is that fear is but faith in a negative result. Good management reallocates faith into a positive result.

THE VULNERABILITIES OF *GUANXI* AND THE BAMBOO NETWORK

It is illuminating to tap into http://www.cbn.com.sg/, the website of the World Chinese Business Network. The WCBN is one of the world's most powerful political and financial networks, more cohesive than Davos and far more interesting than the annual ASEAN golf match. It is the brainchild of Singapore's Lee Kuan Yew, one of the world's better-known business networkers.

The overseas Chinese number about 55 million, including 22 million in Taiwan, 6 million in Hong Kong, and 3 million in Singapore. Although this is less than 10 percent of the population of East and Southeast Asia, this community dominates the commercial life of the region. They are nine out of every ten of the region's billionaires, control two-thirds of retail trade, and have access to an estimated $1 trillion in liquid assets. The overseas Chinese have invested far more in mainland China than all the companies from the United States, Europe, and Japan combined.

Most of their firms, huge though they might be, are still family-run. They have all the trappings of a modern corporation such as professional management staffs, stock market listings, public relations and human resources departments, and in-house design staffs to draw up product logos and produce newsletters, on-line and in print. Yet the old ways—the ways of the first-generation founding fathers who carved empires out of *guanxi* or ancestral village ties—still persist, even though it is their sons who mostly do the managing and investment these days. This second generation, the Bamboo Network of agglomerative patriciate Chinese, are cut very much from the same cloth as their fathers. Many were educated abroad, though in the 1960s when business schools in universities were preoccupied with the mechanics of the conglomerate, the "Organization Man" personality, silo management ideas, and information gathering and analysis that proceeded without computers.

These sons were well into their advanced managerial years by the time computers came along in force and changed business school thinking about personnel management, investment, cash management, and mergers and acquisitions. They were filling their fathers' vacating shoes at the top when the Internet came along, and with it many of the ideas about business communication, marketing, product creation, and graphics presentation that have arisen straight out of Internet-mindedness.

There is an enormous generation gap between the founding fathers and the Bamboo Network generation, and the young managers coming up today who talk about MBAs, entrepreneurial clusters, M&A analysis, product morphing, ultra 3-D in product architecture, virtual communities, and the Japanese design theory of *heihaku tansho* (light-slim-short-small), in which the reality of the space crunch in Asia's cities and homes results in ever smaller cassette players, calculators, cameras, cellular phones, and laptops.

It is the business practices of the second-generation Chinese that largely shaped modern Asia as we know it and had a key role in the 1997 crisis. This generation regards www.cbn.com.sg/ as a culture pulpit as much as a meeting ground. They also make the majority of long-term investment decisions in Asian business today. It is too early to say how their thinking has been affected by the obviousness of their planning failures in the harsh glare of 1997, but the habits they are beginning to question include:

- ferreting the best assets away in mazes of private companies and trusts;
- keeping decision making hierarchical and centralized;
- managing their competitive environment with secrecy and denial;
- using boards mainly to rubber-stamp the decisions of the founder or immediate family.

To give the mind-set of this generation a touch of picturesque realism, their board meeting agendas are often faxed to their secretaries at the home office scribbled on the back of an in-flight menu.

While it most certainly does not show up on www.cbn.com.sg/, control of the Bamboo Network is now passing from its founders to the Chinese third generation. There is a great deal of anxiety in Asia's business and political communities about the significance of this transition.

The third generation of Chinese business people was educated largely in the mid-1980s through the Internet era. Instead of their fathers' preoccupation with break-even analysis, cash-flow projection, benchmarking, and critical path analysis, this generation is thinking about objects, applets, linking and embedding, cluster management, virtuality, and morphing.

Not much of this comes as cheering news to the Bamboo Network. For one, an old Chinese proverb says that new wealth does not last for more than three generations. The Chinese sense that the generation just now arriving into management ranks with their MBAs and all that virtuality talk may not be up to the job of running a company that has employees, competitors, and delicate political dependencies. In the shadows of their legendary fathers, the second generation was cautious. They consider today's blithe risk-taking of the M&A and venture capitalism type as too airy to be reliable.

They are also running up against one of the lurking dangers of family-owned business empires: the fact that family fights get embarrassingly public when squabbling members own different parts of the same empire. The point where the family ends and business begins is often hard to discern when all is well, but painfully astigmatic in messy divorce cases. When relatives are sprinkled into the management ranks regardless of talent just to give spare sons a dignified job, hired managers soon bump against the limits of their authority and come to believe that, however well they perform, they will never acquire a significant stake in the business. The second generation was as tight-lipped as the first, but their third-generation progeny most definitely are not. They have seen a lot more of Oprah than they have Judge Pao, the popular Hong Kong series. Half-hearted attempts to separate management from ownership have created dangerous tensions from sons who feel (often rightly) that they are being summarily excluded from the riches they have become accustomed to.

In another example, a three-year feud involving the second- and third-generation family owners of Yeo Hiap Seng, a Singaporean food company, ended in 1996 with the firm being taken over by outsiders.

A principal cause of disputes—hauntingly reminiscent of the warlord empires of long ago—often is bypassing a rightful, but dreadfully ordinary, first-born heir to promote a second- or third-born son who is brighter. Although the Chinese value their eldest sons highly, they do not inherit automatically. In 1996, Winston Wang, the heir apparent to Taiwan's Formosa Plastics, was exiled to America for a year by his family after an alleged extramarital affair. Shares in the group fell as investors worried whether any of the eleven other children of eighty-year-old Wang Yung-ching would vie to take Winston's place (they didn't).

Sometimes, lacking a male heir, a tycoon will adopt one. Before his death, Sir Y. K. Pao, the Hong Kong shipping and property magnate, divided his empire among his four sons-in-law. In Manila, Henry Sy, a Chinese emigrant to the Philippines who now owns half the country's shopping malls, is giving a daughter rather than one of his sons the lead in running that family business.

Into these already insecure empires the upcoming third generation is a very big question mark. The way they are groomed for the top job mixes the old system of filial piety with modern MBA professionalism. Typically, after the MBA in a Western business school, they start work in their mid-twenties as executives in a prominent division of the family firm. This is the point where the entrepreneurially minded among them often decide to do their own thing. Sometimes the results are good. Li Ka-shing, Hong Kong's best-known tycoon, installed his two American-educated sons, Victor and Richard, on the boards of his two main companies. Richard went off to do deals on his own. He started Star Television, a pan-Asian satellite-television business, and as of late 1997 was building up a Singapore-based group, Pacific Century.

However, most sons turn their professional training into the first stage of a long management preparation under their father's eye. Sometimes even these submissive sons bring just a little too much of the Western deal-making mentality back with them from the Western school. The Lippo Group, the large Jakarta-based conglomerate, is being run by the politically indelicate James and Stephen Riady, who tried to spread the ownership of Lippo's businesses through stock market listings and brought professional managers into the highest ranks. When they overreached themselves in the U.S. political arena, their father, Mochtar Riady, who founded the firm in the early 1960s after his parents had emigrated from China's Fujian province, had to step back onto center stage to calm investors' fears.

Asian governments came to realize that one consequence of '97 is that they must free up their domestic economies, particular the vastly underexploited middle-class consumer market. The Bamboo Network is not sensitive to this market; the younger set practically lives in it. When the old *guanxi* began to need alliances, they invented the Chinese agglomerative patriciate. Now the third generation comes along with international mindedness and says that being a Chinese counts for less than being an MBA.

To build on their inheritance, the next generation of leaders will have to develop contacts of their own, and how they will do this is a great big enigma in Asian management circles. Unlike their fathers, the third generation tends to trust the alumni of a western business school more than they trust cousins and friends of no particular qualifications beyond being sons of their fathers. Bangkok Bank was founded by an ethnic-Chinese rice trader, Chin Sophonpanich, who lent only to people he knew, usually on trust or in return for a favor. His western-educated son, Chatri Sophonpanich, modernized the bank and attracted customers from far outside his father's circle. Some older Chinese say this may stifle enterprise. An elderly ethnic Chinese businessman who started his business with a loan from Chin Sophonpanich big enough to establish several factories, would not get the money were he starting in today. Younger Chinese say that theory is hooey; if the business plan is a good business plan, the project gets the money.

A number of ethnic Chinese are experimenting with divorcing ownership from management altogether—a major shift in Asia business thinking. First Pacific, a Hong Kong-based conglomerate with businesses from telecoms to banking, is owned by Indonesia's Salim family but is run entirely by professional managers led by a Filipino managing director, Manuel Pangilinan. Stan Shih, the founder of Taiwan's Acer Computers, is breaking his firm into a federation of companies each with its own management and stock market listing (see below).

Still, even in 1998 after the economic debacle, these are exceptions. Most families appear unwilling to even consider selling their majority holdings or putting their trust in professional managers. Some will not sell even a loss-making subsidiary lest it be seen as losing face. There is also a theory emanating from locations as disparate as Mumbai (Bombay) and Hong Kong that a family-run business becomes structurally unstable when it reaches a critical size. The idea is that when highly centralized companies amass thousands of employees across different countries, lines of communication first attenuate and then break down. (This theory is likely to dwindle faster than the firms it describes as the Internet and corporate intranets become more refined and put into the hands of able corporate managers.)

The most likely future for the Bamboo Network is that it will enter cyberspace and not so much weaken as become so different that its slow vanishing will never be noticed. Nearly everyone is unaware how strongly having broad Internet access is likely to fill Asian business offices with the same complex mix of information and imagery that is presently working in the West. The biggest problem Chinese family empires face with the information and e-commerce age is not knowing what to do with it.

Many Chinese family firms will never reach that point. Adhering to long tradition, they will be divided up to enable sons and daughters to inherit or they will break up through takeovers or family feuds. That may prevent many businesses from growing into the sprawling multinationals they have the potential to become. It will also give Chinese entrepreneurialism its golden opportunity.

IT, E-COMMERCE, AND ASIAN MANAGEMENT IDEAS

The IT organizational style of entrepreneurial clusters based on trust makes old-line Chinese management theorists go weak at the knees. "I can't think of an organization where in-fighting is more rife than in the family-owned company," says one Chinese business owner. "How do these new module-enterprise systems propose to do any better? Have they ever thought through what happens when nobody agrees with the way things are being done and everybody has a different idea how to do it better?"

The Asian family enterprise system is based on friendly dictatorships. This is perfect for real estate deals where a handshake can clinch a deal. It also allows firms to change direction quickly. One cautionary that should interest IT and e-commerce marketers moving into Asia is the ubiquity of fly-by-nights in the Chinese SME world. Companies making wigs, plastic flowers, Barbie-doll ripoffs, fashion knockoffs, or cheap radios rent a space, make their profit, and disappear. This may sound dreadfully banal until you realize how much of Taiwan got started (and still operates) this way. The Chinese talent for seeing and responding to a quick buck is as much a problem as it is a virtue.

Critics point out that, unlike the Japanese and the South Koreans, the non-mainland Chinese have had relatively little success in long-term consumer products companies and poor success outside Asia. Many Chinese companies turn to "structure" empires as opposed to product empires, meaning that they assemble opportunities—say, franchise groups—rather than creating internationally competitive products or services. People like Stan Shih of Acer are the exception, not the rule.

What all this means to IT innovations that are marketed by e-commerce is a very open question. The field is too new for any kind of meaningful database to have been built up.

One useful point of comparison is the marked difference between the business thinking of traditional Chinese business owners and the thinking of technocrats in government. Singapore's National Computer Board is a good example. The NCB is perhaps the most technically competent and future-minded business-related organization in Asia. As we saw in chapter 9, the applications conceived and implemented in the NCB are consistently in advance of any other IT organization in Asia, including many multinationals and consulting firms. Yet the NCB is a government think tank that opts out of the profit-and-loss hassles of the business world in order to do R&D at what amounts to a giveaway.

In contrast, to most Asian private businesses, particularly SMEs, the term "manufacturing" means using cheap hands to assemble borrowed technology. The second-generation agglomerative-patriciate style of business is far more adept at organization than it is with ideas. There is tart truth to the observation that a family company of the old school is probably organizationally incapable of building something like an auto manufacturing firm, given that sophisticated autos require coordination and decentralization, bosses who trust their employees, and marketing, production, and design departments that have to make their own decisions. Vaguely defined responsibilities delegated to eldest sons just won't do.

These reasons are why so many Chinese firms are into finance, property development, and gambling; and why young Chinese men are the most voracious readers of the latest management theory books from America and Europe. Few bright managers want to work for an organization that will never give them a role in company strategy. One 1996 survey in Hong Kong found that young Chinese professionals preferred to work for Western or Japanese companies—anything but a Chinese company.

Others argue the entire issue is moot because the autocratic, agglomerative second generation will die off just as the empire builders of the first generation did. They were important as long as business acumen was furthered by striking deals instead of investing in production, but today Asia's economies are shifting towards consumer markets, not export markets; high-priced services, not low-cost products. Most Asian economists believe that the globalizing tendencies of the market economy will erode homegrown empires out of existence. Businesses have to create new products or offer good services if they are to survive, and the second-generation family empires never focused on that. Markets, the glib quip goes, last longer than politicians and bureaucrats.

Well, maybe. There is also a case to be made that it is the countries with small home markets that have to change most adeptly the way they do business. This may be why Singapore and Hong Kong are so good at it. In a much quoted 1996 speech, David Li of the Bank of East Asia warned business people against assuming that there was a uniquely "Asian way" of doing business. Rewarding employees well or building up a core of professional managers, he said, is not "Western"; it is simply good management. However, this does not mean that Western management ideas can be superimposed on Asian business structures at will. For example, reengineering is good at reducing overstaffing in mature industries, but in markets growing as quickly as Asia's, large staffs are necessary.

One problem with this entire subject is that there is a fairly substantive body of example about what does not work but much less about what does work. One company that successfully applied Western management methods to an old-line Chinese business is Li & Fung, a Hong Kong trading house. Founded in Guangzhou in 1906, the company is now run by the founder's Harvard-educated grandsons. IT and e-commerce experts might well take note of this company. Its main expertise is network management in labor intensive industries. Li & Fung makes nothing itself; it acts as a value-chain coordinator linking different suppliers together, designing products, finding customers, and sometimes financing them.

Another role model for analysts of Asia's potential for IT and e-commerce development is Stan Shih of Taiwan's Acer Computers.

Mr. Shih was primed to embrace the entrepreneurial cluster model of enterprise organization because in his early years he watched a foppish family drain the good assets of their family business in order to pursue luxury lifestyles and expensive hobby businesses. Mr. Shih sees the entrepreneurial cluster—invented in the United States—as the best solution yet to many Chinese family-business failings.

Stan Shih's Archipelago Model

Mr. Shih's disdain for the family-style Asian business was shaped by his experience with a traditional secrecy-obsessed, dynastically operated family company. It collapsed because no one was allowed to criticize the family and because most of each company's money was siphoned off into personal family ventures.

The result was Shih's decision to align his Acer Computer Company into a network of loosely allied companies, each with its own boss, personnel system, and salary structure. This structure yields a great deal of autonomy to each company to make its own decisions. Shih's "archipelago" model of corporate structure reflects his lessons from an expansion strategy that was forced by the management of a conglomerate on its subsidiary businesses and which ended up hurting the subsidiaries but not the misjudging top company.

Shih has separated twenty of his business units into individual listed companies united under the aegis of Acer as headquarters company. Acer itself will employ only about eighty people and draw its revenues in part from dividends from its stakeholdings and in part from management and service fees charged to the individual entities. If individual companies buy products or services from any of the others, they pay market prices. If any division decides to spin itself off completely and leave the group (a decision it could make on its own) it would simply have to drop the Acer name. The Acer parent company can either retain or sell its equity holdings at the time of the spin-off.

Mr. Shih's model—and his application of it to his own business—could not have come at a better time for Southeast Asian business managers. Already worried by the clear signs of the "Third-Generation Slide" in Singapore (see the next section) and seeing it just beginning to show up noticeably in Thailand, Malaysia, and Indonesia, some managers believe that third-generation Chinese just entering management ranks today are likely to prove more of a problem to the long-term economic health of Southeast Asia than the losses suffered by the banking and real estate sectors in 1997.

Others say this generation is no better or worse than any other. Until the verdict is clearer, we can draw four observations from the responses of Li & Fung, Stan Acer, and a handful of other companies:

- Family firms need to move more quickly into the service sector.
- Companies will benefit most from building expertise enterprises in well-researched niche markets.
- Young management talent needs to be seen in terms of an investment strategy, not a dynastic perpetuation tool.
- In rapidly developing markets the agglomerative approach may still yield a few success stories, but companies that want to be internationally competitive in the IT/EC era must focus on a few good core businesses.

INHERITOR ANXIETY IN TODAY'S THIRD-GENERATION CHINESE

MBAs and the Internet notwithstanding, the third generation of today's Chinese family empires is the most uncertain generation in many decades. As grandchildren of the region's wealth builders they suffer from a painful inheritor mentality. They will acquire vast wealth and social standing they haven't earned for themselves. They don't have the conquer-all drive of their parents. In comparing themselves with their parents they often experience low self-esteem. It is hard for them to take much satisfaction in their own accomplishments. In part that is because they can't see themselves building the empires their parents did. Sometimes if they do, they fear it will turn out badly.

They read *The Economist* and *Asia, Inc.*, and they set themselves up by the images they find there. They secretly know that the reputation of their own names is due to the wealth and position of their parents.

Many lack motivation. They already have what most people strive for in life, so what's the use of the long hours and shallow personalities that typify their parents. What's the point of it all? This sublimates into a guilt complex their parents never dreamed of. They feel guilty about accepting fortune without merit. Since the Western philanthropic do-good-for-others safety valve is not part of their culture, they worry that they're unworthy of everything they have.

The Chinese culture is based entirely on money and visible signs of success. Their emotions and educations are aimed primarily at those values. So while they may be whizzes at computers and business deals, they have little familiarity with the arts, much less the spiritual values behind art and religion. To them religion is a series of formalities like a business deal. Education has to be something expensive so others will be impressed. They live almost exclusively in the world of the material. They can't understand why the vacuum in the spiritual half of their beings makes everything in the material part seem so empty.[2]

This alienates the third generation from earlier generations. The wealthy Asian inheritors think others admire them only because they are rich—and often they are quite right. They often have opulent homes built for them by their parents but meet their friends in clubs or dance places instead of inviting them to their homes. Often they don't make friends at all and sit around bored to death playing with their toys. Inheritor Chinese are the most addictive computer game players in Asia, although they rarely turn to other addictions such as alcohol or drugs. Those are a lower-class phenomenon.

Underlying all this is their fear that they will lose their patrimony somehow and end up disgraced with no job skills. They live in great fear that their parents' tearing apart the land and fisheries and events like the "haze" problems that deforest more and more of the region every year will end in an economic collapse in which they'll be hated by society and unable to support themselves.

No one in Asia's business world is confronting the fact of this generation's anxieties, much less providing meaningful alternatives. It is useless to speculate on the downside of this neglect, but the upside is a considerable opportunity for businesses that are sympathetic to the behavioral patterns of young Chinese and can turn this into entrepreneurial businesses and cluster-style empires they can use to create identities of their own the way their forebears once did.

NOTES

1. Not all of them may have come directly from Master Kung himself. Asia—hardly unique in this—has a long tradition of spin-doctors rewriting history to suit the views of their own times. Buddhism today is so remote from what the Buddha said it is hard to recognize anything but his name in what passes for his views. Five centuries of oral tradition

have taken their toll. Similarly, the views of Master Kung were refined and reformulated many times before they reached the form we know today.

2. There are clear signs that Singapore is making the transition from a culture self-defined by business prowess to one defined much more broadly via the socially expressive venues of the various arts. More than any other city in this writer's experience, Singapore resembles Paris just before the *Salon des Refuses* that introduced Impressionism and its major shift of the sociology of art. Two of the Singaporean arts arenas where this is showing up most clearly are fashion design and interior decoration. Aptly enough, both are middle-class art forms in which money and taste can be readily displayed without imposing too much of a constraint on one's budget. Several Singaporean fashion designers have the most interesting ideas about the art of cultural definition that this writer has encountered in many years of producing art books. There is a vital nexus forming in Singapore as wealthy individual art collectors who at one time doted on antiquarian pieces now turn their financial support toward younger generations seeking to blend the old with the new. Any reader who really wants to know the future of Asian cultural thinking as an indicator of the future of market demand could do well by paying a lot of attention to the Singaporean arts and fashion scenes.

25

Malay Male Psychology and Behavior

Traditional Malay socialization begins in an environment that is strongly influenced by the mother and has relatively little contact with the father. As living spaces are considered the preserve of the women and children, in traditional homes the husband stays away from the house from the end of early morning prayers until the last prayers in the evening. Modern middle-class homes are a little different in that the father comes home earlier, but the idea is the same: the woman rules the home.

Hence a child experiences nonstop close physical association with the mother. Weaning does not take place until well into the second year. At the age of five or so, the male child is abruptly sent off to the all-male environment of a *pondok* or Islamic religious school in more conservative traditional areas, or to simpler religious training in modern urban areas. Whichever the early schooling, the boy must learn to make his own way in circumstances that combine stern teachers with the intimidations of older children. Brotherhood comes to be seen as both enemy and friend. The desire to recapture the happy security of early years results in narcissism, a romanticization of one's past life as simple, serene, comforting, uncomplicated. Anyone who threatens to take that away is *derhaka*, a treacherous person. Treachery is the most vile force that can be imagined; one must avoid it all costs. Hence life must be built upon harmonies, agreeabilities, concordance, consensus.

One can see in this thread of romantic idyllization the root of the phraseologies associated with the MSC—all the promises of that which can be, will be, should be, might be. There are no unforeseen contingencies; everything is proceeding well; there are no problems. It is only those who oppose us who cause difficulties. *Malaysia Boleh* (Malaysia Can)!

As the individual's personality matures, it acquires the conviction that only the self is good; the world is unpredictable, arbitrary, and suspect. The self, on the other hand, deserves to be honored. The honor of others similarly must be acknowledged. The self, and the brotherhood of other selves like it, did not deserve their separation from the comforting forces that they were once able to command. All who separate the self from its securities are enemies who exercise their power by diminishing the quality of our selfhood.

Hence when thwarted by external circumstance like the 1997 Asian bubble bath, the reaction of Prime Minister Mahathir was perfectly Malay: We did not deserve this injustice forced upon us, it was those big boys with the money who hurt us, took away our identity, our achievement. We did not deserve to be separated from the economic forces that we once controlled so well, so we will set things up our own way all over again, this time shutting out all those big boys and their power.

One sees the ambivalence of this point of view clearly in the Malaysian government's vilification of the British colonial era while benignly accepting the fact that the Japanese have treated Malaysia pretty much the same way the British did, as the origin of cheap products of great use to the home economy without entailing any particular demand for the quid pro quos of technology transfer.

But the Japanese are members of the Asian brotherhood, the brotherhood that Malays are told by their political leaders the British and now the West in general have always exploited. The fact that Prime Minister Mahathir considers Japanese economic exploitation as OK while British exploitation was "colonizing" comes from the ambivalence Malays develop towards the brotherhood of other humans. As the child develops, he sublimates his ambivalence about the concept of brotherhood—unifying on one hand, treacherous on the other. As an ideal, brotherhood is an alternative to the ties with the mother, but in practice other males cannot really be treated as true brothers; they can be pals one minute and bullies the next. When race enters into the issue—and race enters most every issue in Malaysia—it is easy for the British to be cast as the bully and the Japanese as the pal.

This ambivalence is resolved in the brotherhood of Islam, *ummah*. In *ummah* leaders and followers share a common destiny, Islam, and are united both religiously and psychodynamically in the ties of spiritual brotherhood. The Malay political cultures in Southeast Asia share the same concept of leadership: Leaders see themselves as uniquely virtuous and are distrustful of outsiders. They suspect that outsiders do not appreciate their superior worth. They need the assurance of acclaiming followers. They depend on symbols of great achievement—the taller and grander the better—to impress those followers. Pomp is more important than productivity. Their followers are swept into this dependency relationship by their need for the security of an understanding leader who embodies Islam's romanticized brotherhood.

BROTHERHOOD INTO AUTHORITY

The Malay image of authority is a blend of traditional Southeast Asian sentiments of deferential accommodation, Islamic norms of fatalism and commitment to ideals, and British aristocratic standards of fair play reinforced by status barriers. The basis for social relations is respect for social distinctions. This is hardly unusual in Asia, where on the Western end of the region one has India and its thousand-strata caste system, and on the other China with its highly stratified sequence of personal relationships.

The Malay preoccupation with deference springs from their basic early socialization process, which does not provide sustained or predictable support and affection from the parents but does stress punishment and harsh discipline. The combination of casualness and heavy-handed treatment prepares the Malay for service in disciplined, hierarchical organizations such as the army, police, and bureaucracy. The facades of macho competitiveness Malays see in the Western multinational companies seem to have no place for the vital sense of brotherhood Malays crave. The tendency in the Malay office is to be lax whenever possible but to accept sudden, even arbitrary, disciplinary treatment—with the understanding that one will be taken care of in the end in a paternalistic way. Concepts like "firing" or its euphemism "downsizing" are anathema, nearly inhuman. The Malay ideal of authority calls for sternness, dignity, and paternalistic concern. Everyone understands that those in authority can become angered and do irrational things, but compensate by not taking away one's means of survival in the form of firing someone from his job for a trivial thing like not performing up to expectations.

Hence to Malays it is imperative not to provoke authority but rather to stay out of its way. Idealism has always gone hand in hand with noncompetition. Rather than expecting that correct conduct will be rewarded (which is the reward mechanism in Chinese business culture), Malays tend to behave as prudently as possible. It is important to avoid conspicuousness by focusing one attentions on the rituals of routine. Having been socialized to expect uncertainty and unpredictable treatment by superiors, Malays respond in ways that minimize contact with them. On the other hand, one will always be taken care of, even though there may be some bad events in one's work performance.

Thus Malay culture has incorporated many of the behavioral mechanisms common to a culture of low self-esteem, in which people believe there is a rigidly fixed, rather ponderous social order in which their part is small. Attitudes of distrust and feelings of ineffectuality are found even in well-to-do Malays who have had generous support in their education and have moved into the ranks of the elite. The most visible response is overcompensation via image asseting. The foreign investment capital that flowed not into the production economy where it was intended but into the image economy of luxury lifestyles and gigantesque projects was not a manifestation of greed so much as it was a testimony to insecurity.

MALAY GOVERNANCE

In the Malay countries, most members of the civil services and upper management ranks come from well-to-do or aristocratic backgrounds. They believe the self-congratulatory character of their conspicuous consumption signals Malay affirmation. This explains the poorer Malays' great pride in the country's expensive monuments despite the poor quality of the overall public infrastructure. People take them to be assertions of racial pride and government competence, an illusion the image conscious press is not loathe to reinforce. To outsiders these have the appearance of asserting power to intimidate competitive forces such as the overseas-educated progeny of the rising middle class.

There is a good deal more complexity to the Malay elites' assertive consumption than these few examples, but the overall picture is one in which the Malay elites do not welcome synergy from outside their own ranks, not because it is economically competitive but because it is imagistically competitive. One result is the attitude that outsiders are enemies, not potential energy inputs. When Prime Minister Mahathir railed so sharply against the possibility of IMF intervention in Malaysia's economy, it had as much to do with his unwillingness to let the IMF alter the Malay's long-standing *bumiputera* system of racially-based economic preferences as it did with the defects in the IMF's fix-it strategy. The Malaysian government would have loved the IMF's money, but not the image it would have conveyed that they were not quite competent.

This in turn points to the Malay belief in a zero-sum or fixed-pie view of economic life, in which assets change around within the system but the total value of the system itself does not appreciably change. This is one reason why the Indonesian and Malaysian Malays regarded external investment from Japan and the West as a kind of free money to be divvied between the power elites as they desired. A very small proportion of the enormous amounts of capital invested in Malaysia and Indonesia went into civil infrastructure like reliable electricity, clean streets, proper drainage, public transport, better schools, or a better-trained bureaucracy. Much was reexported out of the region into investments in real estate and luxury lifestyles abroad. Driving over the Causeway to clean, efficient Singapore was a vivid illustration of the difference in social energy levels between a society based on feelings of inadequacy, and a society based on attitudes of rising expectations, permanent conditions of opportunity, merit, and due diligence.

The low level of reinvestment in one's milieu—implying a low level of trust in it—is consistent with Malay socialization practices. Malay children are taught to have pride and to maintain their personal dignity. But their world is filled with specters of unseen dangers in the form of this-world enemies (bullying companions) and other-world spirits. Long before religious training begins, the Malay child is exposed to the idea that invisible forces are constantly at work in the environment. At the village level the *bomoh*—a combination of ritual healer, sorcerer, shaman, and medicine man—is there to perform feats of magic and exorcism. The Malay child is taught (even in urban environments) that life's uncertainties come from the workings of "bad magic" and that two persons' magic is greater than the magic one can accomplish alone. The fixed-pie orientation to economic thinking assumes that there is little likelihood of change and that the outcome of one's position in life is fairly fixed. Hence one acquires power from those more powerful.

One result is a low level of interest in self-improvement. In response to the inadequacies of the school system, a host of *tuisyen* (tuition) centers and private individuals (usually retired schoolteachers) have come into existence to tutor children in things like maths (mathematics) and English. The students are over-whelmingly Chinese; very few Malays are found. Nor does one see people reading in those public circumstances, like waiting for the bus or riding one, where bore-dom and wasted time are inevitable.

In the Malay culture people are taught that unexpected events are a sign of dan-ger. They grow up believing that supernatural forces can turn somebodies into no-bodies in the wink of an eye. The physical world is governed by social forces that someone with the right magic can turn into miraculous redemption. The magic world is no less treacherous than the physical one. It is filled with Muslim spirits (*jin Islam*), pagan spirits (*jin kafir*), guardian spirits *(penunggu)*, ancestor spirits (*datuk datuk*), the shepherd of the black tiger (*gembala harimau purun*), vampire cricket banshees (*pelesit*), flying ghouls (*langsuyar*), devils (*iblis, setan*), Shiva (*Hantu Raya*), and many more.

The distant origins of these invisible spirits is the rice culture and its alternating cycles of overwork and indolence, combined with the animism of a jungle culture in which the world beyond the rice paddy is unpredictable and extremely danger-ous.[1] The worst is always ready to happen, and then again it may never happen. Hence the *bomoh*.

The Malay concept of power is one in which cause and effect are not governed by rational orderliness. Malay fiction—notably the vivid descriptions of Malay po-litical and family life by the novelist Che Husma—is filled with the workings of supernatural forces and the whimsical surprises of a people who are still close to nature. Malays are brought up with stories of the incredible feats of *bomohs*, whose abilities to perform the unbelievable are so widely accepted that it is com-mon to believe in the impossible. This is why Malays had no trouble believing that Malaysia could go it alone with no help from the IMF because there is always the Sultan of Brunei.

The belief that real power is invisible creates great uncertainty whenever cir-cumstances call for competition. Malaysian and Indonesian government officials dispense a good deal of rhetoric about *muafakat* ("decision making by agreement," although the term also means "decision making by arrangement"). In actual prac-tice decision making is more often accompanied by power struggles and long-lived, deeply suppressed resentments.

There is a basic ambivalence inherent in the Malay attitude toward power. On one hand, power is seen as meriting reverential deference. On the other hand, very often power holders become so giddy with their status that they cross over into pretentiousness so pompous it becomes transparently silly.

The opposite of the tendency to see power as unpredictable and basically malev-olent is the Western tradition of treating power as orderly and manageable. Any suggestion that the sultans be dispensed with runs into opposition from people who see the sultans as a force for maintaining the status quo. Although the sultans were originally conceived of as champions of Malay interests and defenders of Islam, today they have developed so many economic interests of their own that they are more sympathetic to overseas commercial interests than they are to

Malaysia's economy. The sultans are quite secretive about this. The Malay ideal of authority is that the supreme figure of the sultan will always rise above immediate satisfactions and act with a blend of impartial detachment and Malay-centeredness. One has only to see the ghastly levels of deforestation practices going on in places like the Losing Highlands and other remote areas of Peninsular Malaysia to realize that the sultans selling their timber concessions are hardly acting in Malaysia's interests. The Malay sense of responsibility is akin to *noblesse oblige*, except that it makes more of the *oblige* than it does the *noblesse*. Malays have a long-inculcated sense for the finest gradations of hierarchy and rank, but they are much less certain about to what purposes power should be applied. While ideals of cultural cohesion are very strong, translating those into social munificence and betterment is another matter.

ASIAN ISLAM

Islam has received an unjustly bad press in the Western popular and business media. The Western powers turn a blind eye to their own and their allies' religious and power excesses while vilifying similar excesses when they originate in Islam. After all, it was the West that invented and first used poison gas and the atomic bomb, not Iraq. The press points fingers at Iranian zealotry while barely even looking into the appalling attitudes and behavior of Christian missionaries in the remote fastnesses of Irian Jaya and New Guinea. Much is made about the *fatwa* condemning Salman Rushdie but much less about the corpses of journalists in Brazil or Mexico. The Western intelligentsia ignores a magnificent cultural and intellectual heritage originating in Islam while playing up its own similar achievements. For example, how many Westerners have any idea how much social and economic reconstruction the Muslim societies of Central Asia, India, and Western Asia accomplished in the century after the depradations of Tamarlane, and what a pacific cultural renaissance the Muslim fourteenth century was when compared to what went on in Italy? Few Westerners know that the Black Plague which so devastated Europe between 1348 and 1352 did even worse damage to the Middle East and Levant.

One can go on and on how neglected Islamic culture has been in today's times of political tilting and the smugness of the rationalist-scientific mind. But the sum of the discussion is that Islam affects the thoughts and behavior of many millions of people, and the West ignores those feelings to its long-term peril. Religious specifics aside, Islam is a culture, and if any culture in the world deserves to be considered a better friend than it has been allowed to be, that culture is Islam.

All world religions have basically similar values of human relations and interaction with nature. Buddhists call them *pançasila* or "The Five Virtues" of no killing, lying, stealing, infidelity, or intoxication. Hebrews and Christians have the Ten Commandments. Hindus obey the laws of *puja* and *jati*; Master Kung Fu-tzu (Confucius) originated the ethical goal "Do to others as you would that others do to you." There is the nontheistic secular term "holistic behavior" and its reformulation of Confucius, "Say about people today what you want to hear them say about you tomorrow."

Although case-by-case phraseology may differ, these values are quite alike in spirit of intent. The term for this intent is ethical universalism. The Islamic version of this universalism is *ummah*, the unity of belief with the spiritual, the intellectual, and the physical. Early Islamic society's most notable hallmark is the way it integrated its spiritual values with material well-being and scientific exploration. A list of words contributed by early Moslem culture to the vocabulary of the West hints at the level of Islam's cultural sophistication: bazaar, caravan, tariff, and traffic; sloop, barge, cable; guitar, lute, mandolin; orange, lemon, sugar, syrup, sherbet, julep, jar; mattress, sofa, muslin, satin—not to mention the names of most of the visible stars—Altair, Aldebaran, Deneb, Rigel, and Vega, just to name a few. It was the Muslims who discovered the relationship between science as pure inquiry and technology as application to the betterment of mankind.

Early Islam enjoyed unprecedented success as it was prosyletized throughout Arabia, Persia, Northern Africa, and Spain. The only other world religion to experience such quick and widespread acceptance was Buddhism during the third century B.C. in northern India. Buddhism's attraction was its rejection of a stupefying caste system imposed a millennium earlier by Aryans who invaded from north of the Caucasus.

Unlike Buddhism, however, Islam was proactive rather than reactive. One reason for its popularity was that it cut through the disorganized array of confusing tribal and caravan-route gods with the obvious fact that the cosmos's existence made sense only if originated by a Creator force that destined every fragment and every instant to a sublime purpose. The social facet of this Creator, which Islam calls *Allah* or "The Way," is that all humankind is one brotherhood.

Early Islam was based on these ideas as revealed to the prophet Mohammed, which were then written down in the *Qur'an*. The civilization that arose from these revelations was not simply a theocracy. Its spiritual truth was balanced by a quest for the truths of creation. The result would be a more profound regard for the Creator. Early Moslems discovered that creation could objectively be described by scientific investigation, just as they discovered that the beauty of Allah's creation could be hymned through poetry and music.

People steeped in the Western historical tradition are rightly proud of their scientific method's achievements, but neglect that it was Islam's four centuries of scientific inquiry that laid the foundation for the West's scientific era many centuries later. The origin of words like alchemy, alembic, algebra, azimuth, zenith, and nadir often are overlooked in school texts while Greek and Latin etymology is explained at length. The famed Western scholars Thomas Aquinas, Roger Bacon, William of Ockham, and many others relied on Greek translations of Arabic scientific and astronomical literature. The eighteen-year cycle of the eclipses, the twenty-seven thousand-year precession of the equinoxes, the optics of the rainbow, ground glass lenses, the astrolabe, and the mathematical concept of zero are all Moslem contributions that primed the pump of Western science and technology.

Islamic intellectuals advanced the fields of administration, development, agriculture, industry, engineering, defense, mathematics, shipping, navigation, medicine, and many other fields of knowledge. Higher institutions of learning, laboratories, and libraries were founded from Spain to the Middle East. Ancient knowledge from Greece and Rome was studied and new findings documented. Islamic civil engineers built roads, water supplies, buildings, walls, and towers, public markets, lodging, houses, and the other necessities of an advanced civilization.

This gift was not acknowledged very graciously. The exquisitely cultured Caliphate of Seville was rudely pushed across the Straits of Gibraltar by a general who didn't know how to read and a queen who viewed the New World to the west as a source of quick gold. The splendid Mosque of Cordoba found itself with a gloomy gothic chapel carved into its middle, and the abundance of quick gold induced a two-century era of uncontrolled inflation that ruined Spain's economy. The Portuguese converted the West Coast of India, Ceylon, Malaya, Sarawak, and Macau with bloody mass baptisms presided over by soldiers. The result was a fabulously wealthy Christianity so corrupt that people turned away from spirituality altogether under the impression that spirituality and religion were the same thing. The seventeenth-century Enlightenment that accompanied the Scientific Revolution was in part motivated by the desire to throw religion out of secular affairs altogether.

These cannot be dismissed as cultural aberrations from history long gone. The superiority complex of nineteenth-century Protestant missionaries eradicated the native cultures of the Pacific and Asia, just as international finance today is eradicating many developing nations' sense of being in control, for better or for worse, of their own economic fate. When Aristotle opined that the worst government of all is that of the rich, he could not have foreseen what could happen when the world's richest cultures decided they should be the world's policemen. The West still has a cultural predisposition to decide how others should live, coupled with a tendency to ignore problems at home by exporting them elsewhere. Two lessons to be drawn from this are: (a) the long-term effects of short-term thinking are almost always negative, and (b) the results eventually harm the perpetrator more than the victim.

In Islamic countries the response to these facts has been twofold. Arabic Moslems are preoccupied with a generalized sense of cultural inadequacy that is ironically at variance with their actual cultural achievements. Asia's Moslems, on the other hand, show an increasing tendency to turn their backs on the past to build a future according to their own design. This explains why the preponderance of Moslem fundamentalism lies in Arabia and Africa where economic opportunities are limited, compared with fundamentalism's minimal influence in Asia, where economic opportunity is encouraged.

Moslem fundamentalism is hardly unique: Christianity in Europe, Hinduism in India, and Buddhism in Sri Lanka are all witnessing portions of their societies adopt a fetal-ball approach in response to change from outside. One reaction to feelings of social or economic impotence is to revert to "fundamental" values—most often devotional symbols that emphasize ritual. Underlying their extravagant tantrums of bombing, burning, and throat cutting, fundamentalists of all creeds feel trapped in a revolving-door economy in which they are on the way out. Fundamentalist Islam's problem with the West is largely linked to the West's fundamental problem with Islam: it judges too much and invests too little.

Asian Muslims are cheered by the fact that they are in a unique position to address many of these disservices. By nature Asians prefer building consensus to waging *jihad*. Islam, for all the skewed representations that come from the American press and *The Economist*, is in fact based on tolerance, justice, and brotherhood and great portions of the faithful behave that way, just as great portions of Christians live, as best they can, the Golden Rule. Moslems regard the diversity of nature as one of Allah's greatest gifts, for the diversity of nature reveals the complexity of Allah. Hence tolerance, justice, and the absence of concern about skin color are fundamental Islamic beliefs.

Despite the enormous increase in media coverage of Islam and Muslim politics since the Iranian revolution, the contributions of the Muslims of Southeast Asia have been all too ignored. Today this is changing dramatically. Globalization, the emergence of Asia as a powerful—if volatile—market economy, and the information revolution have triggered a "rediscovery" of Asian Islam. In a world where conventional wisdom has it that Islam is incompatible with modernization and democracy, Southeast Asia offers a proven alternative—for example, the quite intelligent local solutions to local conditions that are coming out of Islamic banking.

Southeast Asia is more multireligious and pluralistic than any other Islamic region. The result is a sizable spawning of Islamic schools, banks, social welfare agencies, and publications; and a modern and educated Islamic elite. In Southeast Asia there is a dynamism and prosperity that surprises anyone who considers Islam regressive.

BUT ASIAN ISLAM IS UNEASY

On the other hand, Asian Muslims live in considerable unease about a fundamentalist surge in the region. The sociology is twofold.

One group is rural believers who are distressed about modern society, who interpret the inroads of Western culture as bringing vice and corruption, and who crave to recapture the communal bliss they—rightly or wrongly—nostalgize as Asian village life.

The other is the wealth-chasing Muslim political and business leadership whose hidden corruption and mediocre governance were exposed by the media attention following the 1997 crisis. The Muslim populaces of Asia realize on one level or another that the ROI they have gotten for their sweat equity is pathetic compared with what their political leaders have gotten. The easiest response is to blame scapegoats, and the Chinese are easy targets.

Once the ghastly bloodshed is over, Muslims will still have to face up to the internal contradiction they had before the riots, between absolutist ideals and democratic *ummah* or community. Islam has an ambiguous ideal of what a good leader should be.

On one hand, the image of the Prophet and of those who spread the Word of Allah by word or deed suggests that a person's deeds are what earn respect. Southeast Asia's Muslim politicians converted the idea of moral deed into the display of wealth, much to the misgivings of the pious. The tepid acquiescence of the *ulama* (religious leadership) was overlooked when everyone was doing well. But when government corruption resulted in many people out of work, tolerance quickly reached its limits.

On the other hand, Islam encourages the ideal of the upright person being willing to sacrifice for the community. A Muslim public that sees its income and its values threatened by modernization is in no mood to embrace the ideal of *'nchallah*, tranquil acceptance of Allah's will.

There is potential for violence in the sharp line drawn by Islam between good and evil. Muslim standards of personal conduct are very difficult to attain, so many people compensate for personal failings by righteous indignation toward those who know they should do better. Modernization easily raises this ire. When the Minister of Education shows up at the golf club in a Lamborghini and the mosque in a Proton, people wonder who he is serving. The insecurities and corruption that accompanied rapid social change have brought many Muslims to romanticize an earlier traditional order and to see what is happening to their culture as a demonic event. The commercial world is especially suspect because many of its products—fashion, perfumes, sexually frank advertising—are identified with the West. The more economic and social change pulls Muslims out of their *kampungs* and *desas* (villages and farms), the more urban unhappiness is able to shed its timidity and burst into rage.

Surprisingly, Asian Islam's poor are more likely to remain docile than the newly well-off middle class and intelligentsia. It was university students, not the older generation, who first demanded stricter Islamic rules. Until quite recently, Malay women did not wear *tudong*s (the characteristic Malay head scarf) or worry about their hair showing. Now few dare to go without it. In the early 1980s university students on home campuses—and even more so overseas—began to demand separate dining facilities and partitions in classrooms to separate men and women. University administrators and government ministries were not quite sure how to handle these religiously inspired demands. To be unsympathetic could have opened the authorities to the charge that they were champions of Western values, yet to give in too easily could have opened the way to escalating demands. These in turn could be endless since there are no clear Islam mandates for the running of a public institution in a multireligious society.

One unforeseen consequence of the 1997 crisis was that Islamic fundamentalists and the region's political leaders have exacerbated each other's shortcoming and thus limited each other's room for maneuver. The eventual victims are likely to be local Chinese, not corrupt politicians or the markets for Western consumer products. The dilemma over what the standards of a modern Islamic society are will likely be a persistent problem for quite some time.

THE VIEW THAT SOCIAL ILLS ARE MODERNITY SHOCK

Islamic government officials have a different view of things than religious leaders. They tend to believe that the social ills besetting the Malay community are caused by their inability to cope with culture shock from the nation's rapid economic progress, whose direction is largely dictated by multinationals and investors. Dr. Megat Junid, Malaysia's Domestic Trade and Consumer Affairs Minister, said that the country's Malays were being poorly prepared to face the challenges of the modern-day life, especially compared with the Chinese:

The escalating social problems affecting the country, especially among Malay and Indian youths, are due to culture shock. They have to compete to improve their lot but are not prepared to cope with the many challenges that come with development. The Chinese community, on the other hand, is used to the idea that challenge leads to improving one's lot. They are used to living in the busy lifestyle of towns, which is usually associated with improving one's socio-economic position. To them, these are nothing new. There is often competition among husband and wife to boost their incomes, resulting in their children being neglected. The majority of youngsters caught committing various social ills claim lack of parental attention and love. This problem also affects many middle- and upper-class Malay families, who often leave their children in the care of foreign housemaids. We must never neglect our cultures and religions while we strive for greater economic progress. The Malays are plagued with numerous social problems including dumping of newborns, dadah (heroin) abuse, rape, and AIDS. The country is calling on all UMNO [Malaysia's largest political group] to help fight these problems.

The salient point to be drawn from the above is not so much that values change and become corrupted, but Dr. Megat's view that Malaysia's social problems are imposed by outside forces and that the solution is a political party matter.

This is a revealing attitude. No one knows how many drug addicts there are in Malaysia, but around fourteen thousand *new* addicts are reported each year. The great preponderance, estimated at between 75 and 90 percent, are Malay young people. Approximately 35 percent are students, factory hands, fishers, and people on government subsidies. The recent shift to designer drugs like Ecstasy affects the more affluent young people who frequent night spots. While Malaysia's drug laws prescribe death for people trafficking in more than 15 grams (0.53 ounces) of heroin and 200 grams (7.05 ounces) of cannabis and more than one hundred people had been executed for drug-related offenses, the country's police nonetheless seized more than 220,000 pounds of dangerous drugs and arrested 3,248 people in drug-related charges between January 1995 and August 1997. The country's addicts spend nearly RM1.25 billion a year ($500 million at the August 1997 exchange rate) to support their addiction. That is an astonishing figure from a highly controlled populace in a nation of only twenty million.

The notion that problems like this can be fixed by a political party hints at the high level of grandeur that exists in Malaysia's political establishment. If the idea of political control is being applied like this in the matter of drug abuse, what are the Malaysian government's attitudes about information it doesn't like?

We saw above how the combination of upbringing, attitudes towards authority, and religious values have conditioned the Malay response towards romanticization and suppression. How is this set of values likely to respond to the enormous influx of information that the MSC represents, particularly (as is likely) if much of the MSC's information that ends up being delivered to the populace at large comes to them through their TV, not a PC?

INTERNATIONAL DOMINANCE OF THE MEDIA
AND FEAR OF CULTURAL EROSION

Asian governments are not happy that the media bring into their homes material that does not reflect their cultural sensitivities. Americans watch so much of their own media that they no longer see how brutal and dehumanizing much of it is in the eyes of cultures who have seen too much of the consequences of brutality to regard it as a desirable tool to advance a plot or ratings. Asians see international media's casual message that brutality is part of everyday life, and they don't want it in their lives.

Material that exacerbates political hostility is also a concern, although many governments are far less sniffy about it when it advances their own causes. Attitudes of Asian governments range from quite concerned to ambivalent about politically inexact material being carried on the media and the Internet.

However, the issue of multinational media dominance influencing local content runs deeper than these two sets of issues. It is in part concern over the threat to cultural values (particularly on the subject of gratuitous sex) in specific programs, but much more so the management and control exercised over the media by distant powers unsympathetic to—and even ignorant of—Asian identity. Media barons act as though the world should think in ways that help sell the products of their clients, but much of Asia does not see it that way.

Malaysian academic Zaharom Nain, in his essay, "The Impact of the International Marketplace on the Organisation of Malaysian Television," typifies Asian unhappiness at the preferential treatment multinationals get as they become allied with Asian political interests. He fears the increasing drift of Asia into the international media market "will all too likely further marginalise alternative explanations, forms of television content, and forms of expression which are not deemed to be commercially viable." This is particularly touchy in a Muslim country, where feelings already run high over the one-sided portrait Islam gets at the hands of the American media.

Others worry about the cultural impact on Asia of the ramifications of the Uruguay Round of the General Agreement on Tariffs and Trade (GATT). By linking trade and communication, some Asians feel the GATT agreement poses a danger that within GATT's global trade culture, television is just another commodity; as unfettered by community cultural values as the trade in wheat is unfettered by local bread-baking styles. Asians say that their values aren't wheat. There is unhappiness in some quarters that proponents of global culture talk about respecting local values but behave as if their own values are what should be defined as local. To many Asians, media multinationals purvey little more than a form of sitcom colonialism.

John Ure, in his 1995 book *Telecommunications in Asia*, is skeptical about permanent damage caused by tension between government objectives, multinational expansion, and domestic business networks. The Singapore government, he points out, attempted to counteract the attractiveness of satellite broadcasting by developing its own national system which offered alternative programs in lieu of overseas material they considered unacceptable. Singapore's Minister for Information and Arts put it, "As satellite dishes got smaller with higher power satellites and clearer signal processing, it became impossible to stop alternative television from being received. We had to change so we got into international broadcasting ourselves. The best defence was a good offense."

This view summarizes the positive solutions in the issue of who controls what. At one time the question was, "Should governments retain some form of control over information content for what they feel is the common good of their people, or should they accept whatever the Internet sends down the wire and what the media barons and corporations want to transmit?" This question was divisive when it was typified by the conflict of values between the violence of Hollywood and the saccharine of Bollywood, but it became less difficult when Singapore began to create offerings that were clearly aimed at self-improvement rather than entertainment. Singapore adroitly redefined the issue into the positive terminology of how to make infotainment as appealing as entertainment. Singapore's reaction was what competition is supposed to be all about: stimulating opportunities and discovering how to better serve the market.

Malaysia and Burma might do all they can to keep unwanted facts out of the heads of their citizens, but Singapore is tackling the free-speech issue right where it should be tackled: on the level of originating a better product. The days are near done—at least in Asia—when free speech proponents can propose a melting pot of universal values which on closer inspection are their own values (or at least those of the culture that spawns the technology), not the values of locals. That *is* neo-colonialism, and the Singaporeans are showing how at least some Asian values might actually be more enriching than many of the West's. The West's habit of defining truth and beauty to benefit its own vested interests eventually constricts their own perspective more than anyone else's. Who has ever seen an action film sequel that was less violent and had a better plot than the original?

Malaysia's Mr. Zaharom sums up the issue benignly: "I do not want my house to be walled in on all sides and my windows to be shut. I want the winds of cultures of all lands to blow about my house freely. I just don't want to be blown off my feet by them." Unfortunately his open-mindedness contrasts sharply with Malaysia's Minister of Education's telling academics to not discuss the country's haze problem (as much due to local pollution as fires in Indonesia) because to discuss the issue might deter foreign investment.

Asia's IT future is confronted with several options in response to the internationalization of the media in general and the Internet in particular. One is Singapore's route, to opt for the upscale, turning out a better product for local needs. It was late off the blocks with television programming but is far ahead of Asia (indeed, most of the world) when it comes to superior on-line offerings. Indonesia has done little beyond allowing its citizens to buy whatever satellite receiver they like. Malaysia's practice is to demonize values the government doesn't approve of, then to paternalize on behalf of its people by access restrictions.

None of these responses respond to the commoditization problem inherent in satellite- and Net-delivered media with the oft-successful solution to oversupply: focusing on niche markets and building premium brands. It is indeed the myriad niche markets of Asia where the long-term profitability of the region's IT and e-commerce lies. The penetration of the Net into Asia is roughly what television was thirty years ago. The Net is far better equipped to work with niche markets than other media. The trick is turning a good product chain like one finds on SingONE and China's *My Computer Family* computer-awareness campaign into a profit chain.

MALAY PROTECTIVENESS AND "BAD INFLUENCES" ON THE NET

In February 1997 Malaysia's Information Minister Datuk Mohamed Rahmat stated, "We may have to look into issuing licenses to Internet subscribers and those with home pages so that we can have better control on the materials that appear in the Net."

The number of Internet subscribers was about eighty thousand when the minister made his statement. At that time MIMOS—the Malaysian government body controlling Internet access—was projecting that about 10 percent of the population (roughly two million) would be on the Net by the turn of the century. Even assuming near unanimity of dissent in a wired culture that is anything but unanimous, 10 percent of the populace seems an unlikely number to overthrow much of anything.

It is hardly news that the Malaysian government is inconsistent on the matter of free information flow in Malaysian society. Ministers like Datuk Mohamed were issuing verdicts for local consumption while the Prime Minister was promising investors whatever would attract capital. Several times during the early courting of investors Mahathir stated that the Malaysian government would not try to control information coming in through the Net. In the 1 January 1996 issue of *Computimes* he said, "If we stop the use of Internet, we will detach ourselves from a source of useful information that is good for us. Whatever we do, the technology will progress rapidly. If we block it at one source, it will come from another." In the 31 January 1996 *New Straits Times* he repeated, "I do not think you can really regulate the Internet as information will be flowing across borders that nobody will be able to control. The only control we can have is intrinsic . . . one's own self. This is the discipline we have to develop among Malaysians. This is what we need to implant in the minds of the people, because it is almost impossible for anybody to try to sieve and censor things that come into the Internet."

This inconsistency is illusory. The Malaysian government does indeed want the free flow of information coming *in* on the Internet, they just don't want it to flow *around* Malaysia once inside the country.

There are two aspects to the matter of Malaysia's duplicity in public statements about fact flow within the country. The first is the government's poor record at controlling genuine social evils like heroin flow in the country. The second is that the government takes the dangers of information to be much more grave than the dangers of heroin, especially when the information reflects on the quality of the government.

The blunt fact is that the Malaysian government is arbitrary and inconsistent on issues related to what it perceives as socially dangerous, and despite what it says, there is no firewall or safety net if information the government doesn't like flows freely within the MSC and is "disseminated" into Malaysian society at large.

Let us examine two examples: (a) pornography in the country's video stores, and (b) the Murray Hiebert case.

MISHANDLING THE PORNOGRAPHY PROBLEM

A number of schemes have been advanced throughout Asia for restricting pornography. Chief among the regulatory approaches is the idea that governments can control content by controlling access to the content. One way is government mandated "national servers" like jaring.my and pacific.net.sg. These have failed to curb the availability of pornography, in part because the Net is so porous. However, the chief cause of failure is easy access to alternative delivery vehicles that have a much larger user base than PC ownership. X-rated material was available on many of the pirated CDs to be found in video and computer stores in even small rural towns but concealed in such a way that governments didn't know it was easily found. There was no end of "Nighthawk" (hint, hint) types of video games that were regular video games on the surface, until buyers put them into a computer and accessed them via CD "movie player" software. When they did, their porn content became available.

Herein lies a contradiction. Heroin is clearly far more dangerous to Asian society, but you don't hear the ASEAN leaders talking about controlling its flow the way they try to control porn. The reason is that almost all of Asia's heroin comes from Burma, a fellow ASEAN member and recipient of sizable Malaysian and Singaporean investments. Just why Malaysia so adamantly defends a government so inimical to Malaysian interests as Burma is a mystery, but Malaysia is paying a terrible price in addiction statistics. The great preponderance of users are young Malays.

The basic problem is that the national consensus on what is bad for society being set by the government and the government—or at least its Prime Minister—is inconsistent and unpredictable. It appears there will be no change in this scenario for the near and middle term (meaning the likely shelf life of this book, about four years). What the pornography/heroin issue really demonstrates about Malaysia is its poor prospects as a player in the free information economy.

THE MURRAY HIEBERT CASE

The example of what happened to a Canadian journalist for the *Far Eastern Economic Review* shows how the Malaysian government can reveal an entirely different face from its public utterances about information flow on the Net to become extraordinarily punitive over seemingly trifling matters when it affects a politician's or other authority's sense of face. The Murray Hiebert case is not about the rule of law in Malaysia, it is about arbitrariness in the law's application.

In citing the facts of the case, this writer has had to adopt the same careful probity that the consulting firms in chapter 3 used when describing their misgivings about the MSC—and for the same reason. In Malaysia, one aspect of the laws regarding "dissemination" of information is that a person can be jailed for disseminating false statements even when the person merely reports an already published statement, *if* that person does not independently validate and verify the facts of the statement personally. In practice, this means reinvestigating the entire matter by oneself, including interviews with principals. Hence in describing the Murray Hiebert case, this writer will simply reproduce verbatim two reports in the Malaysian press, and let the reader make his and her own assessments. It says a great deal about the state of free flow of information issue in Malaysia that this approach has to be taken.

Court Finds Writer Guilty Of Contempt

SHAH ALAM, Fri.—*Far Eastern Economic Review* correspondent Murray Hiebert was found guilty of contempt of court by the High Court today over an article he wrote about a student who was dropped from his school debating team.

Judge Datuk Low Hop Bing fixed July 14 to hear Hiebert's mitigation before sentencing. Low also asked Hiebert, a Canadian, to post bail at RM100,000 [$40,000] with a Malaysian surety and to surrender his passport to the court.

In his judgment, Low said the article under the heading "See You In Court" written by Hiebert in the Jan 23 [1996] issue of the weekly news magazine was contemptuous as it has scandalised the court.

The contempt proceedings against Hiebert, 47, were initiated by the student's mother, Datin Chandra Sri Ram.

Chandra, represented by Datuk Kam Woon Wah, had applied for the order to commit Hiebert to jail over his article which discussed the merits of a civil suit brought by Chandra against the International School of Kuala Lumpur. The article was written while the case was still pending.

Chandra, the mother of Govind Sri Ram, 17, had filed the suit against ISKL for dropping her son from the debating team which took part in the Southeast Asian Cultural Convention in Taipeh in March 1996. However, the suit was settled after ISKL agreed to apologise in court.

Chandra, 45, claimed that Hiebert could not and had not exercised "an independent mind and view" when writing the article. She maintained that the article, when read as a whole, amounted to a serious contempt of court and an unwarranted attack upon the Malaysian judiciary and that Hiebert should never have written the article because his wife was a senior employee of ISKL.

In his affidavit-in-reply Hiebert maintained that his sole purpose in writing the article was to present a newsworthy story in a manner which would fairly summarise the arguments of both parties and illuminate the issues and concerns to which the case had given rise.

Low also said in his judgment that Hiebert's article was "calculated to excite prejudice against Chandra in her civil suit and was designed to exert pressure to the court to decide that suit against Chandra."

Earlier, Low dismissed two preliminary objections raised by Hiebert's counsel, Muhammad Shafee Abdullah, at the outset of the contempt hearing on March 28.

Shafee had objected on the grounds that Chandra's application was lacking in particulars and that the contempt proceedings should be initiated by the Attorney-General and not by Chandra as a private individual.

Low said that the application was in good order and that Chandra had complied with all the requirements prescribed by law in initiating this action. He said that Chandra, although a private party, had sufficient interest in the matter and also the necessary legal standing to initiate the proceedings.

Low also said that Hiebert can apply to the court for his passport if he needs to travel abroad in the course of his profession.

Malaysian Court Sentences Reporter

By HARI S. MANIAM

KUALA LUMPUR, Malaysia (AP) [4 September 1997]—A judge sentenced a Canadian correspondent for the *Far Eastern Economic Review* magazine to three months in jail Thursday for contempt of the judiciary over an article he wrote about lawsuits.

Murray Hiebert, 47, of Steinbach, Manitoba, was ordered to remain in police custody until an additional $54,000 in bail is posted. Since his conviction on May 30, Hiebert had been free on $40,000 bail but had to request his passport each time he traveled out of the country.

Judge Low Hop Bing said he was sentencing Hiebert to jail because the "nature of the contempt is very serious." He added, "No apology has been tendered."

The case stems from an article Hiebert wrote in January about lawsuits in Malaysia, focusing on one against the International School by Chandra Sri Ram, wife of Appeals Court Judge Sri Ram Gopal. Chandra sued the school for dropping her 17-year-old son from a debate team that traveled to Taiwan. That case was settled out of court.

Chandra brought the charge of contempt of the Malaysian judiciary against Hiebert, who mentioned in his Jan. 23 [1996] article that her case had moved quickly through the court system and that her husband was a judge.

Hiebert's attorney, Muhammad Shafie Abdullah, said it was the first time in Malaysia that a journalist had been convicted of contempt of court.

Low said the constitution allows freedom of speech but "our country does not permit . . . trial by media." He said the news media should remember that court cases cannot be used for "commercial purposes."

The *Review*, published in Hong Kong, reports on business and politics in Asia, and has a circulation of about 14,000 in Malaysia.

The editor of the magazine, Nayan Chanda, was in court with Hiebert, but said afterward he would not comment.

AP-NY-09-04-97 0023EDT Copyright 1997 The Associated Press.

The Hiebert case raises the "overkill issue" that lies under so much of Southeast Asia's response to dissent. There is an undercurrent of assumption throughout Malaysian life that everything must be done the way the authorities plan it, and that in matters of social behavior the authorities are always right. Unanswered is the question of who is right when the government is wrong or when individual ministers take matters into their own hands. The abuse of land appropriations that financially enriched high state officials and their cronies reached such proportions in mid-1997 that the government finally brought an Anti-Corruption Agency into the picture. This issue was raised not in the press but by many aggrieved parties complaining to UMNO party officials. The Anti-Corruption Agency made a splash of headlines over some illicit property deals in Malacca, then quietly vanished.

Hence the issue of Datuk Mohamed's statement is not his proposed solution, but how deeply a mind-set of authoritarianism runs through those who would control the MSC. The Malaysian government has not reconciled the need for freedom-based economic growth with its response pattern of dictating parent. The government is simply unwilling to let go of control, be it over the squabbles between the opposition and the ruling parties, the awarding of contracts to favored organizations, or what people are permitted to know.

AN ENIGMATIC MIDDLE CLASS

Into this economic gilded cage Indonesia's and Malaysia's quite recent middle classes are quietly originating their own values. They most certainly don't resemble the values the government thinks they should have. Yet this is, by the admission of market and media researchers in Jakarta and Kuala Lumpur, the most underresearched class in Asia. University academics know more about the Penans of Sarawak than they do about the house-buyers of Kebayoran Baru just south of Jakarta and Bangsar just south of Kuala Lumpur. Clothing designers base their trend decisions on what store clerks tell them people are asking for because a systematic study of the garment consumer market has never been commissioned. The reason is no one wants to pay for it.

What is clear is that the Malay middle class is less susceptible to being exploited by religious antagonisms largely because income is their religion. They are invulnerable to political rhetoric because they watch a lot of ads on TV and find them immensely more to their taste than anything the politicians say. Their main social interest is adhering to the international middle-class consensus on family values like shopping frequently and bringing up their children to be polite graduates of acceptable schools. They are impatient for economic growth but terrified of moves that may upset the established order. In short, they are doing everything middle classes are supposed to do.

The Malays' fear-based antipathy towards the Chinese isn't about political ethics, it is about work ethics. Malay politicians have tried to use political patronage to accomplish the same social cohesion the Chinese have achieved with family patronage. But the *bumiputera* system of racial preferences has turned commonwealth into codependency, creating opportunity based on ethnic preference and contacts, not idea creation and economy building. Its main discipline is local feedback loops, not performance in the marketplace.

The economic collapse of 1997 resulted, assuredly enough, from bad banking and investment policies. But the real victimizer was Southeast Asia's information vacuum. Neither side is particularly well informed about the historical basis of the other's behavior. The cause of Chinese assertiveness is not racism as much as it is Chinese overprotecting against a repeat of their historical deprivation. They had not arrived on tall ships, they had arrived as slaves in all but name. Their traditional culture was lost in hardscrabble lives that allowed them but a few moments of joy, none of them particularly edifying. They had to invent a new culture based on sweat and wits.

The Malays do not welcome the notion that they might be as much victims of a modern politics-business social class invented by their leaders as they are of ancient ethnic tensions based on economic fears. The *bumiputera* policy was originally based on a philosophy of eradicating poverty and restructuring society. Instead it was turned into a patronage tool in which a small and closed class of patrons enjoy the plums. The Malays have been brought up shielded from an economy that requires give and take, risk and reward. Their social role models are into sure things, reward that is guaranteed. They have learned that if you can't manipulate an economy you can manipulate the law. In the old Malay culture, law was based on *adat*, the spirit of duty. The foundation stone of the law—articulated many times in the *Sejarah Malayu* ("Malay Annals")—was that the sultan may defile no subject's honor, nor may a subject ever betray the sovereign. Today this has been replaced with the duty to remain silent about the inequities of leaders.

The Petronas Towers and world's tallest flagpole are not a magnificent distillation of cultural continuity, as Sultan Mansur Shah's 1465 *istana* (palace) was. That *istana* reflected an aesthetic sensibility that was also a social sensibility. It set forth in a building the mental processes by which the Malay people transformed raw information into three broad categories: fundamental order, complex mechanics, and appropriateness to surroundings. This also happened to be a remarkably apt definition of good law as the early Malays understood it—indeed, good law happens to be one of the early Malays' great contributions to Asian history.

To understand the thinking reality of Malaysian leaders today, we must pay close attention to their architecture and think of it as an attitude about law. The Petronas Towers in Kuala Lumpur are trying to add social status without adding social value.

The French aristocracy of the *ancien regime* did this too. We adore Versailles but are grateful we don't have to live with the people who created it. That was the seventeenth century. This is now. It is all very nice for Prime Minister Mahathir to point at the West and cry, "You did it first," but that doesn't much help an economy with a python of politicians around its neck.

NOTE

1. One need only read the newspapers. In 1997 a man was suffocated and partly swallowed by a 25-foot python not very far from Kuala Lumpur. That same year this writer saw a 12-foot python wriggling unconcernedly down the streets of the bucolic suburb where he lived. All this may explain why cats stay indoors so much.

26

Indian Psychology and Behavior

It is easy to overdo it when applying Western child rearing and family models to interpret Asian behavior. This is especially true in the case of the Indian peoples, whose culture and civilization are so vast and complex they easily surpass the usual psychological paradigms of the West. The fundamental myths aren't the same, and neither is the psychology.

In India, forget Freud. Entirely different patterns exist that explain why Indian business associates and employees think so differently about authority, job security, responsibility, and candor.

The Indian baby is typically indulged, nurtured, constantly handled. Every whimper brings a caring response from the whole family. Infants quickly learn that the surest way to get attention is to cry.

The technical term for the result is narcissism—the feeling there must be an immediate gratifying response to every wish. Indian narcissism differs somewhat from the Malay form we saw above. Male children are led to feel that they are the center of the universe and deserve their role. The mother-figure is all-nurturing and all-attending. In India people term their country "Mother India" and symbolize her with the sacred cow.

There is considerable separation shock upon the arrival of the next baby. This typically happens about the age of three (most Indian mothers breast-feed until a child reaches that age). Being abandoned in favor of a younger brother or sister is exacerbated by the fact that the child is simultaneously thrust out among the community so the mother can devote her full time to the new one. The child finds his specialness lost. Crying as a bid for attention gets nowhere.

The commonest reaction is withdrawal into being alone, which is more satisfying than the disappointments imposed by others. This habit is reinforced by Hinduism's primordial beliefs in which life's cravings produce nothing but suffering, hence the only worthy goal is to somehow escape existence altogether. The forest hermit and wandering ascetic are in part childhood rejection responses reinvented using the word "enlightenment."

However, the gratifying self-containment achieved in withdrawal competes with the need to be gregarious if one is to get one's fair share. A behavioral pattern develops in which being aloof coexists with gregariousness. For foreigners, the result is difficulty divining the true feelings of Indian associates, especially the intrusion of sudden uncommunicative remoteness into easygoing friendship.

If the relationship with the mother represents bliss and disappointment, relations with the father are even less satisfying. Indian fathers—and Indian men in general—tend to be demanding, not easily satisfied, critical rather than supportive, aloof, authoritarian, self-centered. The negative consequences of not yielding completely to fatherly authority results in unquestioning acceptance of the father's word. Youngsters learn to cry excessively to mothers but not assert any unhappiness to fathers because of the likelihood of an unpleasant response. Authority conflicts with narcissism, and neither wins.

The Indian's historical solution has been to devise escape hatches from reality. If the parental—and later the material—world is a cycle of disappointments, it must be the spiritual world where supreme bliss resides. Indians grow up yearning for a guide who is nurturing, sympathetic, and harmonious. Historically that person has not come in the form of a savior, but in the form of the *guru*, the wise and kindly teacher who has himself escaped from the world's turmoils but lingers on to reveal how others can find the longed-for sense of perfect inner calm.

THE INDIAN FAMILY-BUSINESS TRADITION

Where the Chinese family business resembles a privately held enterprise with an authoritarian management system, the Indian family business resembles a group of joint stock companies. Indian business values, systems, and functional structures are based on mainly Hindu tradition. In Southeast Asia the Indian family's business goals and the means of achieving them are greatly influenced by considerations of family unity, unlike India itself where caste, linguistic, and regional identities come much more into the picture.

Indian family businesses have more of a sense of enduring dynastic character than Chinese family businesses. They are not very much hit by the "third-generation collapse" that besets so many Chinese families. Indians often look to a formidable history—approaching semi-legend status in some areas—of family communities such as the Marwaris, the Khattris of Punjab, the Gujaratis whose sea-trader roots go back two thousand years, North Indian Banias, the Chettiars with their moneylending tradition, and the Parsees who have given India's industrial sector names like Tata and Birla. An interesting phenomenon is how the family and business value systems of all these geographically separated communities intertwine.

The patriarch of a family business has to strike a balance between meeting the financial needs of the existing business and the funding of new businesses set up not for pampered first sons as in the Chinese model, but by worthy siblings and cousins whose aspirations, Indians feel, must be included if the family business is to remain stable. Filial independence is a hallmark of the Indian family, where filial dependence is the characteristic feature of the Chinese. Indian patriarchs see themselves as heads of a conglomerate partnership of family interests rather than heads of single businesses, as in the Chinese system. The Indian patriarch tends to groom his sons so that he can gradually relax his control over the business while they are still in their prime, in contrast to the Chinese system where no one dares do a thing until the "old guy goes," as it is cheerlessly phrased by the would-be heirs.

Few Indian sons join the family business with the idea of inheriting it simply because they are sons. There is a strong entrepreneurial streak in Indians. Sons are more likely to start their own enterprise and then find a way to graft it into the family dynasty. Indians also have a respect for the intellectual professions—law, medicine, engineering, government service—that is perhaps the most profound in the world. In Southeast Asia Indians have come to dominate these professions in much the same way that Chinese tend to dominate commercial businesses and Malays tend to dominate politics. The quality of Indian management is often very high compared with other groups. One consequence is that the father-son tensions that frequently manifest themselves in Chinese family businesses are rare in Indian families. This may be one reason for the absence of the "third-generation collapse."

Another marked difference in Indian family businesses—at least these days—is the remarkable presence of women in professional and directorial roles. Younger Southeast Asian Indian women see themselves as free from the male-dominant traditions imported from India several generations ago when Indians came over as semi-indentured plantation labor. One of those freedoms is from the implied bondage of marriage to a man as *raja*, or "ruler." Educated younger Indian women are hardly running around braless and informing everyone to put the toilet seat down, but they have clearly taken their futures into their own hands. There exists a compensatory mechanism in many young Indian women, in which they seem to feel obliged to make up for their lowly status under the caste system and today's high rates of alcoholism, drug dependency, and narcissistic rebellion among Indian men who haven't yet made the adjustment that happens when they leave the protected plantation and try to make their ways in Asia's uncivil cities. The upshot is that young Indian women often exhibit a combination of high intellect plus compassion that makes them far and away the finest managers in the region.

Although today's highly educated (often abroad) younger Indians tend to think rather differently from their elders, this has not had much of an effect on the cohesion of family dynasties. One secret of the business family's success is its nonformal business links through a community network. Beyond the extended family, the network includes, among others, family menfolk's fathers-in-law, sons-in-law, maternal uncles, sisters' husbands, wives' brothers as well as wives' sisters and the husbands of the latter—plus the local networks around each of these. This resembles the Western conglomerate, with its semiautonomous wholly-owned subsidiaries allied to a parent organization. It is markedly different from the Chinese agglomerate, which comprises a number of dependent operations within a single management tree.

There is perhaps as much internal cross-financing of ventures as there is in the Chinese family business, but Indian businesses tend to be more transparent about their plans. One reason, of course, is that Indian businesses are out of the line of fire between Malay and Chinese interests, so they don't have to worry about politically imposed ethnic partners siphoning away capital. Indians manage quite nicely to skim profits using a different mechanism. A major difference between the Western business and the Indian one is that Indian family owners are also hands-on managers. All the patriarch's sons join the family business, but, as above, not always in a direct managerial role. Indian sons are their fathers' best outsources. This enables them to skim profits by parallel accounting systems using trusted subcontractors and what is daintily phrased as "little documentation." Another financial ploy is to invest via NRIs (Non-Resident Indians, meaning Indians who live outside India itself but maintain strong family ties). This investment path funnels undocumented cash abroad, which is then repatriated through dummy entities created in tax havens.

Hostile takeovers are generally frowned upon by Indian business communities; they "threaten the network." Similarly, Indian family businesses seldom take in nonfamily members on boards of directors because directors are familiar with the internal workings of both the business *and* the family. For the same reason they tend to steer clear of auditing firms linked to international auditing giants. They prefer local auditors who can advise them on how to work around tax codes.

All this sums up a unique quality in Indian family businesses: they consist of two parallel hierarchies—one merit-based and the other loyalty-based. It is a blend Asia could use more of.

THE SIKHS

Southeast Asia's Sikh community is perhaps one of the smallest ethnic groups in the region, but its members can be found in practically every major town. They are easily distinguishable from the rest of the Indian population by their turbans and beards. Some go without the turbans and are clean shaven—though without disavowing the unique religion that binds all Sikhs—and simply call themselves Punjabis.

Sikhism was founded in India by a religious teacher named Guru Nanak (1469–1539) who had been a Hindu. The term "Sikh" means "disciple." The Sikh religion is a combination of Hinduism and Islam. It recognizes only one God, the Creator of the universe.

All Sikhs take the surname Singh (Sanskrit for lion). The men wear "The Five K's"—*kesh* (uncut hair), *kanyha* (comb), *kara* (iron bracelet), *kaccha* (breeches), and *kirpan* (dagger). These days the dagger is more often a symbolic pin attached to their shirt or jacket.

The Sikhs first arrived in Southeast Asia during the latter decades of the 1800s, imported by the British to be members of the police force. It was thought that their height and bearing were intimidating enough to easily inspire law and order amongst the locals.

Other Sikhs found their way into the countryside. Some became night watchmen. A Sikh's *charpoi* (rope bed) placed in front of the main door of a house or estate was reputedly enough to deter intruders from breaking in. Others went into the transport business. They started with bullock-carts but now own bus companies and a good many of Kuala Lumpur's taxi fleets—a pattern their modern Punjabi colleagues in India have repeated in Bombay.

Others became successful moneylenders—sometimes too successful. A Sikh moneylender in Perlis State in Northern Malaysia lent so much money to so many landowners in Perlis that there was a real possibility he would call all his notes in one day and end up owning the entire state. Hence a law was passed to declare all his loans and pledges null and void in the interests of state security. To be on the safe side, the authorities ostracized him from entering Perlis for the rest of his life.

Moneylending is still common among Sikhs. Sikh and Chettiar money-lenders often are not really interested in recovering the principal loan as much as the continual profit in regularly collecting interest on loans for as long as possible—long before credit cards arrived at the same technique.

Today, Sikhs are very prominent in the professions, especially medicine, engineering, and law.

PART V

Asia's Information Future

27
What Now?

Throughout this book we—like just about everyone—have delicately minced our way around a painful fact: The economies that performed the poorest and spurned external remedies most defiantly in 1997 were those dominated by an *ancien regime* Malay cultural ethos, and those that suffered the least and moved ahead the quickest were mainly Chinese.

Yet the Chinese cultural ethos is no less inclined to autocracy, cronyism, and stage-managed democracy than its Malay counterparts. Nor are the Chinese economies appreciably more inclined to separate business from government. Singapore shows just how successful this nexus can be when it is well managed.

One big difference, however, is that the Chinese-dominated economies place a high emphasis on merit and earning one's success in modern terms, while Malay cultures tend to prefer contacts and the traditional Malay values of *muafakat* (consensus) and *mesyuarat* (consultation), which in turn grew out of ancient *adats* (social traditions and habitual practices) from very ancient historical times. As one lives in Southeast Asia today, one finds it striking how the Malay peoples tend to see their identity in the past, while the Chinese tend to see theirs in the future.[1]

Does it then follow that the Malay values of *muafakat* and *mesyuarat* are incompatible with modern economies?

It would be extremely hazardous to try to replace these as a cultural ethos. Yet they have been badly abused by politicians and their cronies to defend the economic aberrations whose net effect has been to turn the commonwealth legacy of the British era into the codependency societies of today. Racial exceptionalism does not make one exceptional. It makes one a victim.

The emperor's clothes reality behind Prime Minister Mahathir's long record of bluster is that the main obstacle to the rise of the Malay people isn't George Soros or the West, it is the Malay elite. The *wayang kulit* mask in Indonesia's cast of villains isn't a Chinese shadow, it is a Suharto family shadow. These two countries' politicians are simply using any rationale they can to keep their friends' fingers in the till. Malaysian and Indonesian politicians have managed to wring the worst out of ancient traditions like *muafakat* and *mesyuarat* which nearly everyone agrees are healthy values in a healthy body politick.[2] Their response to the Information Age has been to turn it into yet another control mechanism to retain their power. This is why Malaysia's Multimedia Super Corridor is the clearest example we have of how to turn an information advantage into an national liability.

GETTING IT RIGHT THE FILIPINO WAY

Several times we have mentioned the countries that were getting it "right." Singapore, Taiwan, and Hong Kong were named. We left out another: the Philippines. Was that because of benign neglect or ignorance?

No.

Time hasn't yet pointed out the direction of the Philippine future. This caveat duly given, the spirit of democratic institutions has done an enormous amount of good in a country that in the Marcos years much resembled Indonesia. Although hurt by currency declines and stock market upheavals, the Philippines has emerged among the healthiest economies in Southeast Asia. This is mainly because reforms were put in place before the crisis began—starting back in 1992. After being elected in that year, President Ramos opened the Philippine economy to foreign competition and dismantled many monopolies. This enabled Filipinos to taste economic progress after many years.

Today the Philippines is a remarkable example of using modern business management and democratic principles to change the path of a badly directed economy. Although the economic verdict on the Philippines wasn't in when 1997 happened and President Fidel Ramos is constitutionally obliged to leave office in 1998, some facts are fairly certain:

- Democratic reform—true democracy, not this anointing of the preselected that masquerades as democracy in Malaysia—is the most likely path to self-sustaining economic progress.
- The Filipinos, in resolutely opting for democracy, proved that open and transparent government is possible even in regimes that look as bleak as the Marcos mess.

In early 1998, economic experts at a forum organized by the World Bank and the Asian Development Bank in Manila validated these views. Among the more notable statements:

- Vinod Thomas, director of the World Bank's Economic Development Institute, said, "Democracy has helped the Philippines ward off the devastating effects of Asia's financial storm. The Philippines' investment in democracy is paying off. Democratic countries like the Philippines tend to have more transparent financial sectors and provide better access to information, reassuring investors by making it easier to detect problems with the economy."

- Chalongphob Sussangkarn, president of the Thailand Development Research Institute Foundation, said, "Democratic countries have checks against official excesses and corruption that authoritarian governments such as Indonesia's lack."

- President Ramos himself said, "We Filipinos have proven that democracy and sustainable development are compatible and indeed go together, and that democracy is the way of Asia's future."

DEALING WITH FACE

The point of an economy isn't growth. It is people. The point of a market isn't a share of it. It is to enlarge people's share.

Asian buyers and sellers alike want information-based products. They will rejoice when acquisition can be managed electronically. But buyers and sellers do not dominate the decisions that direct their economies. Politicians do that. The person to think about in any assessment of the future of an information economy in Asia isn't anyone in the marketplace. It is the modestly powerful local official of no particular moment outside his community and party. Accustomed to being rewarded by the rituals of local politics, complacent in the unquestioning obedience of his wife and children, immured to the larger world by the perks and patronage of awed constituents, his entire life revolves around privilege and certainty. He hasn't a clue what it is like to live in a society in which everyone is privileged. The looming world of reward becoming associated with knowledge instead of conformity is something he only vaguely understands and little appreciates. To him the placidity of the *kampung* and the petty political office are the fruits of his sense of political honor. He is about as prepared for today's business arena as a hamster is for heaven.

Yet from this personality type, Southeast Asia has evolved four power-concentrating traditions:

- A strong sense of religion but a weak sense of spirituality turns humankind's abiding desire for deep meaning into an ethos of contractual obligations.
- Making law inflexible fosters strong government.
- Trusting the effectiveness of traditions more than the effectiveness of government fosters the rise of powerful bureaucracies.
- Tradition conveys legitimacy but legitimacy does not demand effectiveness, which fosters centralized power.

These are economy-immune traditions. What keeps this system intact is a long cultural predisposition to avoiding conflict by sharply defining and micromanaging the minutia of social roles—the mechanism of face, in other words. You can see it in the panoply of Indian gods. You can see it in the complexities of *adat* in the Malayan people. You can see it in filialism in China.

But now times are changing, and face isn't changing with them. In the old Malay culture, governance was centered in *adat*, the spirit of duty; today this has been replaced by manipulating social roles to elitists' advantage. In the old Chinese culture there was little need for the imaginative; there was a need for the traditional within the contemporary. In old Indian culture there was little need beyond *jataka* and *jati* (family and caste), there was a need for connection to place.

Now Asian collective identities are changing under the impulse of information. Television is almost everywhere, although its content is largely controlled by governments. The Internet, on the other hand, can barely be contained even in orderly Singapore, much less controlled.

One result is that the Chinese are moving from family to consumer identity, the Malays from servants of party and government to servants of corporations, and the Indians from old-wave professions like law and medicine to new-wave ones like IT entrepreneurialism.

The chief losers in these transitions are the old-school political establishments. Even now their present image of stultified and corrupt hacks no longer attracts the best and brightest—they are heading into corporations—but it does invite today's crop of stultified hacks.

Asia's real economic problem isn't Asian values. Asian values are, after all

- orderliness
- cleanliness
- respect
- responsibility
- emotional control

Asia's real economic problem is its age-old response to fear—denial, secrecy, authority, and face—in the hands of people who know how to milk money out of them.

The Asian dream has finally caught up with Asian face. The results are hard to predict. Face is essentially a social contract based on denial—"I will be insulted if you say things that aren't what I want to hear, and once I'm insulted I'm going to make you as miserable as I can for as long as I can."

Face is the inability to confront fear. It uses retribution to deny the truth. Parents know they are not perfect but are afraid of what the kids will think if they admit it, so they demand unquestioned obedience. Company directors and bureaucrats fear someone will pull off the mask of their incompetence, so they rule by authority rather than example. Asian governments wanted industrialization to behave like their children: silent, agreeable, productive, profitable. Instead, industrialization brought give and take, risk and reward.

Societies such as Malaysia's and Indonesia's, which were into sure things and reward that is all but guaranteed, quickly realized that you can get what you want by manipulating the law. They invented the privileges of *bumiputraism*. The theory was, you can get what you want if you build your profit margin into the law.

Well, we certainly know how that theory worked out:

- Service sectors arose in economies before they fully achieved their production sectors, siphoning away vital human and wealth inputs.
- Businesses have difficulty innovating outputs that are intangible.
- Professionals came to see their role as situation maximizers, not wealth creators.
- Paternalism, rigid hierarchies, and silo structures dominated offices and directorates.
- Silence and fear shaped an experience base into a series of resentment rituals such as passive aggression, poison-pen letters, and a truly awesome talent at office intrigue.
- Resentment at being ignored and patronized was channeled into social exclusivism.

YOUR COMPUTER CHIPS PLEASE, NOT YOUR POTATO CHIPS

Some countries will emerge from the 1997 crisis to capitalize on the realization that you can't import the technology and efficiency of Western knowledge theory without also importing its insistence on telling the truth.

But is democracy, American style, really right for Asia? The heritage is not the same; the cultural antecedents aren't really relevant. There was no omnipotent, omnipresent church culture that was overthrown by science. Today one of the most remarkable characteristics of Asia is the genuine (vis-à-vis the Sunday morning) strength of its religions in daily life.

There was no renaissance of reason, for there was no loss of reason in the first place. Asians think internally with a number of logical structures that are very different from Western logics—*vaisheshika* and *paticca sammapada* from India, *'Ilm al-Balagha* from Islam, *taoism* from China are just a few. Few Westerners have ever heard of, much less evaluated the utility of, Asian logical systems. They have no idea what products and services might result from learning more about what goes on inside the Asian head. *Vaisheshika* and *paticca sammapada*, for example, respectively predate object/applet linking and virtuality by over fifteen hundred years, and *'Ilm al-Balagha* predates the idea of fractional reality by more than seven hundred.

And, too, there was no Asian scientific revolution—or at least not one that came as a reaction to a blind-faith religious system. India experienced a surge in scientific thinking over fifteen hundred years ago; Islam had a truly noble scientific revolution nearly a thousand years ago; and although China never really devised a purely scientific way of thinking, the Chinese devised a highly sophisticated technology based on pragmatic need.

Hence when the need for democracy does arise in Asia—from within and not just because the United States and United Nations say Asia should adopt it—that democratic ideal will look and behave quite differently from the one Americans cherish as their unique addition to the world stage. What it will be, no one can predict, except that freedom will most likely play second fiddle to authority. The Americans may be loathe to admit it, but in the eyes of other people in the world the American way of life is brutal, banal, and arrogant. The Asian response is likely to be, "Sell us your information gathering tools, but don't tell us we should become Hollywood with them."

TURNING BATTLEGROUNDS INTO SUPERMARKETS

The 1997 debacle forced Southeast Asian business people to admit that some kind of build-from-within mechanism must evolve if traditional companies are to develop innovative products and services competitive with those being introduced by foreign companies. This boils down to two fundamental economic challenges:

• Redirecting wealth enjoyment from a political elite to society at large
• Turning SMEs into a primary economic innovator

Asian business people adore Silicon Valley, but for the wrong reasons. They like the enormous capital wealth the Valley generates, but not the changes the Valley suggests for business organization and management. In Asia the secretive, closely owned, silo hierarchy predominates. In Silicon Valley, almost exactly the opposite architecture predominates, the hyperarchy. Whether one prefers the IdeaLab, Cisco, or Thermo Electron models, their common factor is that they organize by clustering business deals around products and services, not patriarchs and politicians. Almost everything related to the information economy has been invented by independent people or small groups whose freedom from the tedious duties of surviving in an organization gave them the freedom to think in new ways.

Silicon Valley devised the entrepreneurial cluster model of organization to handle the kind of part government, part venture capitalist, part entrepreneurial ventures that arose because a lot of technology was being produced by a lot of SMEs. In this milieu, innovative organization and finance are as important as innovative technology.

In Asia the problem with the SMEs' role in IT and e-commerce is that there is so much emphasis on foreign technology coming in at the behest of governments and so much ingrained local SME resistance to taking risks, there is valid fear that many Asian SMEs will vanish out of the picture or be absorbed into overseas companies as subsidiaries. This will have negative consequences in the long term. Bringing in overseas brainware is fine, but the ultimate beneficiary has to be seen to be Southeast Asian entrepreneurs and suppliers developing Southeast Asian products and services.

Taiwan's complex network of business parks, government-sponsored R&D, and its myriad of small companies financed by part government and part entrepreneurial venturing is among the most useful models other countries can emulate. But Taiwan is geared largely toward physical production, not intellectual production. Singapore—especially the thinking at the National Computer Board—is presently taking Taiwan's example into the realm of SME-based knowledge enterprises, but—as of 1998—Singapore is very new at this. Nonetheless, if Asians need role models on how to turn SMEs into the driving force of a consumer economy, Singapore is the place to learn how to do it.

FROM SILICON VALLEY TO CYBERASIA SHOP

Twenty years ago the capitalism issue prompted by the computer was how to reshape the fundamental structure of the corporation without ruining it in the process. By the late 1980s the desktop PC made possible the same streamlining of mid-management that the assembly line made possible seventy years earlier. It made no difference whether the jobs were labor or management, if they were unproductive compared with their cost, they went.

Big companies responded by devolving into smaller independencies, giving more power to local managers while globalizing their operations using standardized assemblies and delivery schedules to cut costs no matter where the plant was located.

Analysts of Asian business typologies point out how long group loyalty has endured in Asia in the form of the patriciate style. The patriciate structure is founded on institutional memory, personal trust, risk avoidance, political protection, and captive markets. The patriciate system is exactly the opposite of what has proved so successful in Silicon Valley.

Yet there are a good many illusions in Asia about just what Silicon Valley really is. Many Asians think Silicon Valley is an exotic economic machine where you pour raw materials and money in one end and Oracle and Cisco come out the other.

True, but one percent true. Silicon Valley is an ecosystem in which money is food and people are grazers. The reason it works so well is that it is sensitive to the complex psychology of market-shapers—popular culture, feedback loops, supply-push, if-you-build-it-they-will-come, mediagenicity, glam-cool, the "it's in the air" effect of intangibles like a popular movie or a TV series shifting taste almost instantly out from under existing product lines.

Without taking into account popular culture, a business structure lives in the past not the future. Beneath Silicon Valley as a high-tech invention center is Silicon Valley as the psychology of public attitude. The product is technology. The financing vehicle is venture capitalism. The fuel is entrepreneurial start-ups. The structure is clusters of many interrelated companies under a financial source that keeps its hands off management.

But the heat engine is the consumer.

Hence the question raised by this book is this: Is the point of information technology in Southeast Asia investing $1 billion in 250-odd SME start-ups that ended up yielding $44 billion in profits off of revenues of $85 billion, the way Kleiner Perkins Caulfield & Byers invested in Silicon Valley SMEs?

Well, yes.

And no.

The unastute among Southeast Asian governments want IT to become the newest route to quick wealth as world demand shifts out of cheap-labor manufacturing into services. They are embracing the notion that future value-addition can come from present-value services. To these governments, that assumption means maximizing technology.

Maximizing technology is simple. The easiest way would be to set up monopolies and enclaves. This is exactly what Malaysia, government and private sector, is doing. Try to buy an Apple in Kuala Lumpur from MacMall in Torrance.

The difficult, but more enriching, approach is to maximize the wealth that IT can create. Wealth-building via IT is not going to come from the R&D-park approach, nor from carving up the IT home market by limiting access to sat dishes, nor from adding a rung for IT technology onto the value-added ladder. It's going to come from marketing the *services* IT can create. Those services need to be:

- original
- useful
- indigenous
- universal

The real investment value in information technology is setting it up as the funnel through which culture flows toward the furtherance of technology, not the other way around. The more human value poured into the services, the higher the return on investment.

In theory, what happened in Silicon Valley should have happened in Asia decades ago: A major university spawns a subculture of technicians who are good engineers but unimaginative financiers. A breed of rule-breaking financiers comes along and devises a new form of capitalism based on equity risk rather than collateral risk. Their idea of risk was based on two assumptions: (a) visionary ideas need visionary managers, and (b) nine out of ten ventures will flop but one will set industry standards and be a money machine till the demise of the technology.

None of this is alien to Asia. Venture capital originated in India and Arabia, though few people realize this. It is the most ancient form of risk/reward financing and came out of Asia's ancient maritime industry. Long before Lloyds of London, Arabic and Gujarati shippers devised the idea of an insurance scheme to share their risk by requiring individual ship owners and each shipper to proportionately share the risk and the reward. The result was an early form of the limited liability venture. Typically their risk rates were: cartel 60 percent, ship owner 40 percent, and shipper the value of the cargo. If a ship went down, everybody lost (though not as much as the sailors!), but usually not enough to wipe any one of them out.

Southeast Asia's newest transitory cargo is information. In the past, economies based on cargo did two things: (a) they built ports wherein goods were received (the ancestral MSC), and (b) they acted as flow-throughs to the local economies surrounding them (SingaporeONE), evolving complex and proprietal infrastructures for distribution and service.

The money to be made out of (a) is peanuts: the MSC as presently conceived is nothing but a port. The economy of (b), however, will come from turning IT in Southeast Asia into the funnel through which technological services invented there are distributed from India to China.

That means investment levels far riskier and greater than anything Southeast Asians are used to. What investment vehicles will work there as venture capitalism worked in Silicon Valley? What organizational structures will replace the family silo with the entepreneurial feedlot? Where's the Sand Hill Road on CyberAsia's map?

GLOOM & DOOM OR GLOOM & ZOOM?

Few now would disagree that as long as companies spend more time attending to internal interests than they do attending to client interests, they will prosper less than companies that don't.

Nor do people much argue with the notion that as long as governments try to dictate to the markets instead of listening to them, there will be more 1997s in Asia's future.

The next phase in Asia's economic expansion is likely to be far more complex, in part because IT will be involved, in part because it will be based less on value adding with cheap labor and more on value adding with intellectual labor. Enough astute company directors have learned what a committed workforce and the power of a good brand can do in the marketplace to aim at the critical mass Asia has so sorely neglected: the pulling power of their own markets.

Yet there are many issues left to resolve. Some of them are still largely unrecognized for the dilemmas they pose. For example, how should a company transfer fiduciary responsibilities to professional and managerial contractors? Most companies take the view that hired labor energy is dispensable, but don't always realize that hired talent energy is not the same thing.

Another issue is how to wean companies away from placing so much value on institutional memory to the neglect of institutional innovation. Many Asians hold the view that people with little sense for the value of the past are insensitive to the value of the future. Job security implied longevity, longevity implied loyalty, loyalty implied certainty. Unfortunately certainty is the mask that hides uncertainty.

Today most managers—though not necessarily directors—realize that companies run from a platform of institutional memory are not likely to be responsive to the market. People are coming to the view that the future of a company is its ability to create value, not its ability to hold tightly to the values of the firm's founder. What was most lacking before 1997 was a sense of genuinely strategic vision. It certainly existed in organizations like Singapore's National Computer Board, but not in those many family boardrooms where it was most needed.

Asia has learned a lot of hard lessons. Will the region now do marvelous things with IT and e-commerce, the way it did with exports manufacture?

Or to repeat: gloom & doom or gloom & zoom?

Both. You get what you ask for.

FLIGHT OF THE PHOENIX

Tomorrow's growth does not come from yesterday's ideas. Most of the media criticism of Asia's 1997 economic debacle dwelled at length on the failure of old ideas in Asia. All too neglected was the emergence of innovative new ones.

Asia is a phoenix. It periodically rebuilds itself out of the ashes of things that didn't work. We now know that the economic failures of 1997 were the best thing to have happened to the region. They revealed deadwood ideas that needed to be cleared away before the long-term process of building a modern society could begin.

What we now need to do is reveal what the new ideas are and who has thought of them. In so doing we can see the legends of the next era—Asia's IT and e-commerce age—being made out of the ashes of old legends that didn't work. The finger-pointing at autocratic governments, denial, cronyism, absence of regulatory restraint, blind development, and the host of other ills that stained the pages of the news have now been discussed to death. The real lesson from Asia's economic performance from 1987 through 1997 is something we all need to remember: closed-loop systems work well from within the loop but poorly beyond it.

Most business people and academics underappreciate the power of legend in Asian affairs. The Chinese, Malays, and Indians each have powerful ancestor and hero myths that recur today in deeply held psychological behaviors—just as the *Hero With A Thousand Faces* that Joseph Campbell wrote about shows up in *Star Wars*, in the American Super Bowl, and in the dynamics of corporate takeovers.

To those who understand the root myths that motivate social thinking in Asia, the 1997 economic debacle was an inevitable outcome of human institutions that behave cyclically. It fulfilled deeply held expectations expressed by the Chinese in the phoenix story, among the Malays in their legend of the epic struggle of the conflict between heroism and loyalty in the Hang Tua and Hang Jebat legend, and among the Indians the god Shiva acting in his destroyer and renewer aspect.

All these are cleansing legends. They stem from a primordial belief conditioned by historical experience in which change occurs as punctured self-satisfaction. And when change comes, it comes as a massive sweeping away of the past so a pristine future may rise.

To put the matter in less literary terms, Asia's economic future will depend heavily on information technology, electronic business, and electronic commerce, just as the economic success of the 1980s and 1990s depended on cheap labor and cheap money.

On one level, the business person's role is to discover where the opportunities exist for economic success in Asia in the era of 1997 to 2005. The usual business information will play its part—demographics, investment routes, markets, and the like.

But we must not neglect the potency of primal matters, the fundamental causes of behavior that recur just as the pheonix recurs:

- power and the myth
- fear and face
- sociology and organization
- power and integrity

All of these vary considerably with their counterpart values in the West. Those who help with Asia's regeneration will prosper with it in more ways than in mere matters financial.

Those who blame and point fingers will end up a speck of dust hovering in the air as the great bird now massing out of Asia's ashes rises and begins to move its wings.

NOTES

1. More interesting than either are the Southeast Asian Indians, who have managed to retain the past (especially religious and family ethos) while embracing the future (replacing the caste system with meritocracy). Lamentably, their numbers are too few politically to do much more than ally themselves with the strongest party and work out their own fortunes privately. Again let it be emphasized that Southeast Asian Indians—especially the professional young women—are among the best managers this writer has come across anywhere.

2. Lest it seem we are unduly harsh on any particular politician or political group, or even Asian politics in general, it is helpful to remember what Aesop said around 600 B.C.: "We hang the petty thieves, but send the grand ones to high office."

Selected Bibliography

WEB AND E-MAIL SITES

International

http://www.minds.com
http://www.broadcaster.co.uk/
http://www.tabnet.com/services/
http://www.ne-dev.com/
http://www.idg.com.au/computerworld/
http://www.newspage.com
http://www.oecd.org/dsti/sti/it/ec/index.htm
http://www.nytimes.com
http://www.nwfusion.com/
http://www.infospace.com/
http://www.cmpnet.com/
http://www.techweb.com/smallbiz
http://www.techweb.com/wire/international.html
http://www.news.com
http://www.dejanews.com
http://www.websitez.com
http://www.edgar-online.com
http://www.frost.com
http://www.ibm.com/e-business/
http://www.forbes.com
http://www.fortune.com
http://www.hbsp.harvard.org
http://www.idg.net/
http://www.idcresearch.com
http://www.aecpii.com/newprod.html
http://www.cdt.org

http://www.cme.org/cme/
http://snyside.sunnyside.com/home/
http://www.osc.edu.eclips/
http://www.ecrc.ctc.com/
http://www.napainc.org/index.html
http://www.economist.com
http://www.feer.com
http://www.the-times.co.uk/news/

SoutheastAsia

http://www.ncb.gov.sg
http://www.tas.gov.sg
http://www.edb.gov.sg
http://www.singlinks.com.sg
http://www.mdc.com.my
http://www.mtdc.com.my
http://www.asiasociety.org
http://www.asiapulse.com
http://www.jaring.my/star/
http://www.bangsar.com/
http://www.asiaecon.com
http://www.asialinks.com
http://www.jaring.my/maybank
http://www.prnewswire.com/asiapulse.html
http://www.asia1.com.sg/
http://www.xtramedia.com
http://www.netiq.com.my
http://www.arthurandersen.com
http://www.cneminent.com
http://www.corpnetwork.com.my
http://www.idm.com.my
http://www.adlittle.com
http://www.cisco.com
http://www.McKinsey.com
http://www.oracle.com
http://www.sun.com.sg

India

http://www.webpage.com/hindu/
http://www.indiaworld.com/open/biz/index.html
http://www.webindia.com/india.html
http://www.stph.net
http://www.indiaserver.com/biz/dbi/MEA2.0.html
http://www.indiaserver.com/biz/dbi/MEA3.0.html
http://www.indiaserver.com/biz/dbi/dbi.html

http://www.globalindia.com/index.htm (still sparse yet)
http://www.indiacomm.com/
http://www.economictimes.com/today/pagehome.htm
http://www.webcom.com/%7Eprakash/ECONOMY/ECONOMY.HTML

BUSINESS AND DOING BUSINESS

Southeast Asia

Asian Development Bank. *Asian Development and Outlook, 1997–1999.* Singapore: Oxford University Press, 1997.
Barabba, Vincent P. *Meeting of the Minds: Creating the Market-Based Enterprise.* Boston: Harvard Business School Press, 1995.
Barraclough, Simon. *A Dictionary of Malaysian Politics.* Singapore: Heinemann Publishers Asia Pte. Ltd., 1988.
Beamish, Paul W., and J. Peter Killing, eds. *Cooperative Strategies: Asian Pacific Perspectives.* San Francisco: The New Lexington Press, 1997.
Bedlington, Stanley S. *Malaysia and Singapore: The Building of New States.* Ithaca: Cornell University Press, 1978.
Block, Zenas, and Ian C. MacMillan. *Corporate Venturing: Creating New Businesses Within the Firm.* Boston: Harvard Business School Press, 1995.
Bowman, Edward, and Bruce Kogut, eds. *Redesigning the Firm.* Oxford: Oxford University Press, 1995.
Choudhury, G.W. *Islam and the Modern Islamic World.* Kuala Lumpur: WHS Publications, 1994.
Culbert, Samuel A. *Mind-Set Management.* Oxford: Oxford University Press, 1996.
Deschamps, Jean-Phillipe, and P. Ranganath Nayak. *Product Juggernauts.* Boston: Harvard Business School Press, 1996.
Ellsworth, Jill H., and Matthew V. Ellsworth. *Marketing on the Internet.* Singapore: John Wiley & Sons, Inc., 1997.
Embree, Ainslie T. *Sources of Indian Tradition.* New York: Columbia University Press, 1988.
Farrell, Paul B. *Expert Investing on the Net.* Singapore: John Wiley & Sons, Inc., 1997.
Forbes, Eric C. *Dictionary of Malaysian Business.* Petaling Jaya: Pelanduk Publications, 1992.
Gomez, Edmund Terence, and K.S. Jomo. *Malaysia's Political Economy: Politics, Patronage and Profits.* Cambridge: Cambridge University Press, 1997.
Guengerich, Steve, et al. *Building the Corporate Intranet.* Singapore: John Wiley & Sons, Inc., 1997.
Hagel, John, III, and Arthur G. Armstrong. *Net Gain: Expanding Markets Through Virtual Communities.* Boston: Harvard Business School Press, 1997.
Hamlin, Michael Alan. *Asia's Best: The Myth and Reality of Asia's Most Successful Companies.* Singapore: Prentice Hall, 1998.
Hills, Mellanie. *Intranet Business Strategies.* Singapore: John Wiley & Sons, Inc., 1997.
Husin, Adinan. "The Transfer of Technology for Production of Agricultural Produce." In *Agriculture Commercialization in Sarawak.* Kuching: Angkatan Zaman Mansang Sarawak (AZAM) and Konrad Adenauer Foundation (KAF), 1995.
Jomo, K.S. *Malaysian Economic Development Policies After 1990.* Townsville, Australia: Centre for East and Southeast Asian Studies, 1994.

Jomo, K.S. and Ng Seuw Kiat. *Malaysia's Economic Development*. Kuala Lumpur: Pelanduk Publications, 1996.

Kakar, Sudhir. *The Inner World: A Psychoanalytic Study of Childhood and Society in India*. Oxford: Oxford University Press, 1991.

Khoo, Kay Kim. *Malay Society: Transformation and Democratisation*. Petaling Jaya: Pelanduk Publications, 1991.

Kotter, John P. *Leading Change*. Boston: Harvard Business School Press, 1996.

Lam, C.K. "The Chinese." In *Jurnal Sekolah AZAM*. Kuching: Angkatan Zaman Mansang Sarawak, 1992.

Maister, David H. *Managing the Professional Service Firm*. Singapore: Free Press Paperbacks (Distributed by Simon & Schuster, Singapore), 1997.

McEachern, Tim, and Bob O'Keefe. *Re-Wiring Business: Uniting Management and the Web*. Singapore: John Wiley & Sons, Inc., 1998.

Mohamad, Taib Osman. *Malay Folk Beliefs*. Kuala Lumpur: Dewan Pustaka dan Bahasa, 1989.

Navaratnam, Ramon V. *Managing the Malaysian Economy: Challenges & Prospects*. Petaling Jaya, Malaysia: Pelanduk Publications, 1997.

Ninan, Sevanti. *Through the Magic Window: TV and Change in India*. New Delhi: Penguin, 1996.

O'Keefe, Steve. *Publicity on the Internet*. Singapore: John Wiley & Sons, Inc., 1997.

Patching, Alan, and Dennis Waitley. *The Futureproof Corporation*. Singapore: Butterworth-Heinemann Asia, 1997.

SarDesai, D.R. *Southeast Asia, Past and Present*. San Francisco: Westview Press, 1994.

Schell, Michael S., and Charlene M. Solomon. *Capitalizing on the Global Workforce*. Chicago: Irwin Professional Publishing, 1998.

Sheppard, Mubin. *A Royal Pleasure Ground: Malay Decorative Arts and Pastimes*. Kuala Lumpur: Oxford University Press, 1977.

Singh, Surgit, ed. *Malaysian Entrepreneurs*. Kuala Lumpur: Malaysian Institute of Management, 1995.

Tapscott, Don. *The Digital Economy: Promise and Peril in the Age of Networked Intelligence*. New York: McGraw Hill, 1996.

Thaib, Luckman. *Political System of Islam*. Kuala Lumpur: Penerbit Amal, 1994.

Vakil, Tarjani. *Achieving Excellence: Case Studies of 6 Indian Companies*. Delhi: Tata McGraw-Hill, 1996.

Walther, Thomas. *Reinventing the CFO*. New York: McGraw-Hill, 1996.

Wiersema, William H. *Activity-Based Management*. AMACOM [American Management Association], 1995.

Yeoh, Sek Chew, and Ng Chai Lee. *ISO 9002 in the Malaysian Construction Industry: Guide and Implementation*. Singapore: McGraw-Hill Book Co., 1996.

Yoshihara, Kunio. *The Rise of Ersatz Capitalism in South-East Asia*. Quezon City: Atemeo de Manila University Press, 1988.

Zainul, Haji Ariff Haji Hussain. "Emerging Social Issues and Problems of the 21st Century." In *Sarawak: The Next Step*, Hatta Solhee et al. Kuching: State Planning Unit and Angkatan Zaman Mansang Sarawak, 1995.

Index

About the Author

DOUGLAS BULLIS is a writer, editor, and current owner of Atelier Books, a full service book production firm serving international publishers with interests in the Southeast Asian and Indian subcontinent markets. Bullis has written and published more than 200 articles on topics ranging from art and cultural history to business, country investment, and technology transfer. He is the author of two previous Quorum books, *Doing Business in Today's India* (1998) and *Selling to India's Consumer Market* (1997).